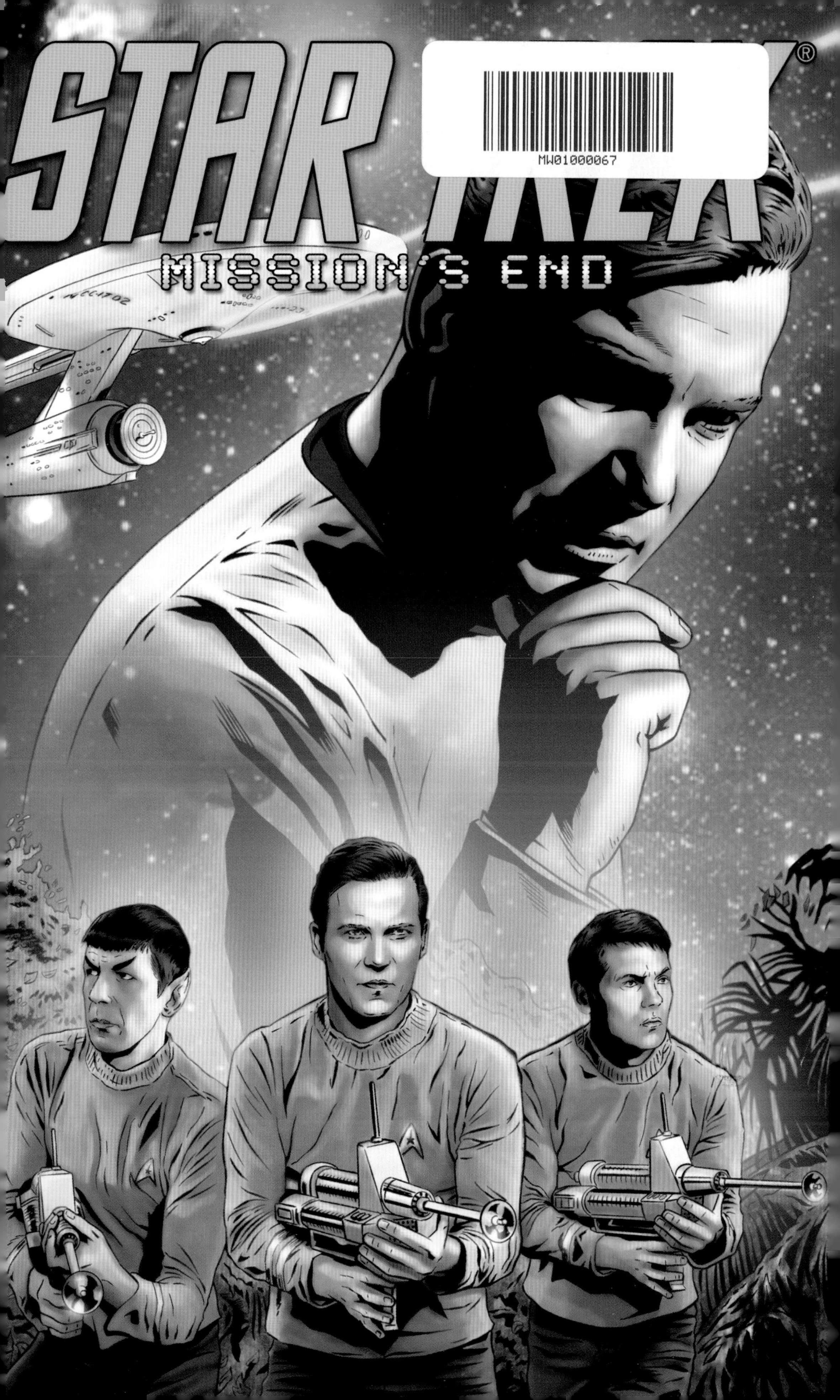
STAR
MISSION'S END

STAR TREK®

MISSION'S END

Story by Ty Templeton

Art by Stephen Molnar

Colors by John Hunt

Letters by Neil Uyetake and Robbie Robbins

Original Series Edits by Andy Schmidt and Scott Dunbier

Collection Edits by Justin Eisinger

Editorial Assistance by Mariah Huehner

Collection Design by Chris Mowry

IDW Publishing
Operations:
Ted Adams, Chief Executive Officer
Greg Goldstein, Chief Operating Officer
Matthew Ruzicka, CPA, Chief Financial Officer
Alan Payne, VP of Sales
Lorelei Bunjes, Dir. of Digital Services
AnnaMaria White, Marketing & PR Manager
Marci Hubbard, Executive Assistant
Alonzo Simon, Shipping Manager
Angela Loggins, Staff Accountant

Editorial:
Chris Ryall, Publisher/Editor-in-Chief
Scott Dunbier, Editor, Special Projects
Andy Schmidt, Senior Editor
Justin Eisinger, Editor
Kris Oprisko, Editor/Foreign Lic.
Denton J. Tipton, Editor
Tom Waltz, Editor
Mariah Huehner, Associate Editor
Carlos Guzman, Editorial Assistant

Design:
Robbie Robbins, EVP/Sr. Graphic Artist
Neil Uyetake, Art Director
Chris Mowry, Graphic Artist
Amauri Osorio, Graphic Artist
Gilberto Lazcano, Production Assistant

www.IDWPUBLISHING.com   ISBN: 978-1-60010-540-1   12 11 10 09   1 2 3 4

STAR TREK created by Gene Roddenberry
Special Thanks to Risa Kessler and John Van Citters at CBS Consumer Products.

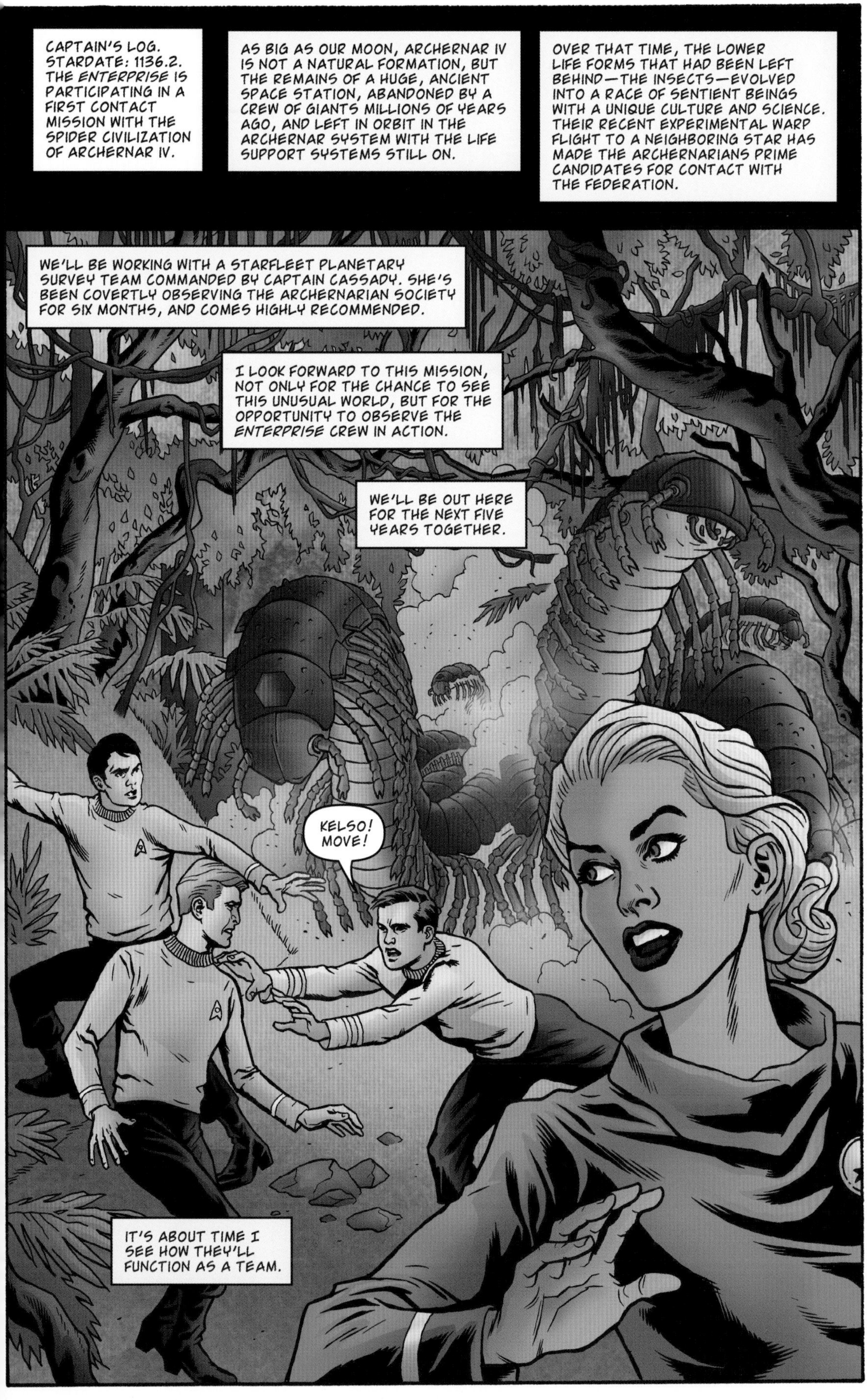
CAPTAIN'S LOG. STARDATE: 1136.2. THE *ENTERPRISE* IS PARTICIPATING IN A FIRST CONTACT MISSION WITH THE SPIDER CIVILIZATION OF ARCHERNAR IV.
AS BIG AS OUR MOON, ARCHERNAR IV IS NOT A NATURAL FORMATION, BUT THE REMAINS OF A HUGE, ANCIENT SPACE STATION, ABANDONED BY A CREW OF GIANTS MILLIONS OF YEARS AGO, AND LEFT IN ORBIT IN THE ARCHERNAR SYSTEM WITH THE LIFE SUPPORT SYSTEMS STILL ON.
OVER THAT TIME, THE LOWER LIFE FORMS THAT HAD BEEN LEFT BEHIND—THE INSECTS—EVOLVED INTO A RACE OF SENTIENT BEINGS WITH A UNIQUE CULTURE AND SCIENCE. THEIR RECENT EXPERIMENTAL WARP FLIGHT TO A NEIGHBORING STAR HAS MADE THE ARCHERNARIANS PRIME CANDIDATES FOR CONTACT WITH THE FEDERATION.
WE'LL BE WORKING WITH A STARFLEET PLANETARY SURVEY TEAM COMMANDED BY CAPTAIN CASSADY. SHE'S BEEN COVERTLY OBSERVING THE ARCHERNARIAN SOCIETY FOR SIX MONTHS, AND COMES HIGHLY RECOMMENDED.
I LOOK FORWARD TO THIS MISSION, NOT ONLY FOR THE CHANCE TO SEE THIS UNUSUAL WORLD, BUT FOR THE OPPORTUNITY TO OBSERVE THE *ENTERPRISE* CREW IN ACTION.
WE'LL BE OUT HERE FOR THE NEXT FIVE YEARS TOGETHER.
KELSO! MOVE!
IT'S ABOUT TIME I SEE HOW THEY'LL FUNCTION AS A TEAM.

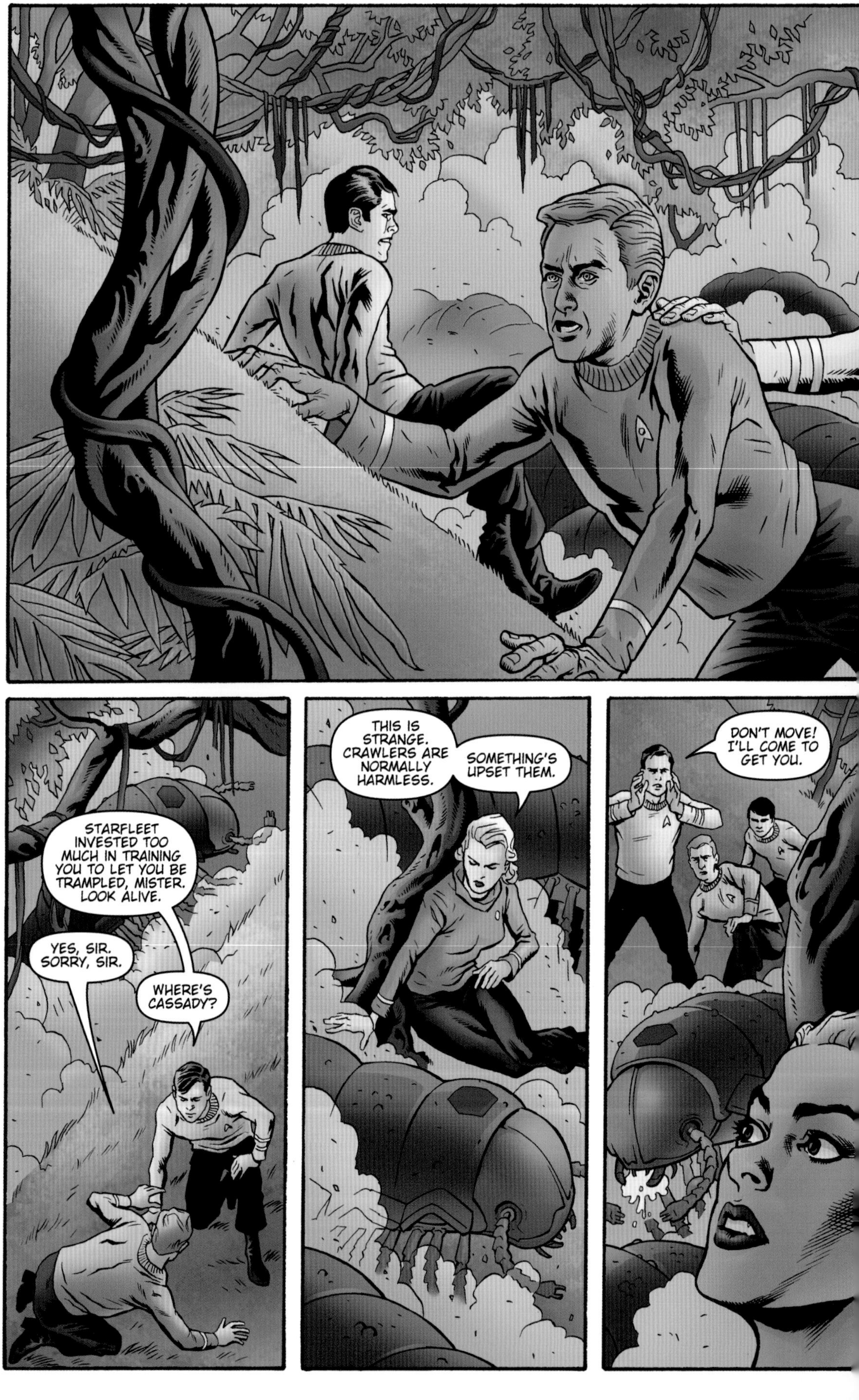
STARFLEET INVESTED TOO MUCH IN TRAINING YOU TO LET YOU BE TRAMPLED, MISTER. LOOK ALIVE.
YES, SIR. SORRY, SIR.
WHERE'S CASSADY?
THIS IS STRANGE. CRAWLERS ARE NORMALLY HARMLESS.
SOMETHING'S UPSET THEM.
DON'T MOVE! I'LL COME TO GET YOU.

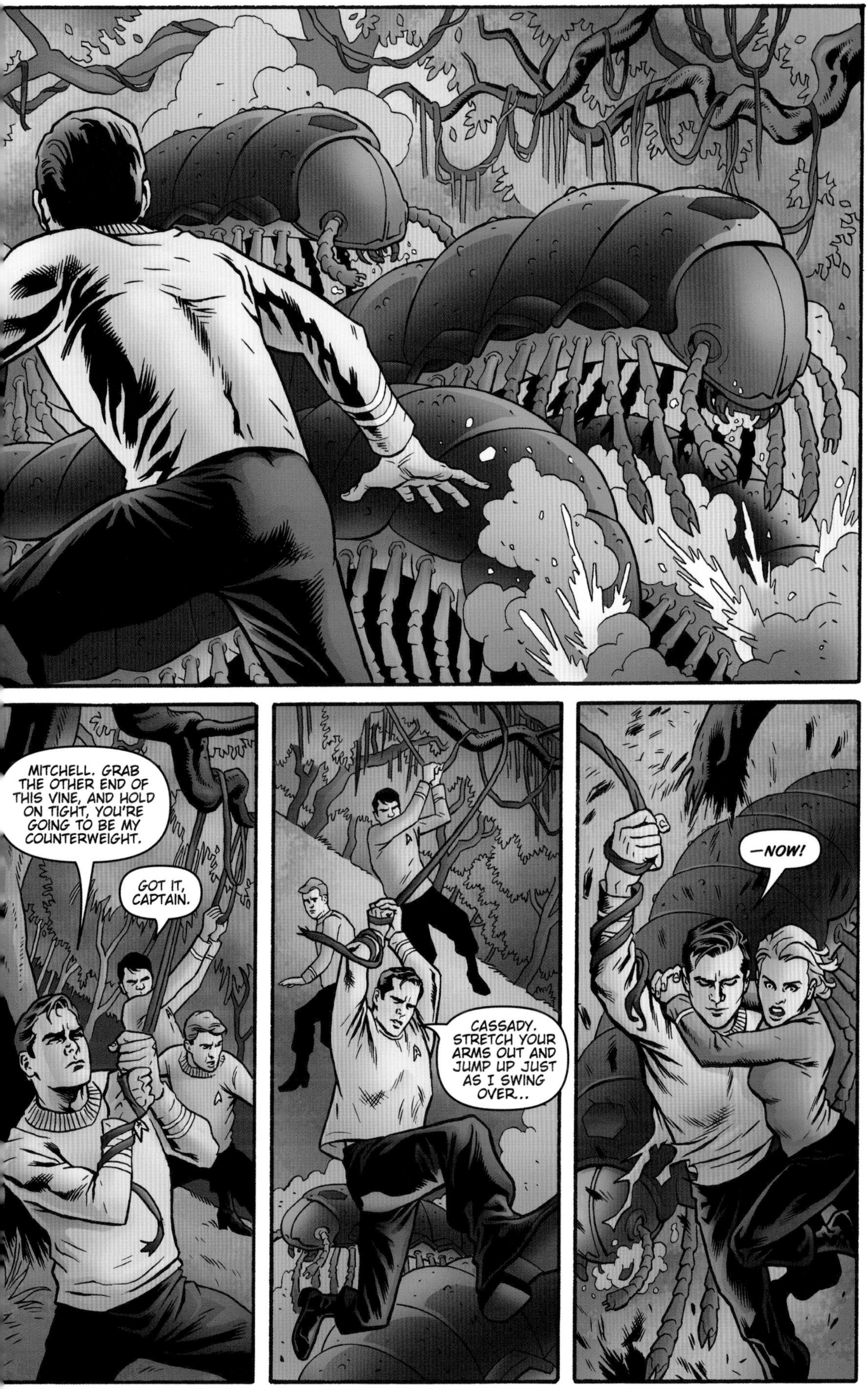
MITCHELL. GRAB THE OTHER END OF THIS VINE, AND HOLD ON TIGHT, YOU'RE GOING TO BE MY COUNTERWEIGHT.
GOT IT, CAPTAIN.
CASSADY. STRETCH YOUR ARMS OUT AND JUMP UP JUST AS I SWING OVER...
—NOW!

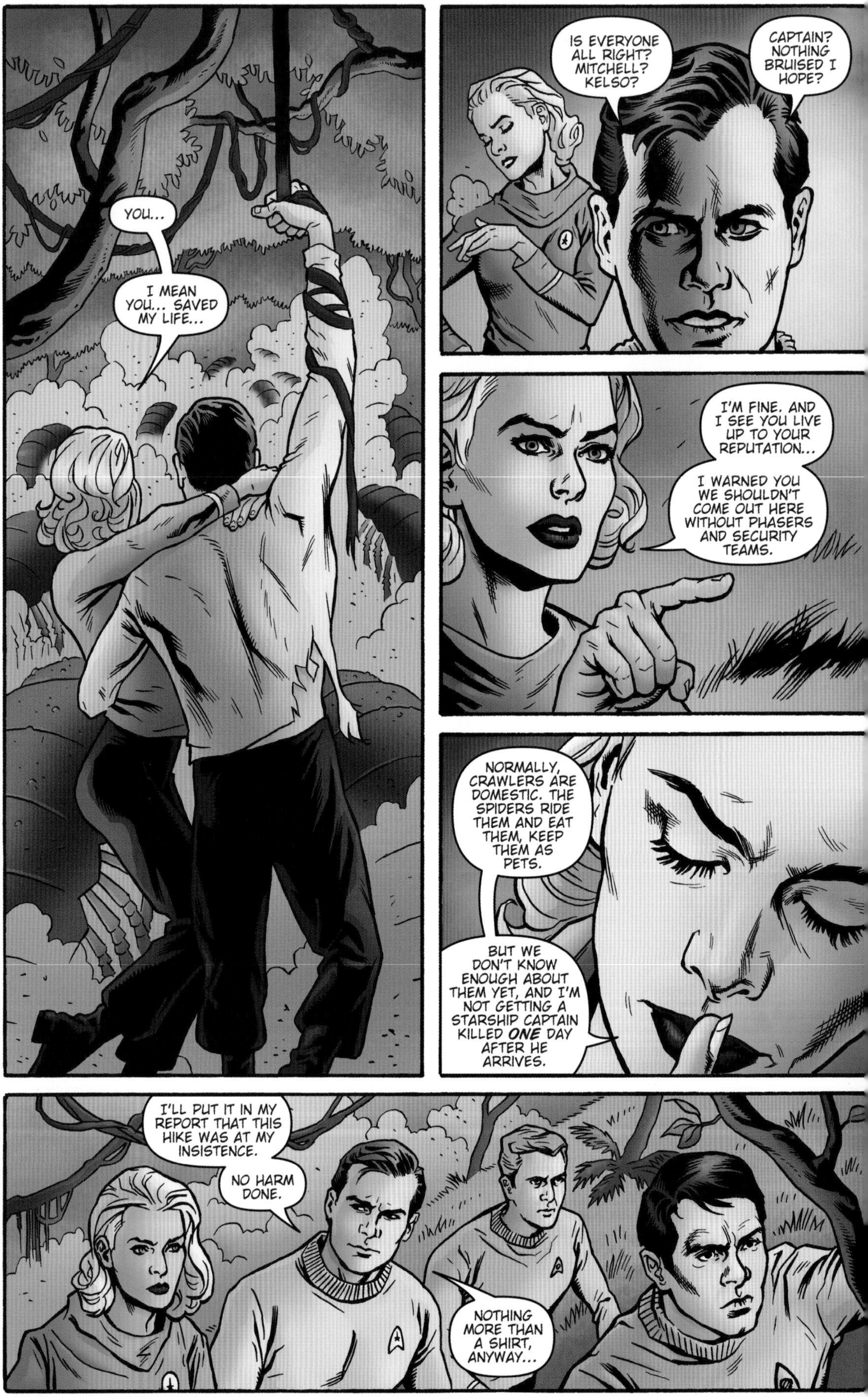

YOU...
I MEAN YOU... SAVED MY LIFE...
IS EVERYONE ALL RIGHT? MITCHELL? KELSO?
CAPTAIN? NOTHING BRUISED I HOPE?
I'M FINE. AND I SEE YOU LIVE UP TO YOUR REPUTATION...
I WARNED YOU WE SHOULDN'T COME OUT HERE WITHOUT PHASERS AND SECURITY TEAMS.
NORMALLY, CRAWLERS ARE DOMESTIC. THE SPIDERS RIDE THEM AND EAT THEM, KEEP THEM AS PETS.
BUT WE DON'T KNOW ENOUGH ABOUT THEM YET, AND I'M NOT GETTING A STARSHIP CAPTAIN KILLED ONE DAY AFTER HE ARRIVES.
I'LL PUT IT IN MY REPORT THAT THIS HIKE WAS AT MY INSISTENCE.
NO HARM DONE.
NOTHING MORE THAN A SHIRT, ANYWAY...

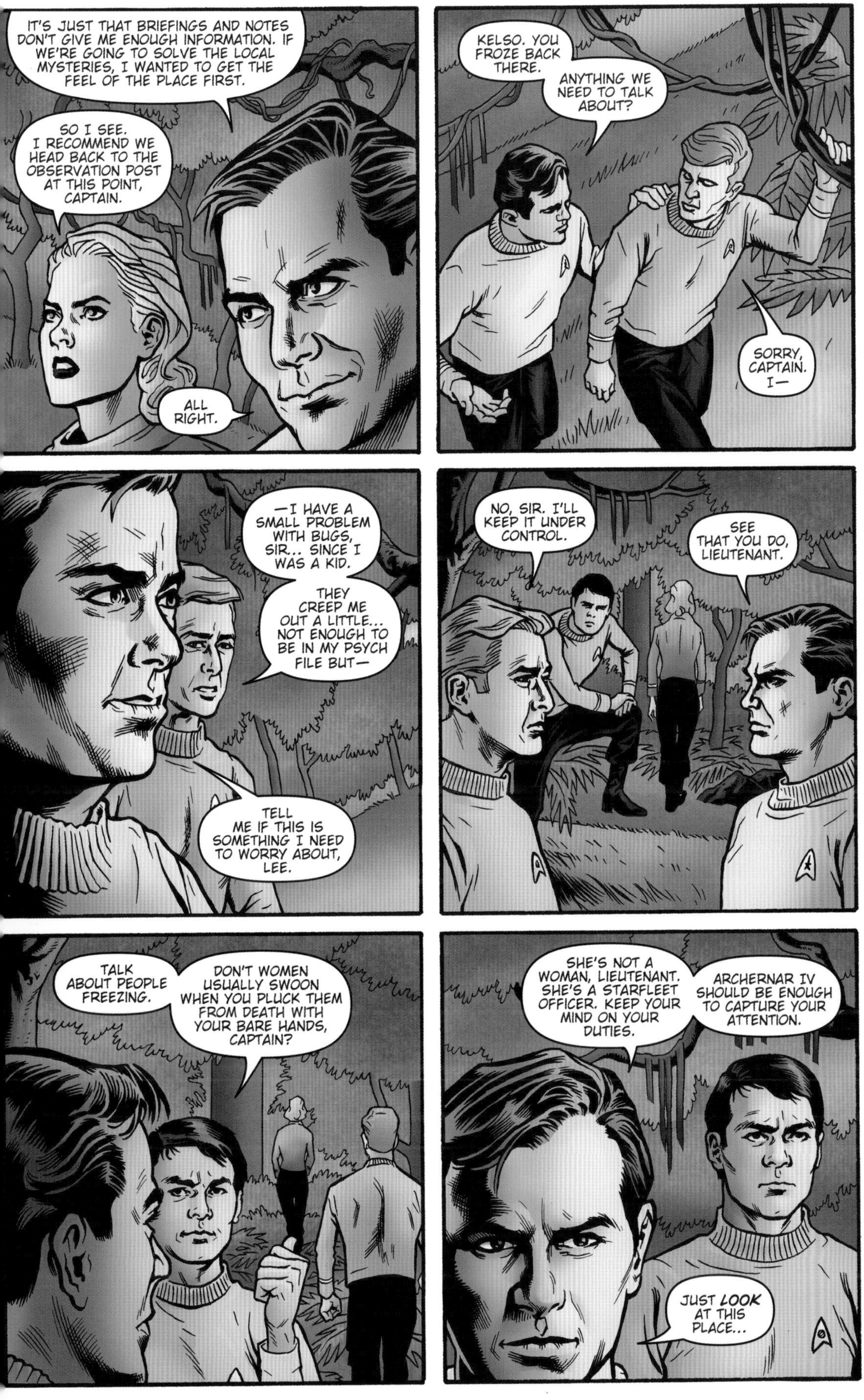
IT'S JUST THAT BRIEFINGS AND NOTES DON'T GIVE ME ENOUGH INFORMATION. IF WE'RE GOING TO SOLVE THE LOCAL MYSTERIES, I WANTED TO GET THE FEEL OF THE PLACE FIRST.
SO I SEE. I RECOMMEND WE HEAD BACK TO THE OBSERVATION POST AT THIS POINT, CAPTAIN.
ALL RIGHT.
KELSO. YOU FROZE BACK THERE.
ANYTHING WE NEED TO TALK ABOUT?
SORRY, CAPTAIN. I—
—I HAVE A SMALL PROBLEM WITH BUGS, SIR... SINCE I WAS A KID.
THEY CREEP ME OUT A LITTLE... NOT ENOUGH TO BE IN MY PSYCH FILE BUT—
TELL ME IF THIS IS SOMETHING I NEED TO WORRY ABOUT, LEE.
NO, SIR. I'LL KEEP IT UNDER CONTROL.
SEE THAT YOU DO, LIEUTENANT.
TALK ABOUT PEOPLE FREEZING.
DON'T WOMEN USUALLY SWOON WHEN YOU PLUCK THEM FROM DEATH WITH YOUR BARE HANDS, CAPTAIN?
SHE'S NOT A WOMAN, LIEUTENANT. SHE'S A STARFLEET OFFICER. KEEP YOUR MIND ON YOUR DUTIES.
ARCHERNAR IV SHOULD BE ENOUGH TO CAPTURE YOUR ATTENTION.
JUST **LOOK** AT THIS PLACE...

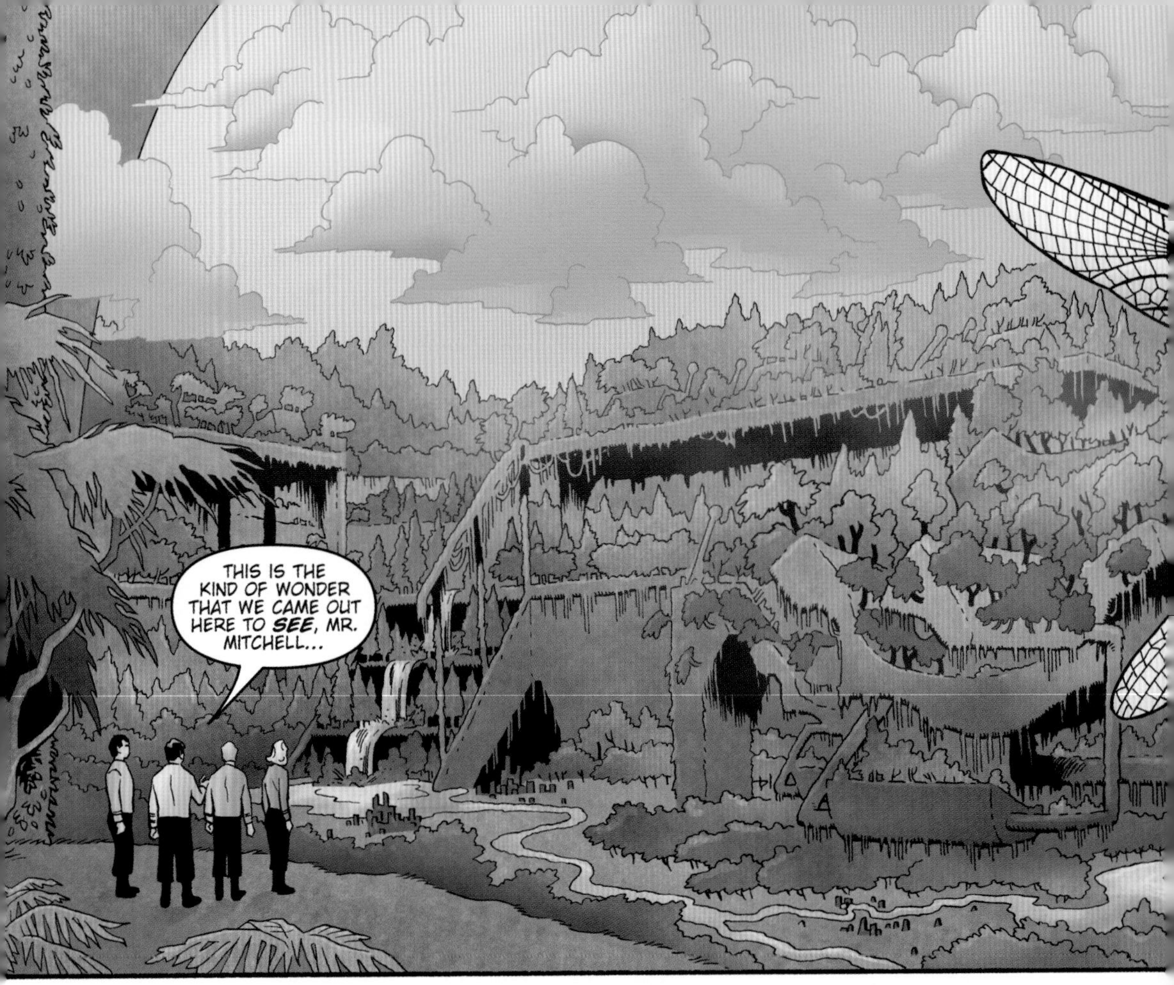
THIS IS THE KIND OF WONDER THAT WE CAME OUT HERE TO SEE, MR. MITCHELL...

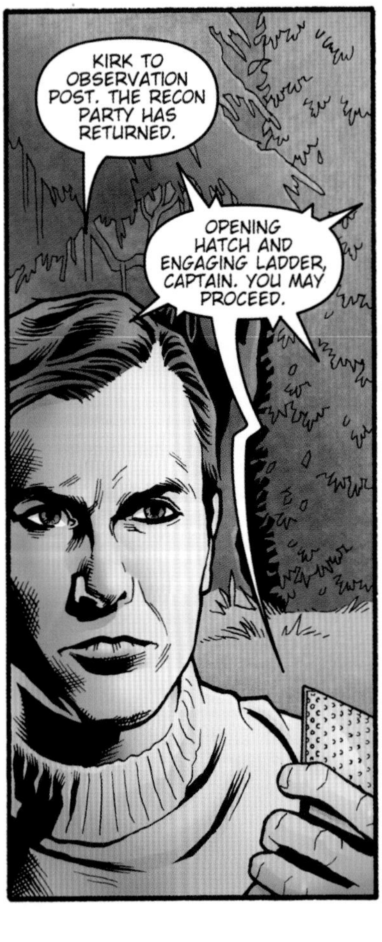
KIRK TO OBSERVATION POST. THE RECON PARTY HAS RETURNED.
OPENING HATCH AND ENGAGING LADDER, CAPTAIN. YOU MAY PROCEED.

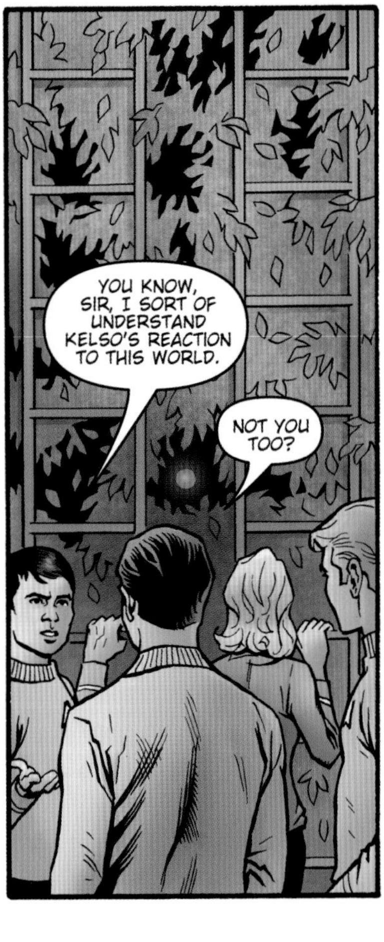
YOU KNOW, SIR, I SORT OF UNDERSTAND KELSO'S REACTION TO THIS WORLD.
NOT YOU TOO?

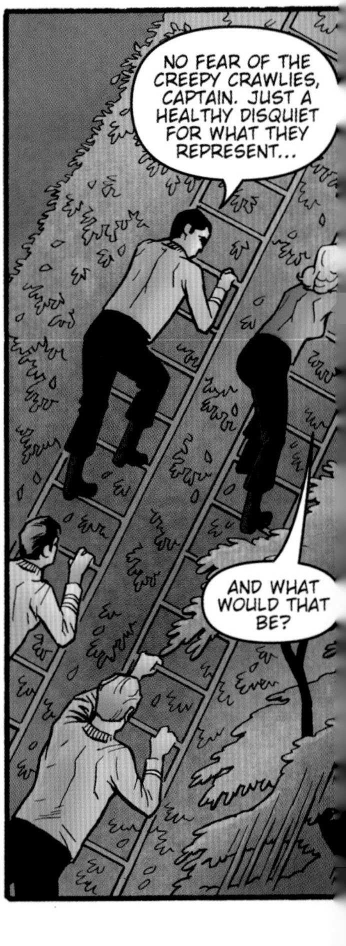
NO FEAR OF THE CREEPY CRAWLIES, CAPTAIN. JUST A HEALTHY DISQUIET FOR WHAT THEY REPRESENT...
AND WHAT WOULD THAT BE?

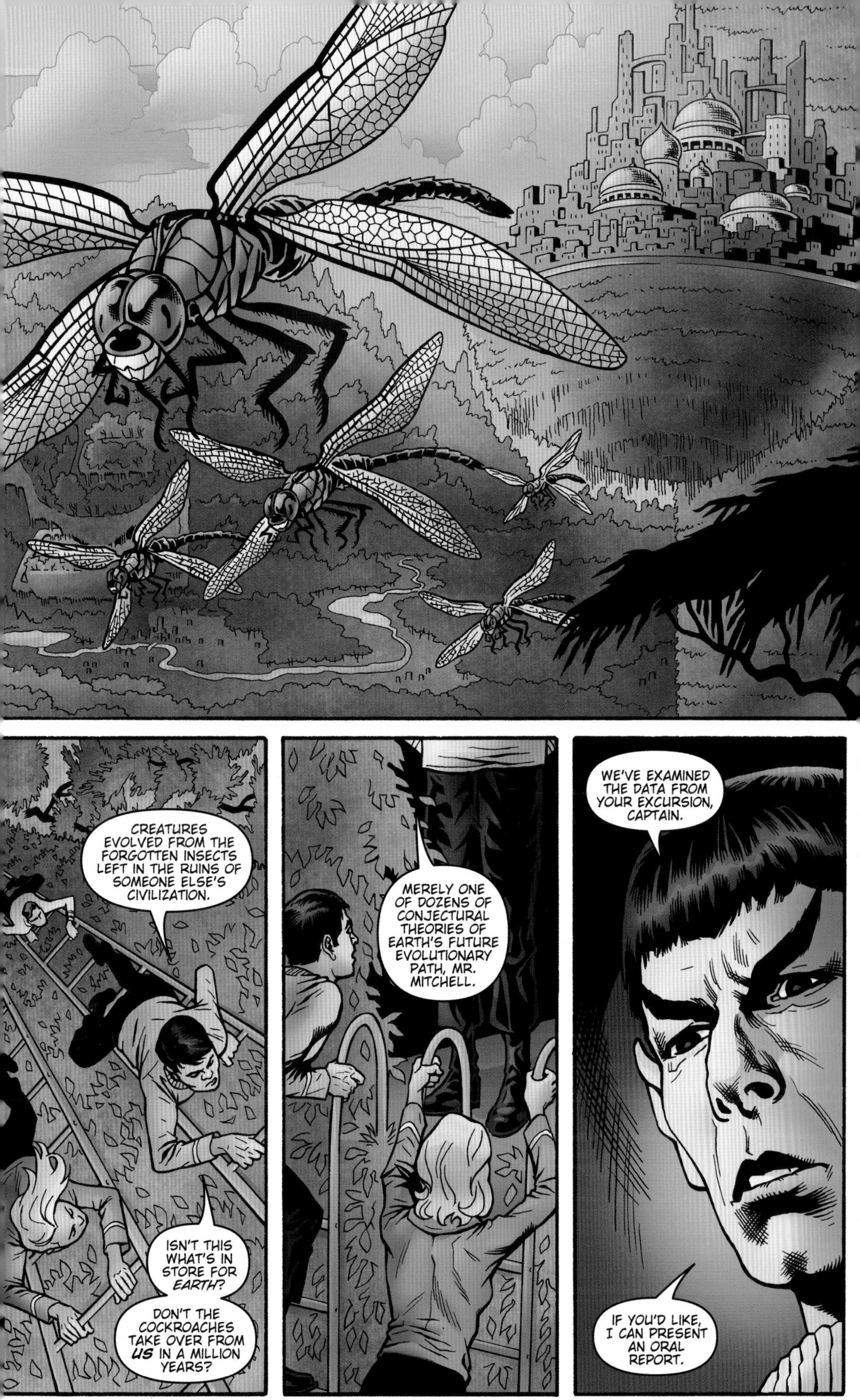
CREATURES EVOLVED FROM THE FORGOTTEN INSECTS LEFT IN THE RUINS OF SOMEONE ELSE'S CIVILIZATION.
ISN'T THIS WHAT'S IN STORE FOR *EARTH*?
DON'T THE COCKROACHES TAKE OVER FROM ***US*** IN A MILLION YEARS?
MERELY ONE OF DOZENS OF CONJECTURAL THEORIES OF EARTH'S FUTURE EVOLUTIONARY PATH, MR. MITCHELL.
WE'VE EXAMINED THE DATA FROM YOUR EXCURSION, CAPTAIN.
IF YOU'D LIKE, I CAN PRESENT AN ORAL REPORT.

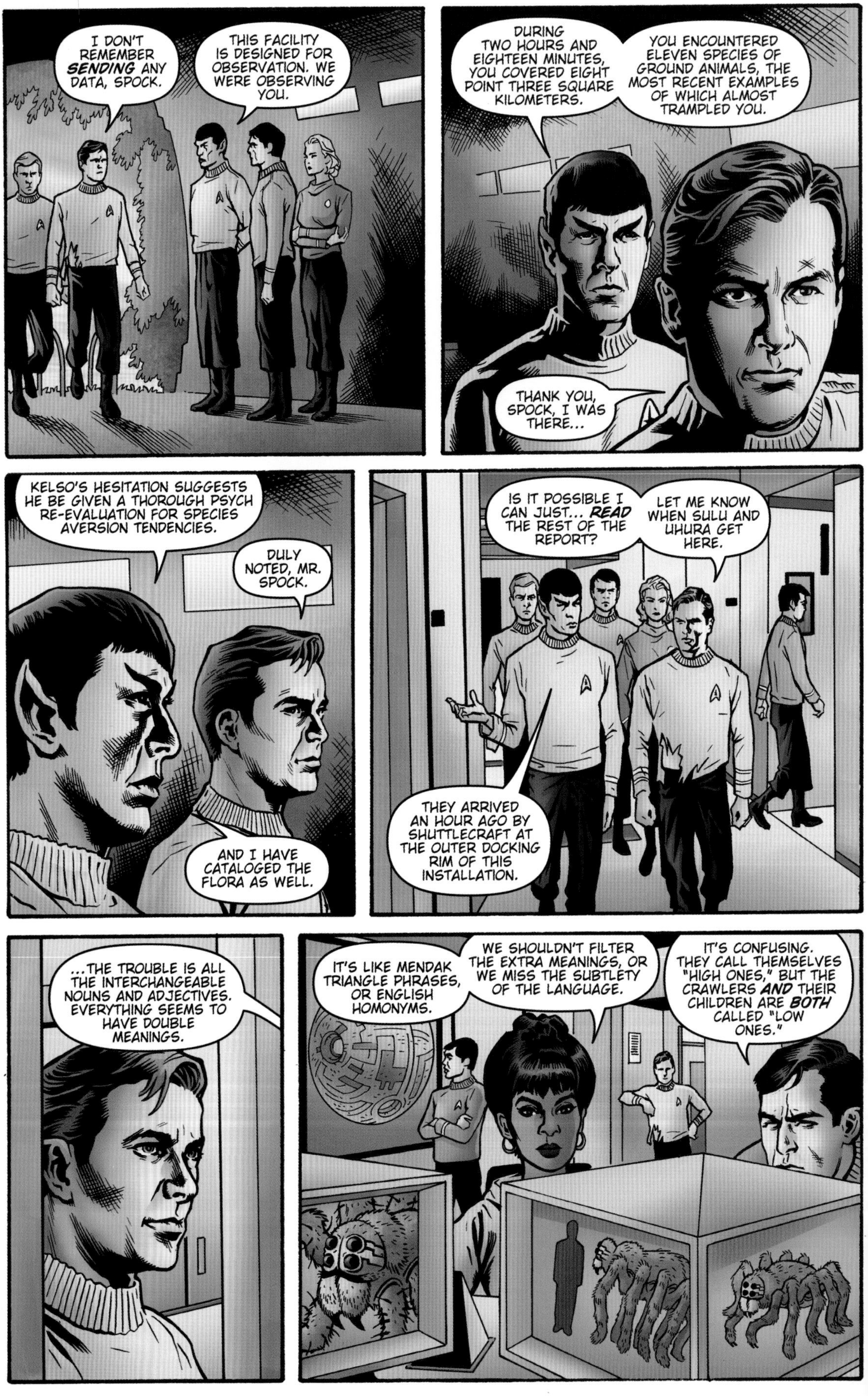

I DON'T REMEMBER SENDING ANY DATA, SPOCK.
THIS FACILITY IS DESIGNED FOR OBSERVATION. WE WERE OBSERVING YOU.
DURING TWO HOURS AND EIGHTEEN MINUTES, YOU COVERED EIGHT POINT THREE SQUARE KILOMETERS.
YOU ENCOUNTERED ELEVEN SPECIES OF GROUND ANIMALS, THE MOST RECENT EXAMPLES OF WHICH ALMOST TRAMPLED YOU.
THANK YOU, SPOCK, I WAS THERE...
KELSO'S HESITATION SUGGESTS HE BE GIVEN A THOROUGH PSYCH RE-EVALUATION FOR SPECIES AVERSION TENDENCIES.
DULY NOTED, MR. SPOCK.
AND I HAVE CATALOGED THE FLORA AS WELL.
IS IT POSSIBLE I CAN JUST... READ THE REST OF THE REPORT?
LET ME KNOW WHEN SULU AND UHURA GET HERE.
THEY ARRIVED AN HOUR AGO BY SHUTTLECRAFT AT THE OUTER DOCKING RIM OF THIS INSTALLATION.
...THE TROUBLE IS ALL THE INTERCHANGEABLE NOUNS AND ADJECTIVES. EVERYTHING SEEMS TO HAVE DOUBLE MEANINGS.
IT'S LIKE MENDAK TRIANGLE PHRASES, OR ENGLISH HOMONYMS.
WE SHOULDN'T FILTER THE EXTRA MEANINGS, OR WE MISS THE SUBTLETY OF THE LANGUAGE.
IT'S CONFUSING. THEY CALL THEMSELVES "HIGH ONES," BUT THE CRAWLERS AND THEIR CHILDREN ARE BOTH CALLED "LOW ONES."

IS THAT ABOUT SIZE OR STATUS? IT GOES TO ARCHERNARIAN PHILOSOPHY.

WHAT PHILOSOPHY DEVELOPS WHEN YOU EVOLVE INTO A WORLD THAT YOU CAN EASILY *TELL* HAS BEEN CONSTRUCTED?

THAT'S WHY WE'RE GOING TO MEET THEM TODAY. TO GET ANSWERS. TO FIND OUT WHY THE LIGHTS ARE STILL RUNNING, AND WHY THIS WORLD EVEN *EXISTS.*

CAPTAIN! I DIDN'T SEE YOU THERE...

THAT'S ALL RIGHT, LIEUTENANT. PLEASE FINISH.

WE'RE WRAPPING UP HERE, SIR. JUST SOME LAST-MINUTE ADJUSTMENTS TO THE UNIVERSAL TRANSLATOR LOGARITHMS.

THEN I'LL SEE YOU ALL WITH MEDI-KITS, HAND PHASERS AND TRICORDERS IN THE *SUTHERLAND* IN AN HOUR.

WE'LL TAKE NO CHANCES, THIS PLACE IS UNPREDICTABLE. BUT PHASERS ON *STUN*, THANK YOU.

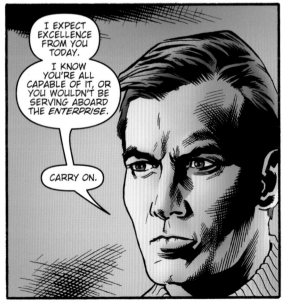

I EXPECT EXCELLENCE FROM YOU TODAY.

I KNOW YOU'RE ALL CAPABLE OF IT, OR YOU WOULDN'T BE SERVING ABOARD THE *ENTERPRISE.*

CARRY ON.

EVERYBODY SECURED?

AYE, SIR.

TAKE US OUT, MR. MITCHELL.

AND LET'S MAKE A SPECTACLE OF OURSELVES.

WE WANT TO BE SEEN IN THE SKIES BEFORE WE ARRIVE AT THE ARCHERNARIAN CAPITAL.

FREE OF GRAVITY AND MOVING OUT. PLEASE REPLY.

Sutherland

NIAGARA IS UP AS WELL, CAPTAIN KIRK.

I'VE BEEN WAITING TO DO THIS FOR *MONTHS*.

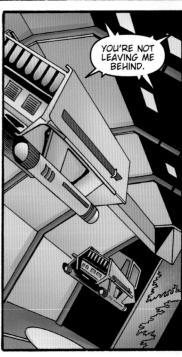

YOU'RE NOT LEAVING ME BEHIND.

Sutherland

WHOOSH

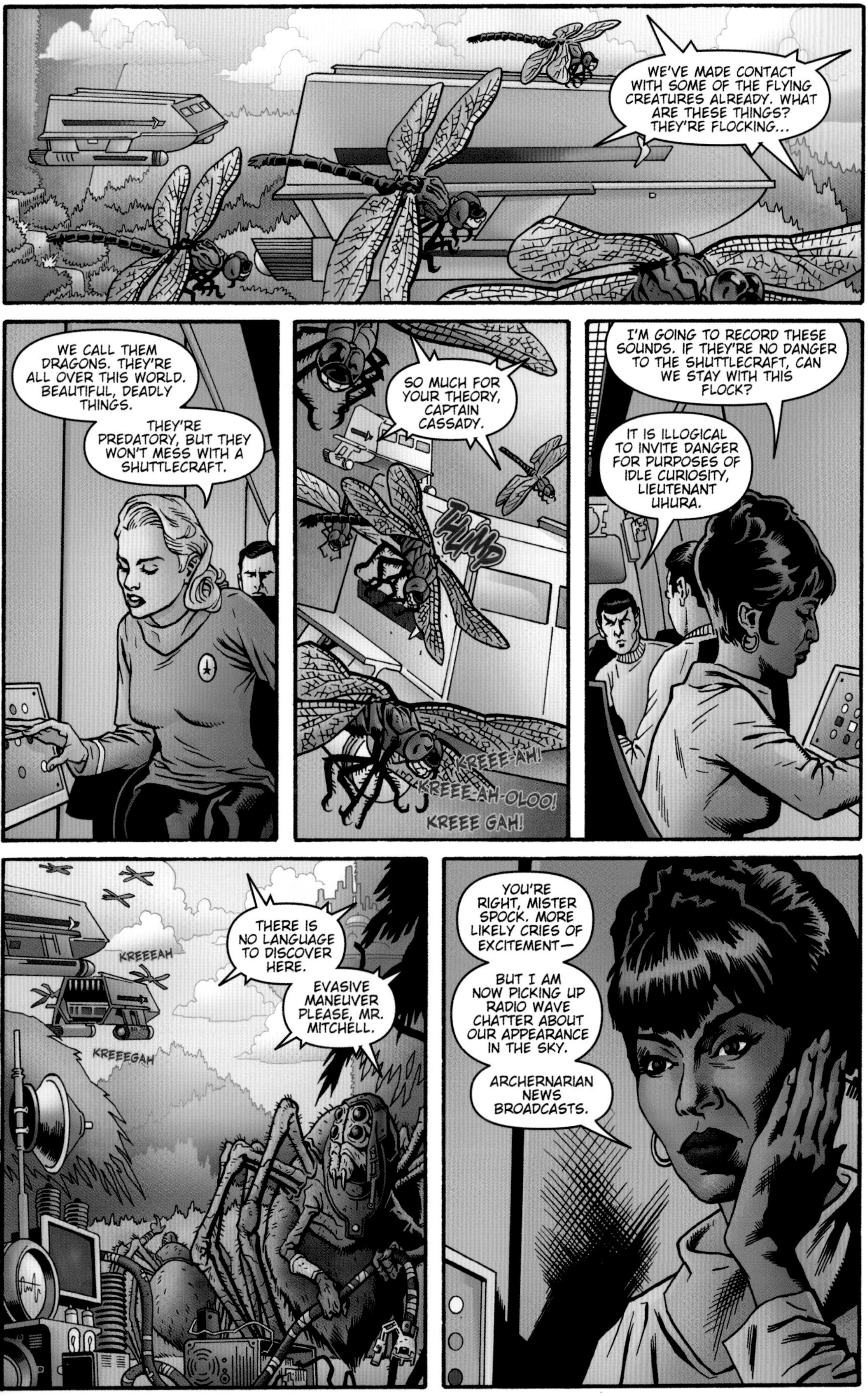

WE'VE MADE CONTACT WITH SOME OF THE FLYING CREATURES ALREADY. WHAT ARE THESE THINGS? THEY'RE FLOCKING...
WE CALL THEM DRAGONS. THEY'RE ALL OVER THIS WORLD. BEAUTIFUL, DEADLY THINGS.
THEY'RE PREDATORY, BUT THEY WON'T MESS WITH A SHUTTLECRAFT.
SO MUCH FOR YOUR THEORY, CAPTAIN CASSADY.
THUMP
KREEE-AH!
KREEE-AH-OLOO!
KREEE GAH!
I'M GOING TO RECORD THESE SOUNDS. IF THEY'RE NO DANGER TO THE SHUTTLECRAFT, CAN WE STAY WITH THIS FLOCK?
IT IS ILLOGICAL TO INVITE DANGER FOR PURPOSES OF IDLE CURIOSITY, LIEUTENANT UHURA.
KREEEAH
KREEEGAH
THERE IS NO LANGUAGE TO DISCOVER HERE.
EVASIVE MANEUVER PLEASE, MR. MITCHELL.
YOU'RE RIGHT, MISTER SPOCK. MORE LIKELY CRIES OF EXCITEMENT—
BUT I AM NOW PICKING UP RADIO WAVE CHATTER ABOUT OUR APPEARANCE IN THE SKY.
ARCHERNARIAN NEWS BROADCASTS.

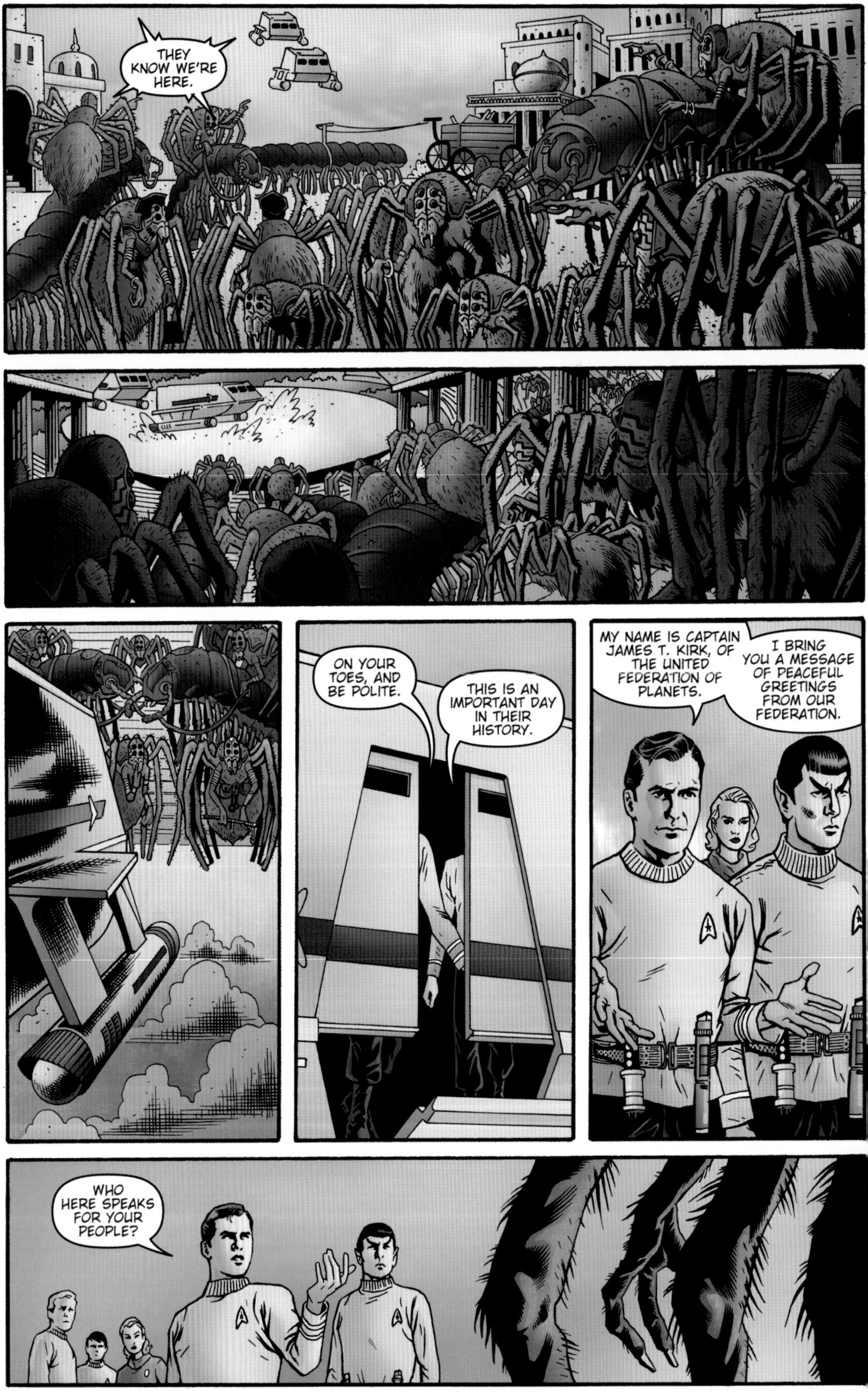
THEY KNOW WE'RE HERE.
ON YOUR TOES, AND BE POLITE.
THIS IS AN IMPORTANT DAY IN THEIR HISTORY.
MY NAME IS CAPTAIN JAMES T. KIRK, OF THE UNITED FEDERATION OF PLANETS.
I BRING YOU A MESSAGE OF PEACEFUL GREETINGS FROM OUR FEDERATION.
WHO HERE SPEAKS FOR YOUR PEOPLE?

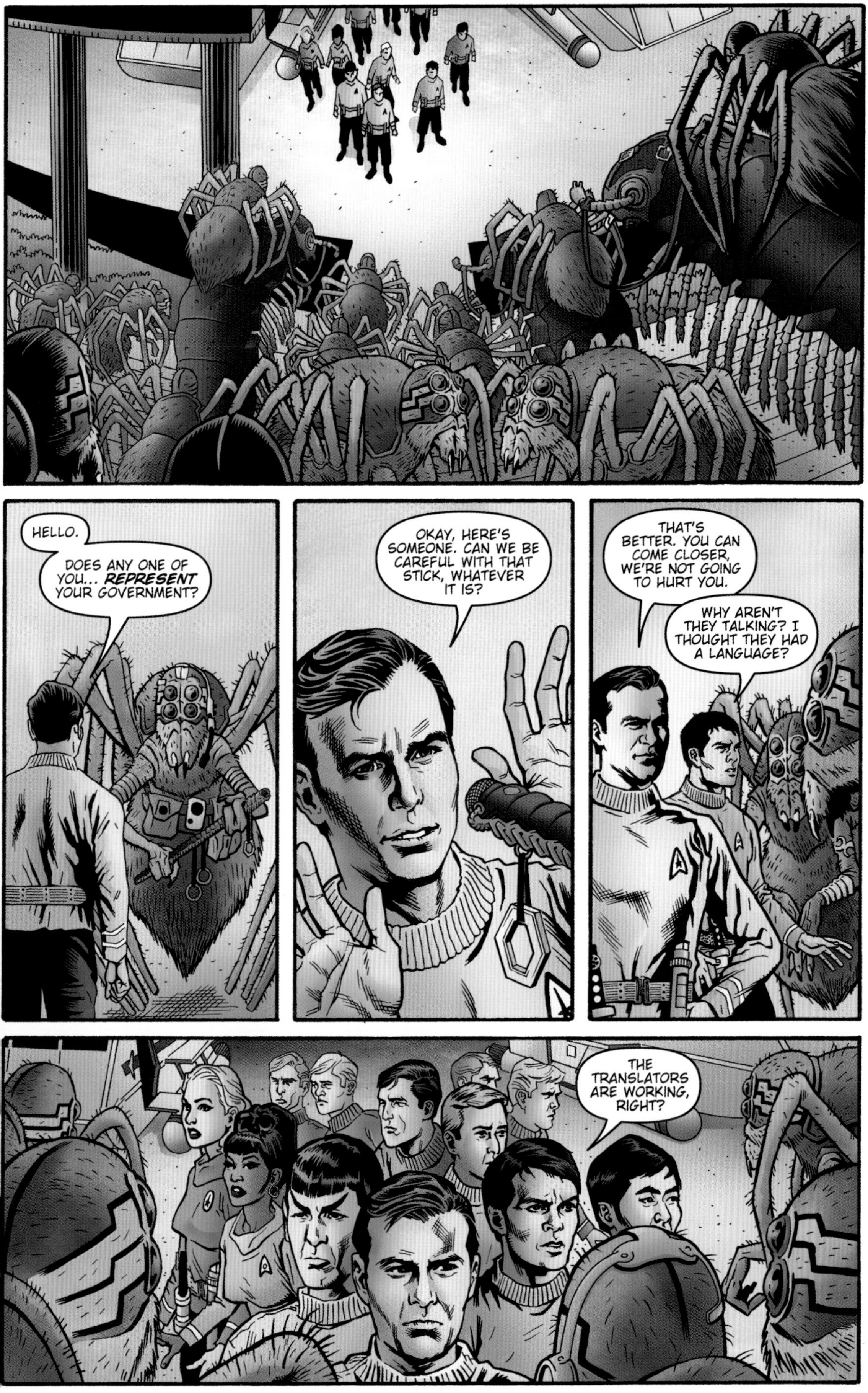
HELLO.
DOES ANY ONE OF YOU... ***REPRESENT*** YOUR GOVERNMENT?
OKAY, HERE'S SOMEONE. CAN WE BE CAREFUL WITH THAT STICK, WHATEVER IT IS?
THAT'S BETTER. YOU CAN COME CLOSER, WE'RE NOT GOING TO HURT YOU.
WHY AREN'T THEY TALKING? I THOUGHT THEY HAD A LANGUAGE?
THE TRANSLATORS ARE WORKING, RIGHT?

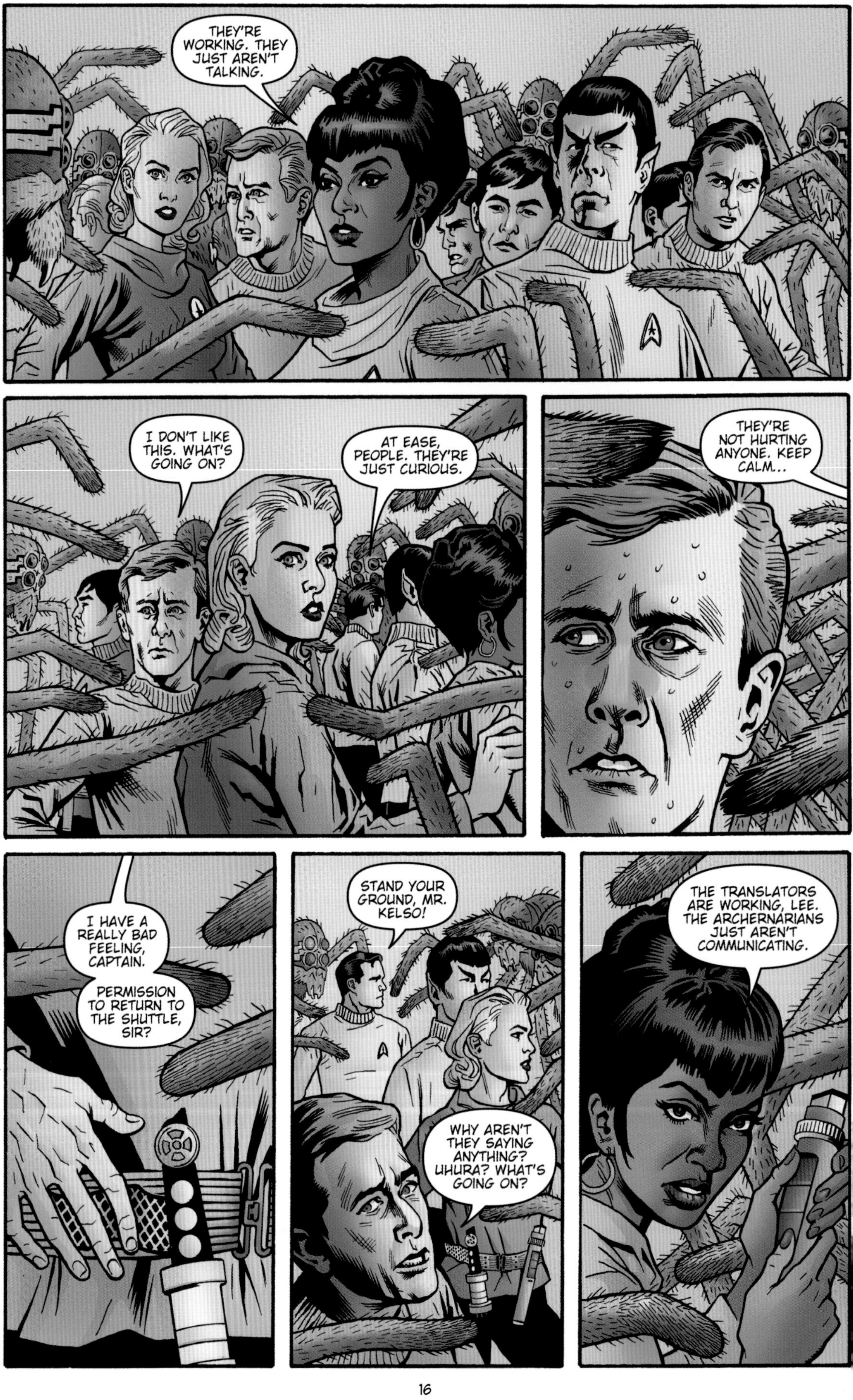
THEY'RE WORKING. THEY JUST AREN'T TALKING.
I DON'T LIKE THIS. WHAT'S GOING ON?
AT EASE, PEOPLE. THEY'RE JUST CURIOUS.
THEY'RE NOT HURTING ANYONE. KEEP CALM...
I HAVE A REALLY BAD FEELING, CAPTAIN.
PERMISSION TO RETURN TO THE SHUTTLE, SIR?
STAND YOUR GROUND, MR. KELSO!
WHY AREN'T THEY SAYING ANYTHING? UHURA? WHAT'S GOING ON?
THE TRANSLATORS ARE WORKING, LEE. THE ARCHERNARIANS JUST AREN'T COMMUNICATING.

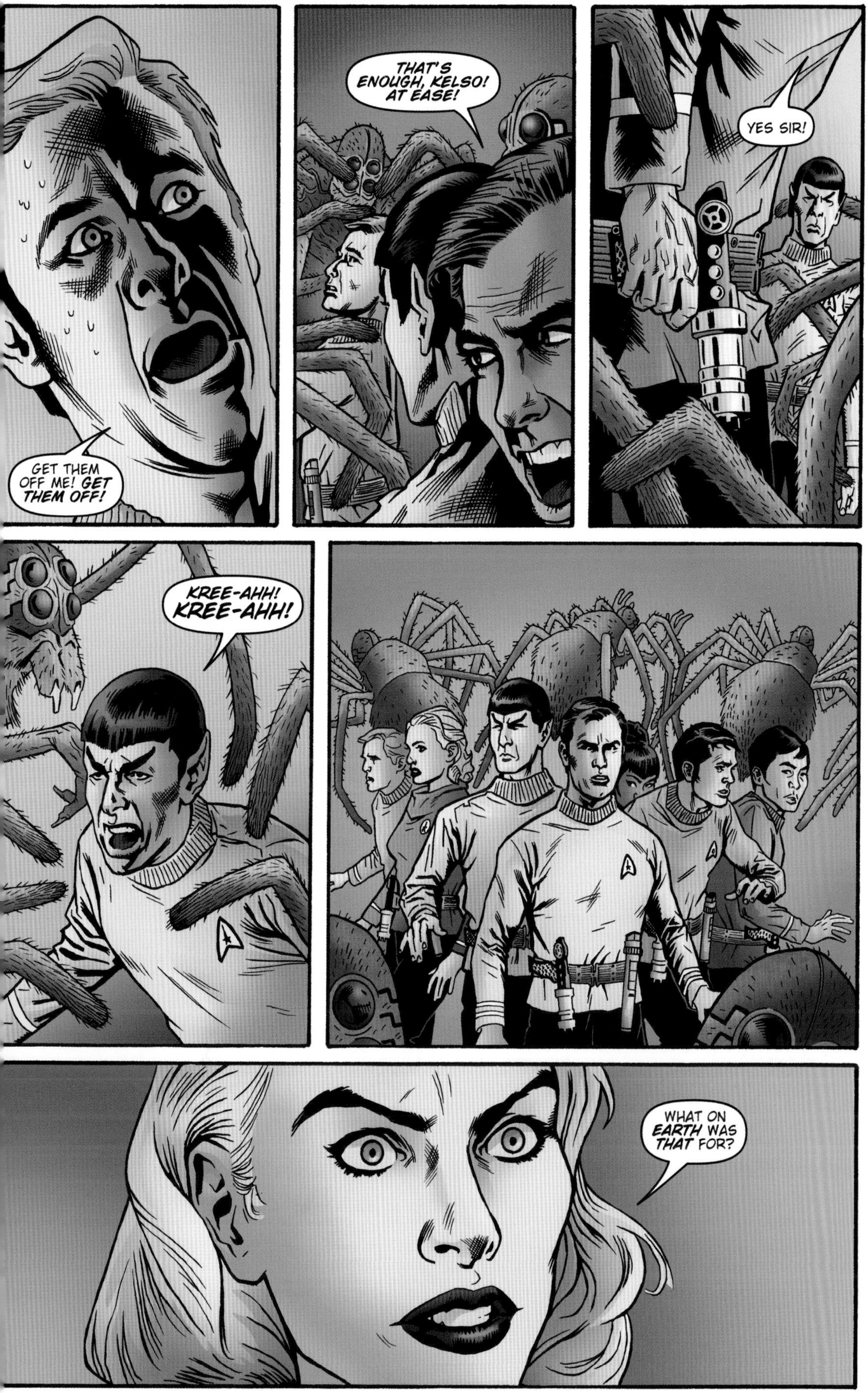
GET THEM OFF ME! GET THEM OFF!
THAT'S ENOUGH, KELSO! AT EASE!
YES SIR!
KREE-AHH! KREE-AHH!
WHAT ON EARTH WAS THAT FOR?

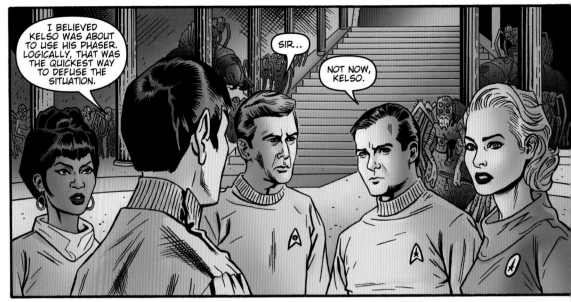

I BELIEVED KELSO WAS ABOUT TO USE HIS PHASER. LOGICALLY, THAT WAS THE QUICKEST WAY TO DEFUSE THE SITUATION.

SIR...

NOT NOW, KELSO.

AND FOLLOWING LOGIC, I APPROXIMATED THE CRY OF THE PREDATORY WINGED CREATURES WE ENCOUNTERED, AS I BELIEVE THAT SOUND TO BE—

NOT *NOW*, SPOCK.

WE ARE CREATURES OF PEACE. FROM THE UNITED FEDERATION OF PLANETS.

SMALL AND LOW ONES IN YOUR EYES. PLEASE FORGIVE US THAT FRIGHTENING SOUND, AND SPEAK TO US.

YOU... ARE LOW? FROM BEYOND OUTSIDE? OTHER WORLDS?

YES, THAT'S RIGHT. WE'RE FROM OUTSIDE THIS WORLD. THERE ARE OTHER WORLDS BESIDES THIS ONE.

FIRST OF GREAT LESSONS SINCE I AM CHILD. WE ALL KNOW. TEN GENERATIONS HAVE SEEN STARS. SHIPS BEEN OUTSIDE.

UNEXPECTED YOUR APPEARANCE IS. BUT WELCOME, ALIEN LOWS.

18

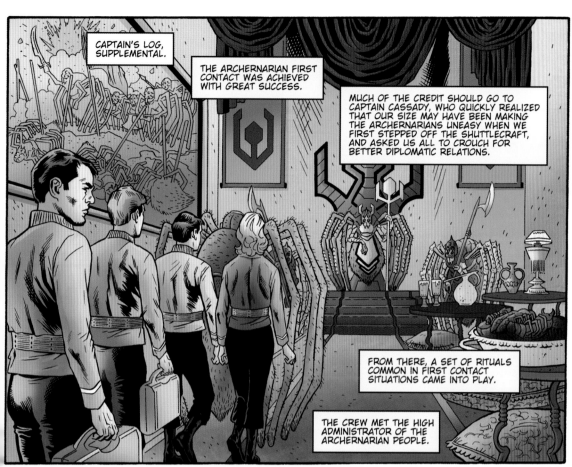

CAPTAIN'S LOG, SUPPLEMENTAL.

THE ARCHERNARIAN FIRST CONTACT WAS ACHIEVED WITH GREAT SUCCESS.

MUCH OF THE CREDIT SHOULD GO TO CAPTAIN CASSADY, WHO QUICKLY REALIZED THAT OUR SIZE MAY HAVE BEEN MAKING THE ARCHERNARIANS UNEASY WHEN WE FIRST STEPPED OFF THE SHUTTLECRAFT, AND ASKED US ALL TO CROUCH FOR BETTER DIPLOMATIC RELATIONS.

FROM THERE, A SET OF RITUALS COMMON IN FIRST CONTACT SITUATIONS CAME INTO PLAY.

THE CREW MET THE HIGH ADMINISTRATOR OF THE ARCHERNARIAN PEOPLE.

GIFTS WERE EXCHANGED...

AND A FEAST WAS HELD IN OUR HONOR.

DOCTOR PIPER EXAMINED THE FOOD AND DETERMINED THAT FIRST OFFICER SPOCK IS ALLERGIC TO IT, BUT THE REST OF THE CREW IS NOT.

SO, TO GIVE SPOCK SOMETHING TO DO WHILE THE CREW ENJOYED AN INTERESTING MEAL, I TOLD HIM TO ACCEPT AN OFFER TO TOUR THE ARCHERNARIAN HOLY SITE—A PLACE THEY CALL "THE HEART OF GOD."

IT WILL DO HIS ANALYTICAL MIND SOME GOOD TO STUDY ILLOGIC AND FAITH FOR A CHANGE.

HE COULD USE THE BALANCE.

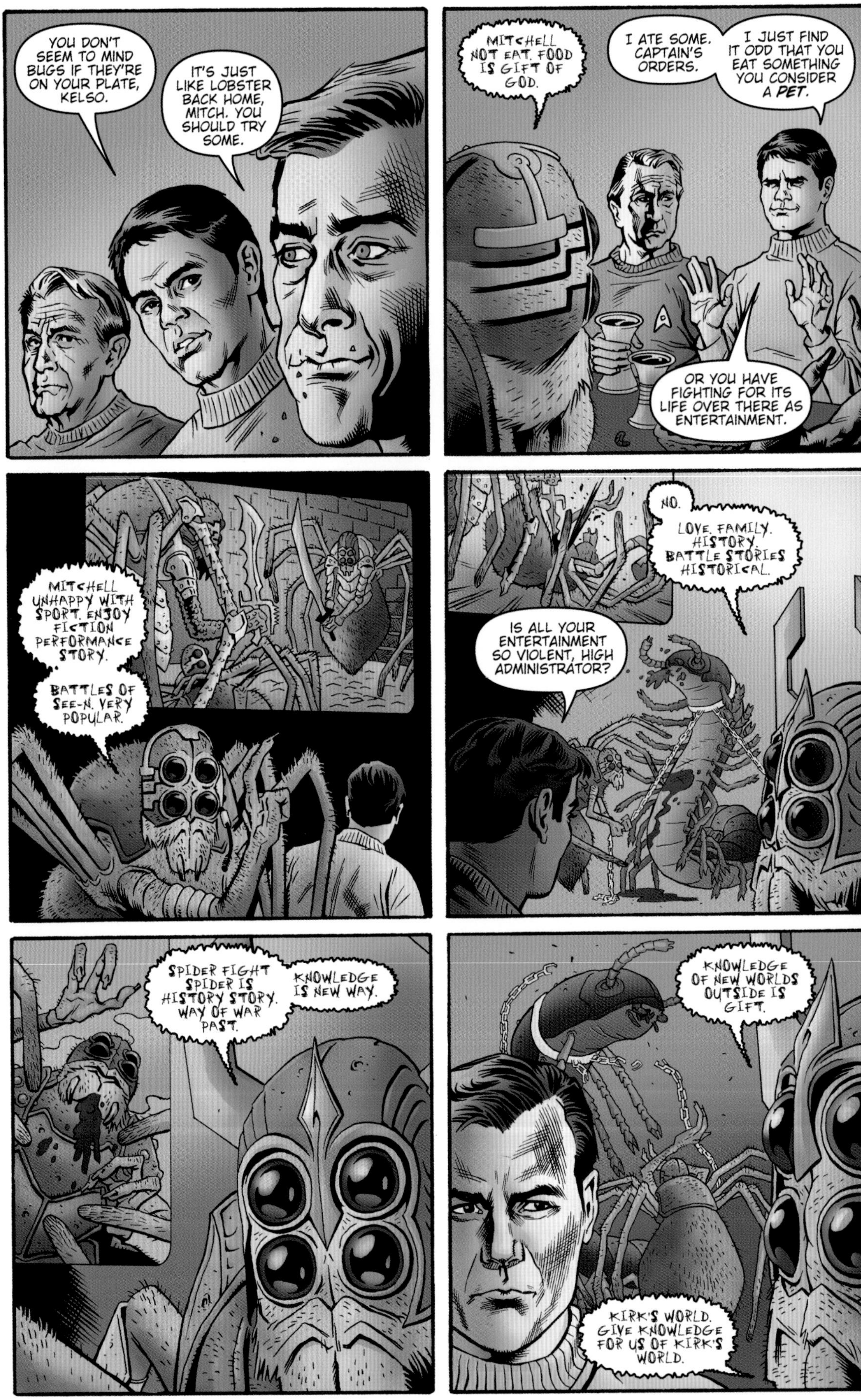

YOU DON'T SEEM TO MIND BUGS IF THEY'RE ON YOUR PLATE, KELSO.
IT'S JUST LIKE LOBSTER BACK HOME, MITCH. YOU SHOULD TRY SOME.
MITCHELL NOT EAT. FOOD IS GIFT OF GOD.
I ATE SOME. CAPTAIN'S ORDERS.
I JUST FIND IT ODD THAT YOU EAT SOMETHING YOU CONSIDER A *PET*.
OR YOU HAVE FIGHTING FOR ITS LIFE OVER THERE AS ENTERTAINMENT.
MITCHELL UNHAPPY WITH SPORT. ENJOY FICTION PERFORMANCE STORY.
BATTLES OF SEE-N. VERY POPULAR.
IS ALL YOUR ENTERTAINMENT SO VIOLENT, HIGH ADMINISTRATOR?
NO.
LOVE. FAMILY. HISTORY. BATTLE STORIES HISTORICAL.
SPIDER FIGHT SPIDER IS HISTORY STORY. WAY OF WAR PAST.
KNOWLEDGE IS NEW WAY.
KNOWLEDGE OF NEW WORLDS OUTSIDE IS GIFT.
KIRK'S WORLD. GIVE KNOWLEDGE FOR US OF KIRK'S WORLD.

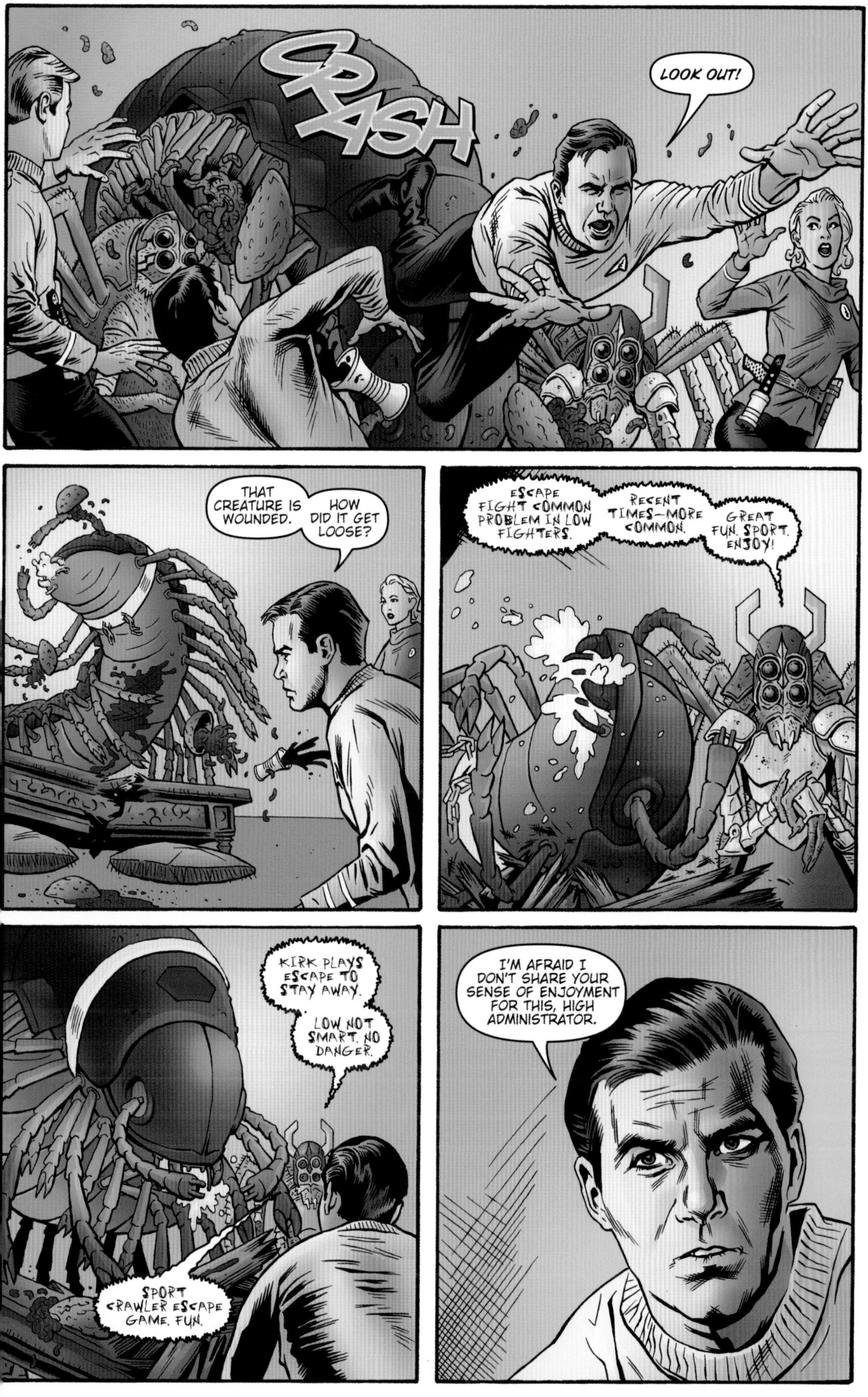
CRASH
LOOK OUT!
THAT CREATURE IS WOUNDED.
HOW DID IT GET LOOSE?
ESCAPE FIGHT COMMON PROBLEM IN LOW FIGHTERS.
RECENT TIMES—MORE COMMON.
GREAT FUN. SPORT. ENJOY!
KIRK PLAYS ESCAPE TO STAY AWAY.
LOW NOT SMART. NO DANGER.
SPORT CRAWLER ESCAPE GAME. FUN.
I'M AFRAID I DON'T SHARE YOUR SENSE OF ENJOYMENT FOR THIS, HIGH ADMINISTRATOR.

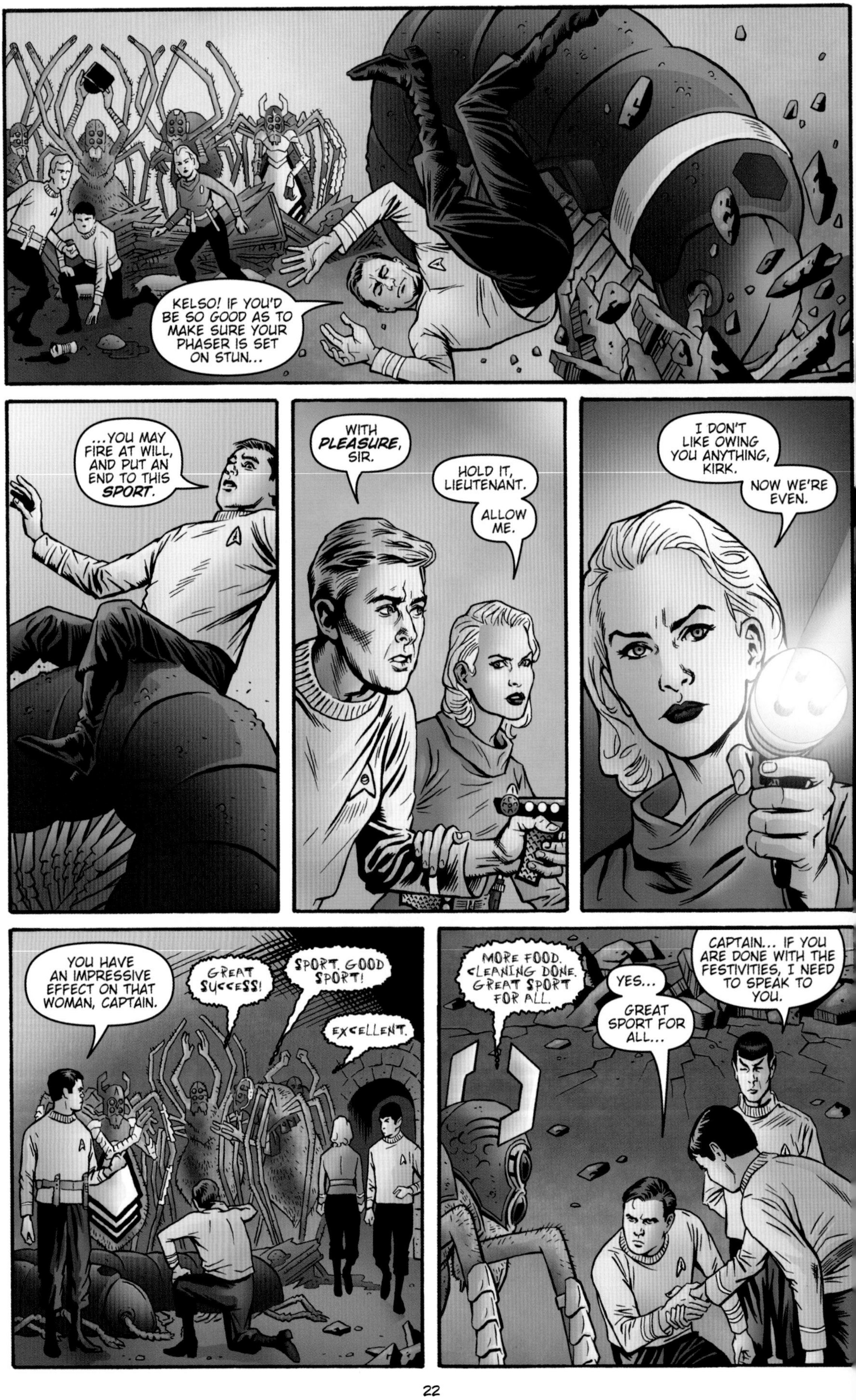
KELSO! IF YOU'D BE SO GOOD AS TO MAKE SURE YOUR PHASER IS SET ON STUN...
...YOU MAY FIRE AT WILL, AND PUT AN END TO THIS SPORT.
WITH PLEASURE, SIR.
HOLD IT, LIEUTENANT.
ALLOW ME.
I DON'T LIKE OWING YOU ANYTHING, KIRK.
NOW WE'RE EVEN.
YOU HAVE AN IMPRESSIVE EFFECT ON THAT WOMAN, CAPTAIN.
GREAT SUCCESS!
SPORT. GOOD SPORT!
EXCELLENT.
MORE FOOD. CLEANING DONE. GREAT SPORT FOR ALL.
YES...
GREAT SPORT FOR ALL...
CAPTAIN... IF YOU ARE DONE WITH THE FESTIVITIES, I NEED TO SPEAK TO YOU.

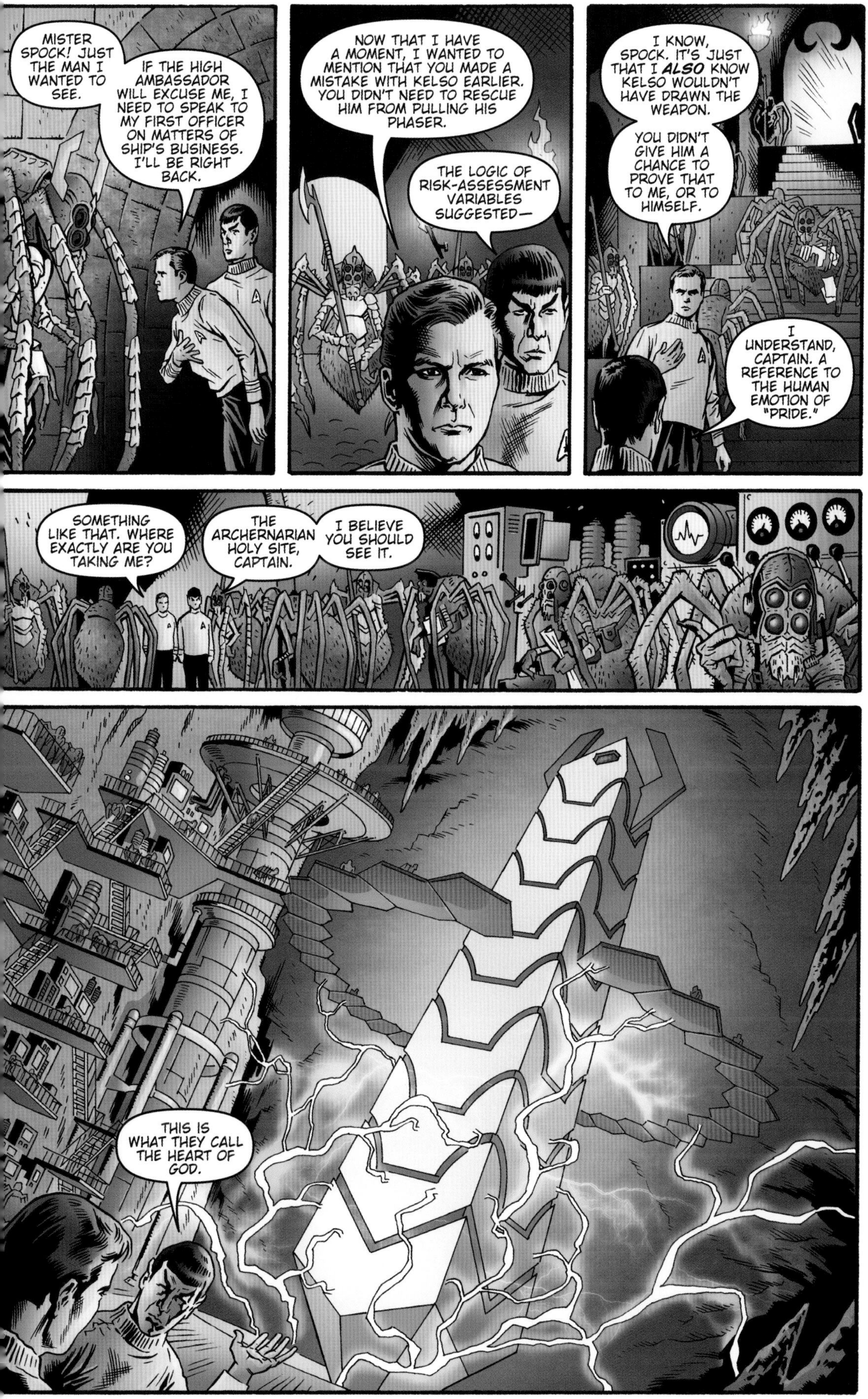
MISTER SPOCK! JUST THE MAN I WANTED TO SEE.
IF THE HIGH AMBASSADOR WILL EXCUSE ME, I NEED TO SPEAK TO MY FIRST OFFICER ON MATTERS OF SHIP'S BUSINESS. I'LL BE RIGHT BACK.
NOW THAT I HAVE A MOMENT, I WANTED TO MENTION THAT YOU MADE A MISTAKE WITH KELSO EARLIER. YOU DIDN'T NEED TO RESCUE HIM FROM PULLING HIS PHASER.
THE LOGIC OF RISK-ASSESSMENT VARIABLES SUGGESTED—
I KNOW, SPOCK. IT'S JUST THAT I ***ALSO*** KNOW KELSO WOULDN'T HAVE DRAWN THE WEAPON.
YOU DIDN'T GIVE HIM A CHANCE TO PROVE THAT TO ME, OR TO HIMSELF.
I UNDERSTAND, CAPTAIN. A REFERENCE TO THE HUMAN EMOTION OF "PRIDE."
SOMETHING LIKE THAT. WHERE EXACTLY ARE YOU TAKING ME?
THE ARCHERNARIAN HOLY SITE, CAPTAIN.
I BELIEVE YOU SHOULD SEE IT.
THIS IS WHAT THEY CALL THE HEART OF GOD.

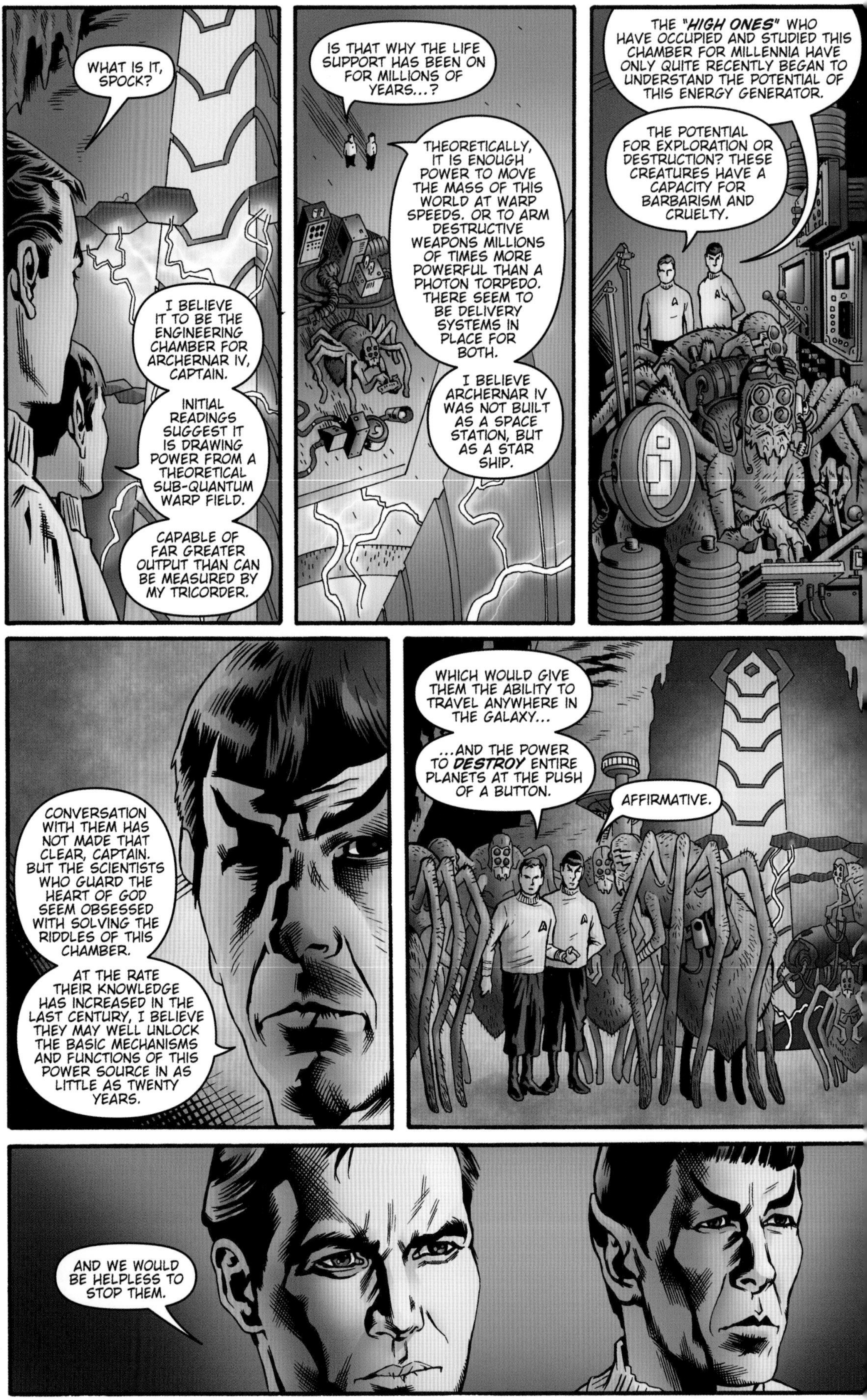
WHAT IS IT, SPOCK?
I BELIEVE IT TO BE THE ENGINEERING CHAMBER FOR ARCHERNAR IV, CAPTAIN.
INITIAL READINGS SUGGEST IT IS DRAWING POWER FROM A THEORETICAL SUB-QUANTUM WARP FIELD.
CAPABLE OF FAR GREATER OUTPUT THAN CAN BE MEASURED BY MY TRICORDER.
IS THAT WHY THE LIFE SUPPORT HAS BEEN ON FOR MILLIONS OF YEARS...?
THEORETICALLY, IT IS ENOUGH POWER TO MOVE THE MASS OF THIS WORLD AT WARP SPEEDS. OR TO ARM DESTRUCTIVE WEAPONS MILLIONS OF TIMES MORE POWERFUL THAN A PHOTON TORPEDO. THERE SEEM TO BE DELIVERY SYSTEMS IN PLACE FOR BOTH.
I BELIEVE ARCHERNAR IV WAS NOT BUILT AS A SPACE STATION, BUT AS A STAR SHIP.
THE "HIGH ONES" WHO HAVE OCCUPIED AND STUDIED THIS CHAMBER FOR MILLENNIA HAVE ONLY QUITE RECENTLY BEGAN TO UNDERSTAND THE POTENTIAL OF THIS ENERGY GENERATOR.
THE POTENTIAL FOR EXPLORATION OR DESTRUCTION? THESE CREATURES HAVE A CAPACITY FOR BARBARISM AND CRUELTY.
CONVERSATION WITH THEM HAS NOT MADE THAT CLEAR, CAPTAIN. BUT THE SCIENTISTS WHO GUARD THE HEART OF GOD SEEM OBSESSED WITH SOLVING THE RIDDLES OF THIS CHAMBER.
AT THE RATE THEIR KNOWLEDGE HAS INCREASED IN THE LAST CENTURY, I BELIEVE THEY MAY WELL UNLOCK THE BASIC MECHANISMS AND FUNCTIONS OF THIS POWER SOURCE IN AS LITTLE AS TWENTY YEARS.
WHICH WOULD GIVE THEM THE ABILITY TO TRAVEL ANYWHERE IN THE GALAXY...
...AND THE POWER TO DESTROY ENTIRE PLANETS AT THE PUSH OF A BUTTON.
AFFIRMATIVE.
AND WE WOULD BE HELPLESS TO STOP THEM.

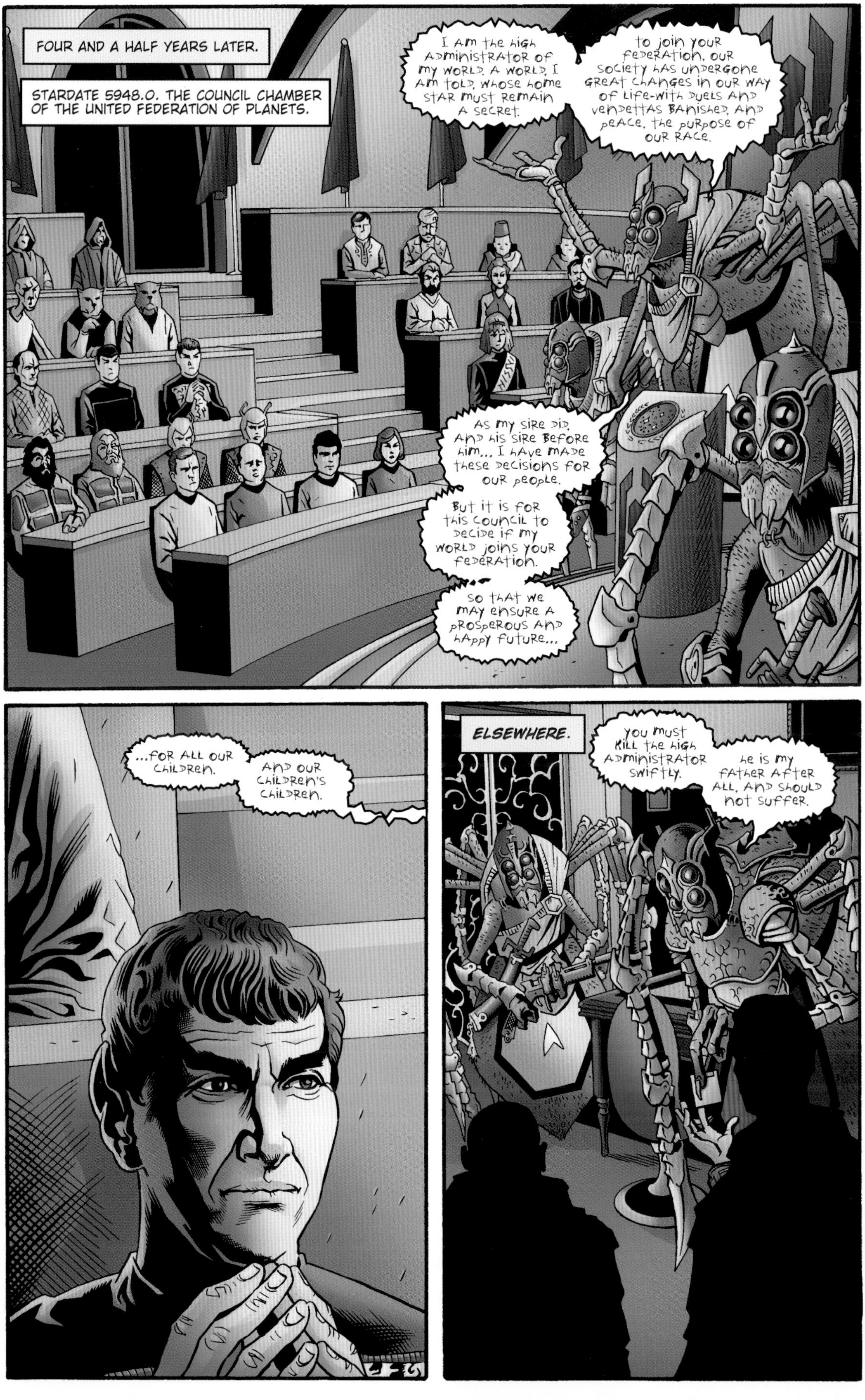
FOUR AND A HALF YEARS LATER.
STARDATE 5948.0. THE COUNCIL CHAMBER OF THE UNITED FEDERATION OF PLANETS.
I AM THE HIGH ADMINISTRATOR OF MY WORLD. A WORLD, I AM TOLD, WHOSE HOME STAR MUST REMAIN A SECRET.
TO JOIN YOUR FEDERATION, OUR SOCIETY HAS UNDERGONE GREAT CHANGES IN OUR WAY OF LIFE--WITH DUELS AND VENDETTAS BANISHED, AND PEACE, THE PURPOSE OF OUR RACE.
AS MY SIRE DID, AND HIS SIRE BEFORE HIM... I HAVE MADE THESE DECISIONS FOR OUR PEOPLE.
BUT IT IS FOR THIS COUNCIL TO DECIDE IF MY WORLD JOINS YOUR FEDERATION.
SO THAT WE MAY ENSURE A PROSPEROUS AND HAPPY FUTURE...
...FOR ALL OUR CHILDREN.
AND OUR CHILDREN'S CHILDREN.
ELSEWHERE.
YOU MUST KILL THE HIGH ADMINISTRATOR SWIFTLY.
HE IS MY FATHER AFTER ALL, AND SHOULD NOT SUFFER.

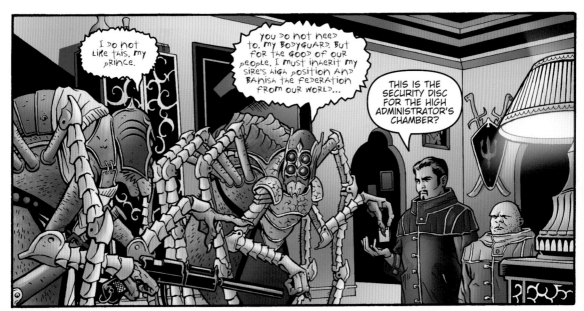

I DO NOT LIKE THIS, MY PRINCE.

YOU DO NOT NEED TO, MY BODYGUARD. BUT FOR THE GOOD OF OUR PEOPLE, I MUST INHERIT MY SIRE'S HIGH POSITION AND BANISH THE FEDERATION FROM OUR WORLD...

THIS IS THE SECURITY DISC FOR THE HIGH ADMINISTRATOR'S CHAMBER?

YES, EARTH-MAN. AND I REMIND YOU, THIS MUST APPEAR TO BE A FEDERATION CRIME.

THE ANTI-FEDERATIONALISTS OF MY WORLD ARE SCIENTISTS AND SCHOLARS, STILL ONLY A SMALL PERCENTAGE OF MY PEOPLE.

BUT IF HUMANS WERE SEEN TO KILL THE HIGH ADMINISTRATOR, ALL MY PEOPLE WILL BE DRAWN TO MY CAUSE.

THAT'S FINE. MY ORGANIZATION BELIEVES THE FEDERATION DOESN'T NEED THE BURDENS OF AN UNDERDEVELOPED BACKWATER RIGHT NOW. IT'S WHY WE *CAME* TO YOU WITH THIS PLAN.

THAT, AND THE HIGH REWARD YOU WILL RECEIVE. BUT OUR WORLD IS NOT SO BURDENSOME AS YOU MIGHT THINK.

YEAH. I HEAR RUMORS.

CLASSIFIED STUFF... DILITHIUM OR SOMETHING. NO ONE'S EVEN ALLOWED TO KNOW WHERE YOUR PLANET IS!

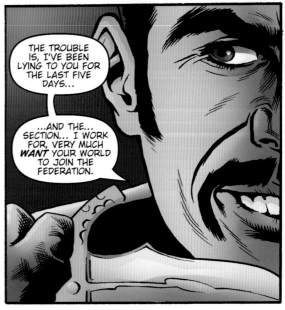

THE TROUBLE IS, I'VE BEEN LYING TO YOU FOR THE LAST FIVE DAYS...

...AND THE... SECTION... I WORK FOR, VERY MUCH *WANT* YOUR WORLD TO JOIN THE FEDERATION.

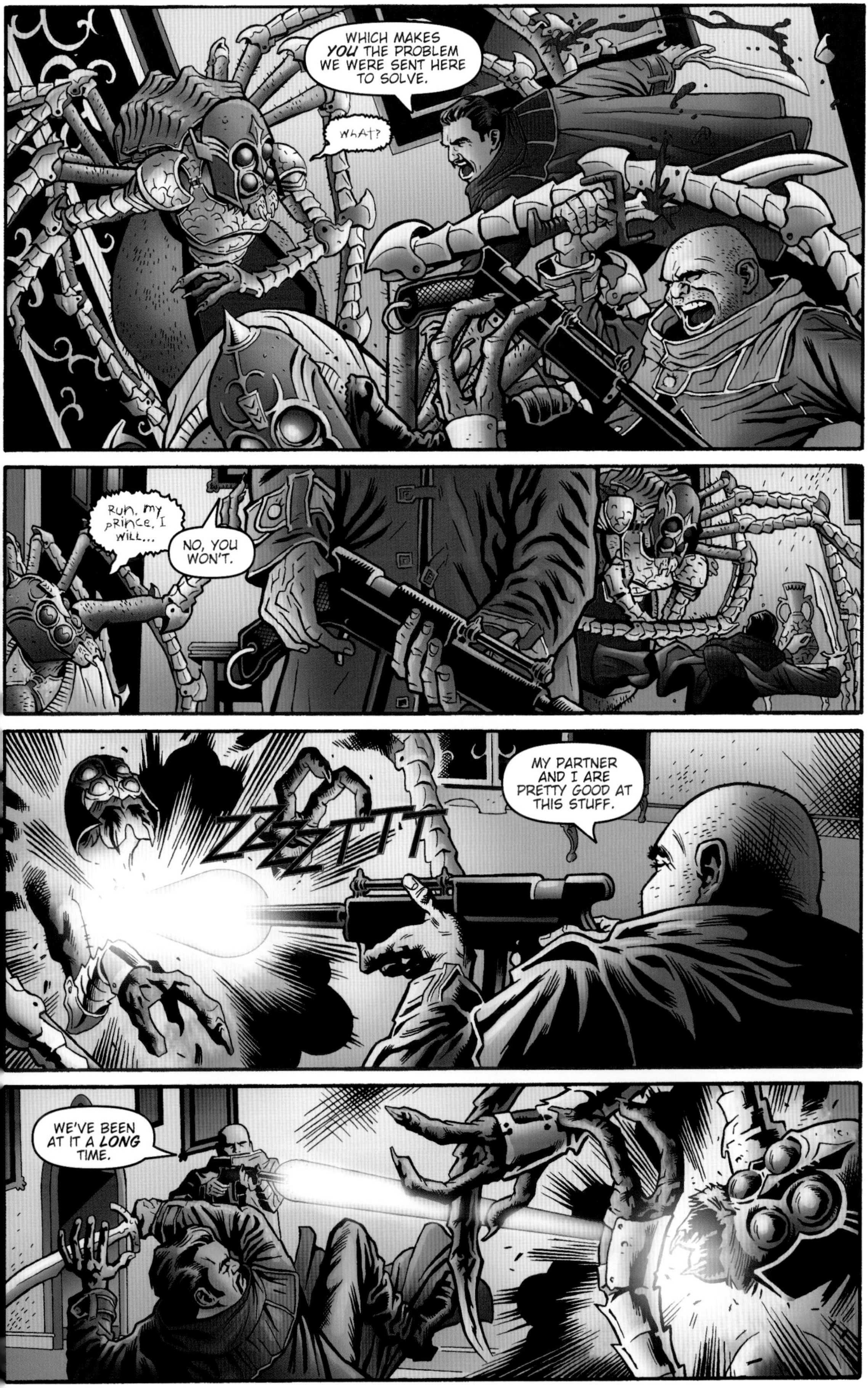

WHICH MAKES YOU THE PROBLEM WE WERE SENT HERE TO SOLVE.
WHAT?
RUN, MY PRINCE, I WILL...
NO, YOU WON'T.
ZZZZTTTT
MY PARTNER AND I ARE PRETTY GOOD AT THIS STUFF.
WE'VE BEEN AT IT A LONG TIME.

SET THAT MESS UP TO LOOK LIKE A DUEL GONE BAD. THESE CREATURES STILL *DO* THAT... WHATEVER THEIR NEW LAWS TELL THEM.
I'M TAKING A QUICK PEEK AT THIS DISC. YOU NEVER KNOW WHAT'S IN THE ROYAL FILES.
OH.
THIS IS *SO* MUCH BETTER THAN A FEW DILITHIUM ROCKS.
REALLY? WHAT DID YOU FIND?
INFORMATION THAT I COULD SELL FOR A *LOT* OF MONEY.
I'M NOT SHARING, I'M AFRAID.
WHAT?
AND NOW THAT IT DOESN'T MATTER...
...I CAN TELL YOU I'VE BEEN SLEEPING WITH YOUR WIFE FOR YEARS.
ZAAP
AHH!

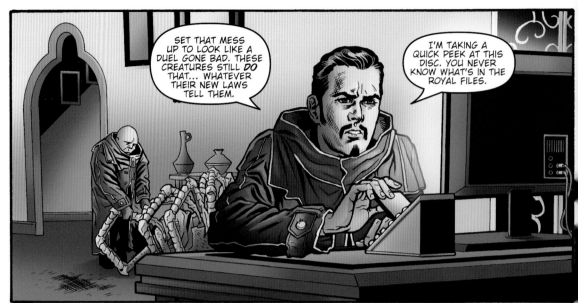

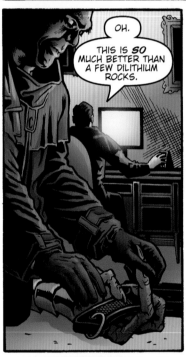

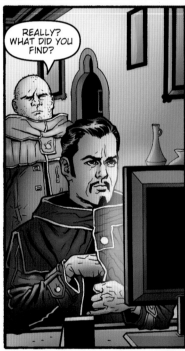

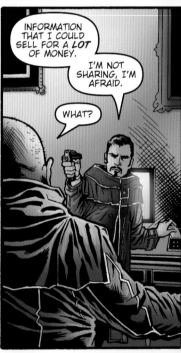

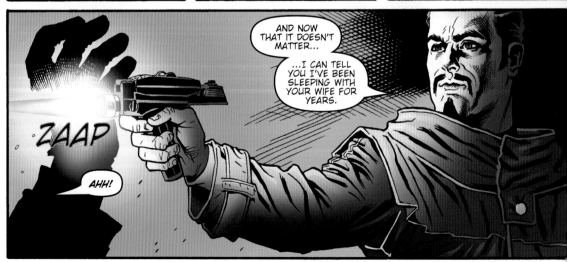

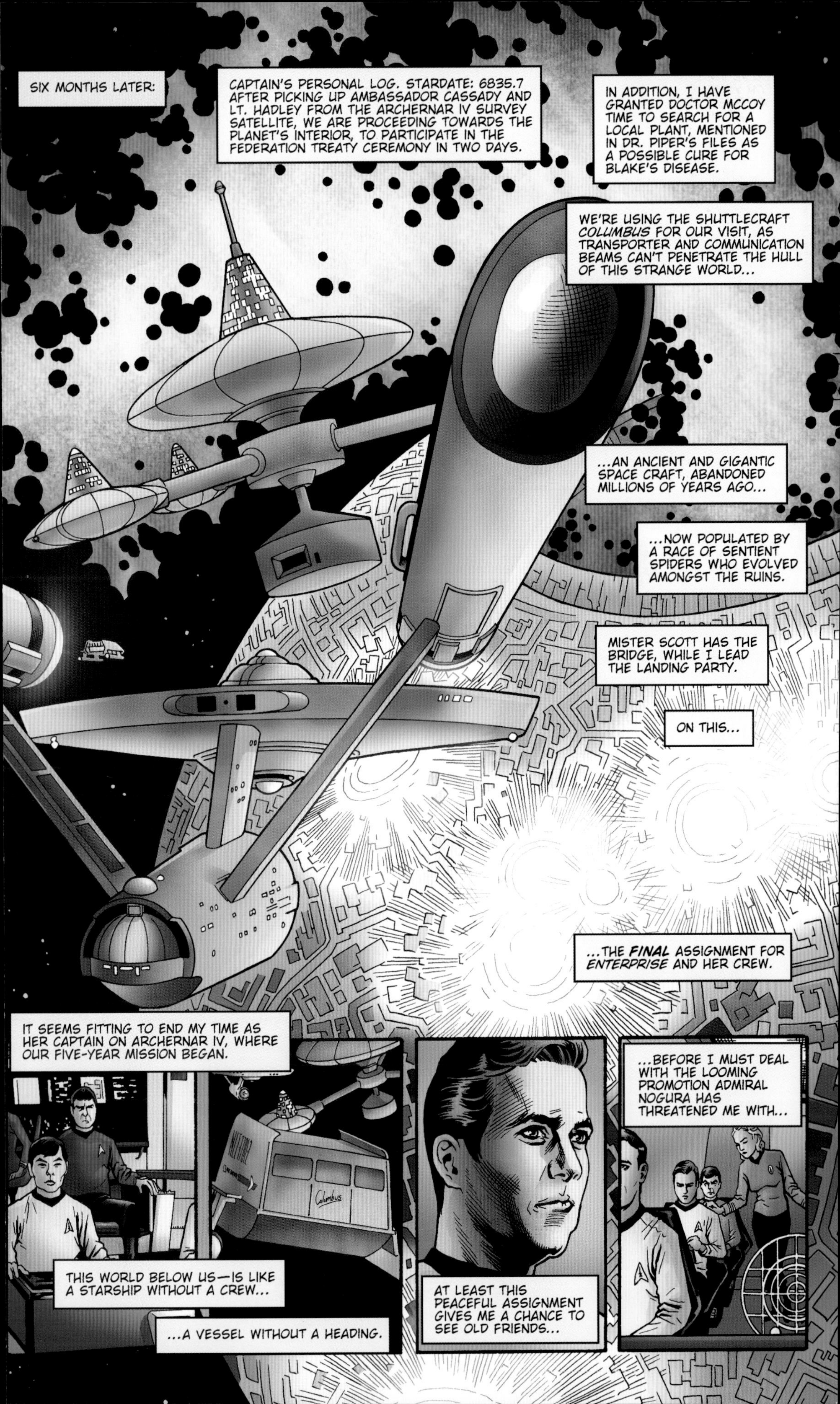
SIX MONTHS LATER:
CAPTAIN'S PERSONAL LOG. STARDATE: 6835.7 AFTER PICKING UP AMBASSADOR CASSADY AND LT. HADLEY FROM THE ARCHERNAR IV SURVEY SATELLITE, WE ARE PROCEEDING TOWARDS THE PLANET'S INTERIOR, TO PARTICIPATE IN THE FEDERATION TREATY CEREMONY IN TWO DAYS.
IN ADDITION, I HAVE GRANTED DOCTOR MCCOY TIME TO SEARCH FOR A LOCAL PLANT, MENTIONED IN DR. PIPER'S FILES AS A POSSIBLE CURE FOR BLAKE'S DISEASE.
WE'RE USING THE SHUTTLECRAFT *COLUMBUS* FOR OUR VISIT, AS TRANSPORTER AND COMMUNICATION BEAMS CAN'T PENETRATE THE HULL OF THIS STRANGE WORLD...
...AN ANCIENT AND GIGANTIC SPACE CRAFT, ABANDONED MILLIONS OF YEARS AGO...
...NOW POPULATED BY A RACE OF SENTIENT SPIDERS WHO EVOLVED AMONGST THE RUINS.
MISTER SCOTT HAS THE BRIDGE, WHILE I LEAD THE LANDING PARTY.
ON THIS...
...THE ***FINAL*** ASSIGNMENT FOR *ENTERPRISE* AND HER CREW.
IT SEEMS FITTING TO END MY TIME AS HER CAPTAIN ON ARCHERNAR IV, WHERE OUR FIVE-YEAR MISSION BEGAN.
THIS WORLD BELOW US—IS LIKE A STARSHIP WITHOUT A CREW...
...A VESSEL WITHOUT A HEADING.
Columbus
AT LEAST THIS PEACEFUL ASSIGNMENT GIVES ME A CHANCE TO SEE OLD FRIENDS...
...BEFORE I MUST DEAL WITH THE LOOMING PROMOTION ADMIRAL NOGURA HAS THREATENED ME WITH...

YOU'VE DONE WELL FOR YOURSELF... *AMBASSADOR* CASSADY...

THANKS... BUT I'M REALLY JUST A SURVEY CAPTAIN WHO'S AN EXPERT ON THIS WORLD.

WHERE ARE MITCHELL AND KELSO? I'D LOVE TO CATCH UP.

DIED IN THE LINE OF DUTY, I'M AFRAID.

I DIDN'T KNOW. I'M SORRY.

SO AM I. THEY WERE GOOD MEN.

I'VE NEVER LOST ANYONE UNDER MY COMMAND. BUT THAT'S A PART OF A STARSHIP CAPTAIN'S JOB. YOU GROW TO ACCEPT, I SUPPOSE.

NO.

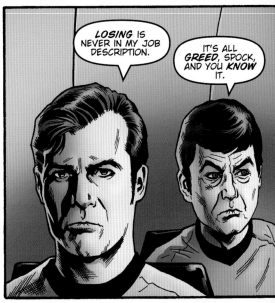

LOSING IS NEVER IN MY JOB DESCRIPTION.

IT'S ALL *GREED*, SPOCK, AND YOU *KNOW* IT.

THESE SPIDER-CREATURES AREN'T READY FOR THE FEDERATION... YOU SAID YOURSELF THEY'RE A BARBARIC SOCIETY. THEY FIGHT DEATH DUELS, THEY MISTREAT THEIR PACK ANIMALS...

BUT WE MAKE THEM A "PROTECTORATE," GIVE THEM FOOD REPLICATORS, ROBOTS, PRECIOUS METALS, AND COMPUTERS...

ALL TO GET OUR GREEDY HANDS ON THE SECRET ALIEN TECHNOLOGY THAT RUNS THEIR WORLD, BEFORE ANYONE ELSE CAN.

TYPICALLY, DOCTOR, YOU FAIL TO SEE THE LOGIC.

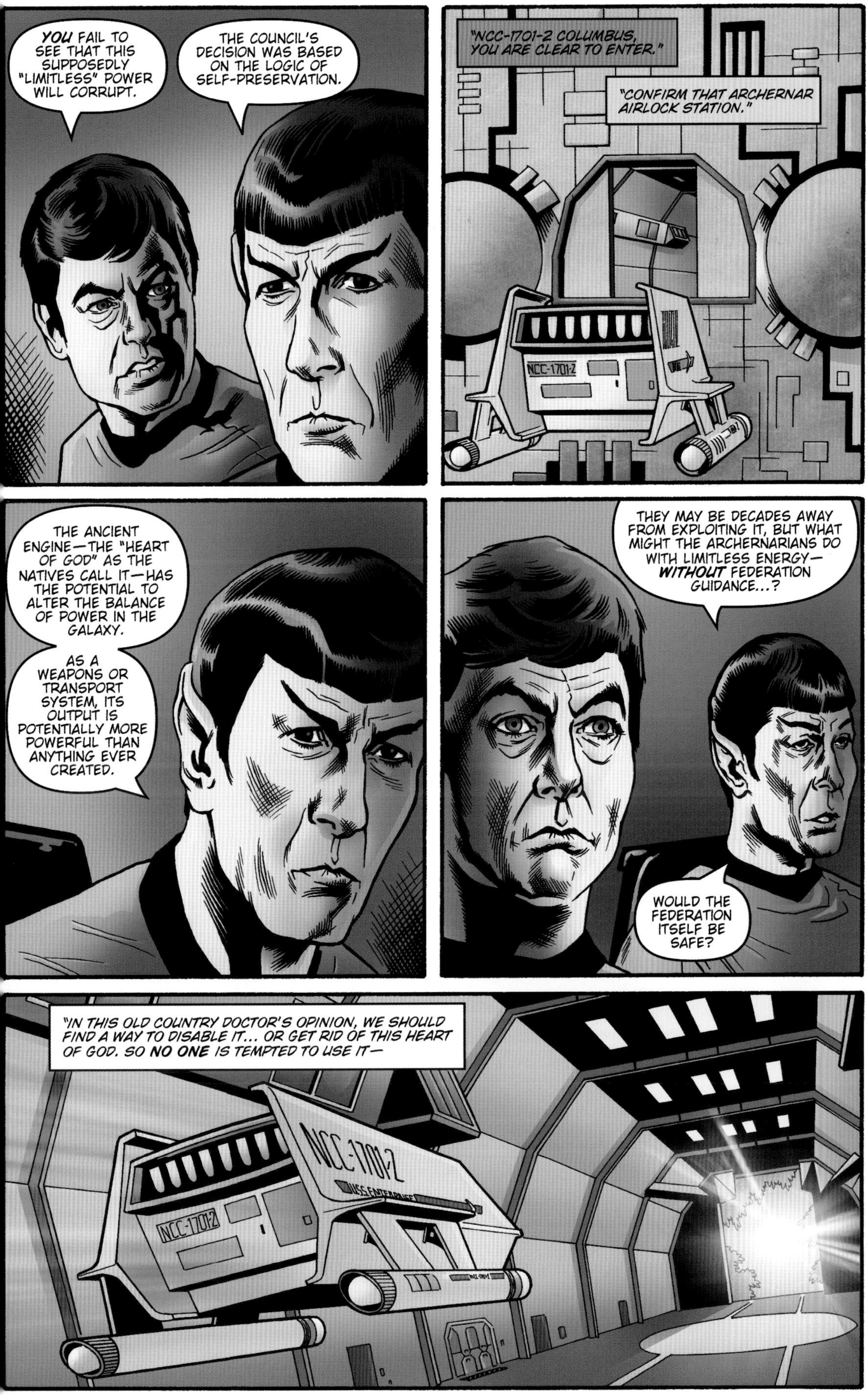

YOU FAIL TO SEE THAT THIS SUPPOSEDLY "LIMITLESS" POWER WILL CORRUPT.
THE COUNCIL'S DECISION WAS BASED ON THE LOGIC OF SELF-PRESERVATION.
"NCC-1701-2 COLUMBUS, YOU ARE CLEAR TO ENTER."
"CONFIRM THAT ARCHERNAR AIRLOCK STATION."
NCC-1701-2
THE ANCIENT ENGINE—THE "HEART OF GOD" AS THE NATIVES CALL IT—HAS THE POTENTIAL TO ALTER THE BALANCE OF POWER IN THE GALAXY.
AS A WEAPONS OR TRANSPORT SYSTEM, ITS OUTPUT IS POTENTIALLY MORE POWERFUL THAN ANYTHING EVER CREATED.
THEY MAY BE DECADES AWAY FROM EXPLOITING IT, BUT WHAT MIGHT THE ARCHERNARIANS DO WITH LIMITLESS ENERGY—WITHOUT FEDERATION GUIDANCE...?
WOULD THE FEDERATION ITSELF BE SAFE?
"IN THIS OLD COUNTRY DOCTOR'S OPINION, WE SHOULD FIND A WAY TO DISABLE IT... OR GET RID OF THIS HEART OF GOD. SO NO ONE IS TEMPTED TO USE IT—
NCC-1701-2
NCC-1701-2

"—THIS IS ONE PARADISE THAT'S BETTER OFF WITHOUT AN APPLE."

IT'S NOT *ALL* CORRUPTION OR CONQUEST, GENTLEMEN. I PREFER TO THROW A LITTLE *HOPE* INTO THE EQUATION.

WE'RE INSIDE THE HULL NOW, CHEKOV. OPEN A CHANNEL.

AYE, SIR.

HIGH ADMINISTRATOR. I BRING GREETINGS FROM EARTH, AND CONDOLENCES ON THE LOSS OF YOUR SON.

CAPTAIN KIRK! THANK YOU FOR YOUR KIND WORDS.

A LOT HAS CHANGED SINCE WE LAST SPOKE TO EACH OTHER.

FEDERATION GENEROSITY HAS DONE MUCH FOR OUR WORLD.

NOW, MAY I PRESENT OUR HIGH MINISTER OF TRUTH AND SCIENCE, KEL-M.

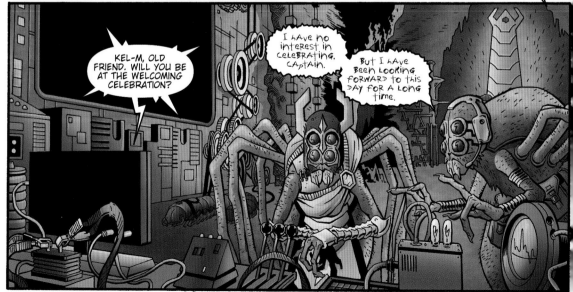

KEL-M, OLD FRIEND. WILL YOU BE AT THE WELCOMING CELEBRATION?

I HAVE NO INTEREST IN CELEBRATING, CAPTAIN.

BUT I HAVE BEEN LOOKING FORWARD TO THIS DAY FOR A LONG TIME.

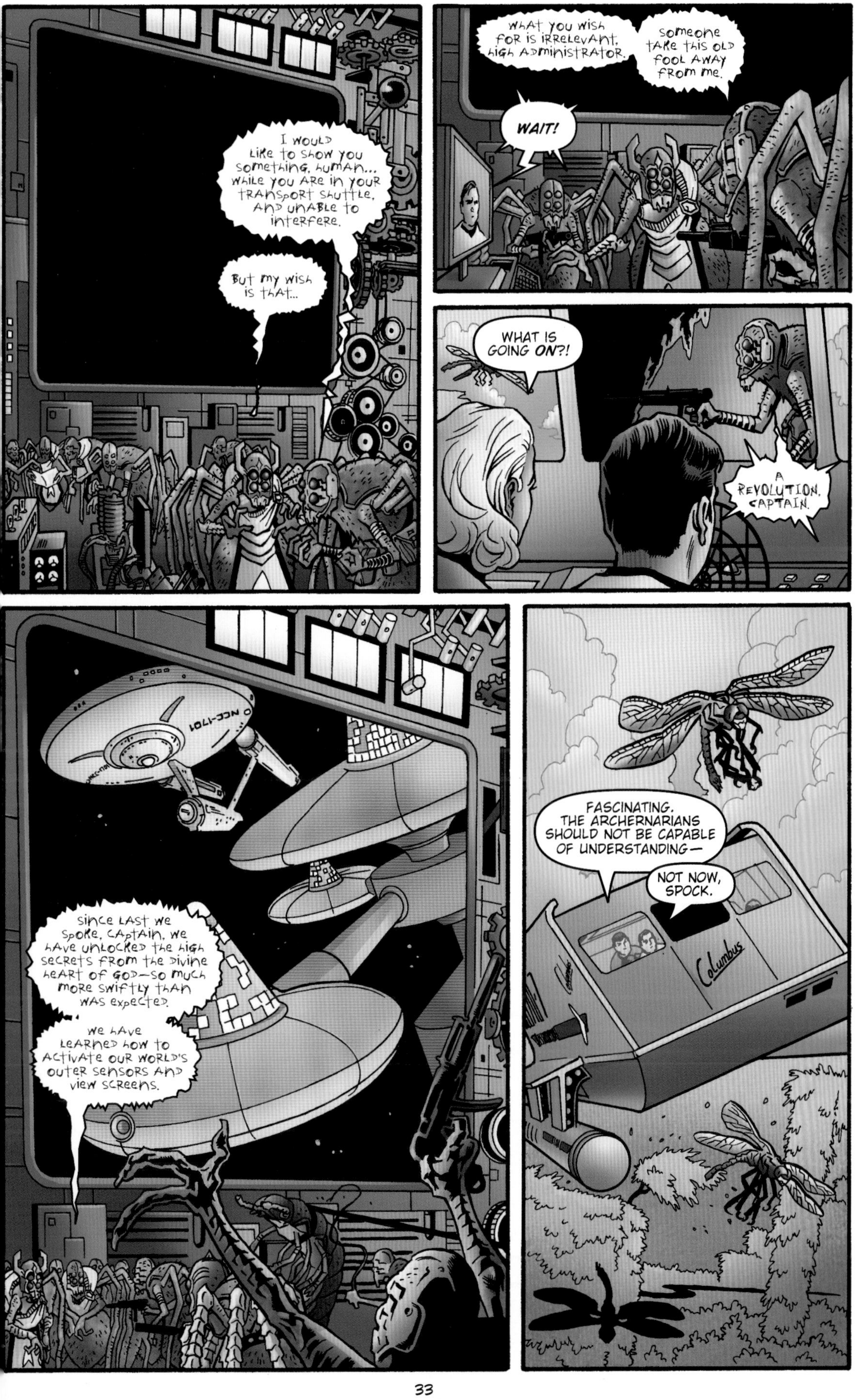
I would like to show you something, human... while you are in your transport shuttle, and unable to interfere.
But my wish is that...
What you wish for is irrelevant, high administrator.
Someone take this old fool away from me.
WAIT!
WHAT IS GOING ON?!
A REVOLUTION, CAPTAIN.
NCC-1701
Since last we spoke, Captain, we have unlocked the high secrets from the divine heart of God—so much more swiftly than was expected.
We have learned how to activate our world's outer sensors and view screens.
FASCINATING. THE ARCHERNARIANS SHOULD NOT BE CAPABLE OF UNDERSTANDING—
NOT NOW, SPOCK.
Columbus

WHAT DO YOU WANT, KEL-M? CAN WE DISCUSS...?

i want nothing more than for you to report back to your federation masters what you are about to see.

ACCORDING TO MY INSTRUMENTS, YOUR SPACE STATION HOLDS ELEVEN BEINGS, AND YOUR STARSHIP HOLDS FOUR HUNDRED AND TWENTY-SEVEN.

we consider this star system to be our sacred territory, and will not tolerate intruders.

and we have far more working than the monitor screens...

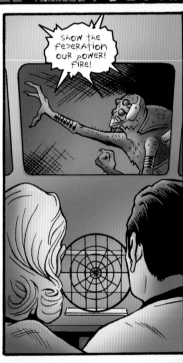

SHOW THE FEDERATION OUR POWER! FIRE!

COMMANDER SCOTT! I'M READING A HUGE ENERGY BURST FROM THE SURFACE, AND GRAVITON FORCE FIELDS GOING UP AROUND THE PLANET.

SHIELDS!

34

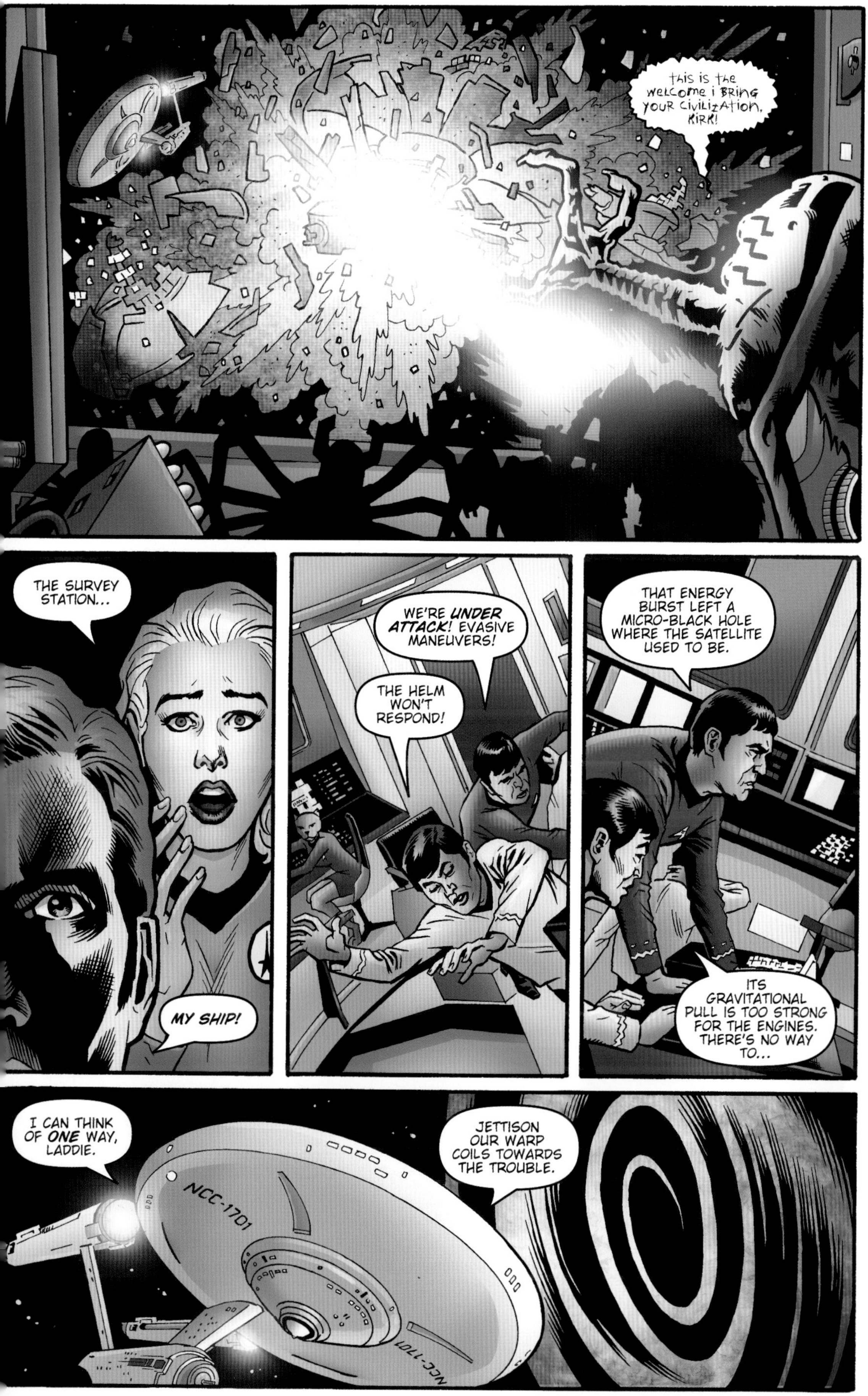
this is the welcome i bring your civilization, kirk!
THE SURVEY STATION...
MY SHIP!
WE'RE UNDER ATTACK! EVASIVE MANEUVERS!
THE HELM WON'T RESPOND!
THAT ENERGY BURST LEFT A MICRO-BLACK HOLE WHERE THE SATELLITE USED TO BE.
ITS GRAVITATIONAL PULL IS TOO STRONG FOR THE ENGINES. THERE'S NO WAY TO...
I CAN THINK OF ONE WAY, LADDIE.
JETTISON OUR WARP COILS TOWARDS THE TROUBLE.
NCC-1701
NCC-1701

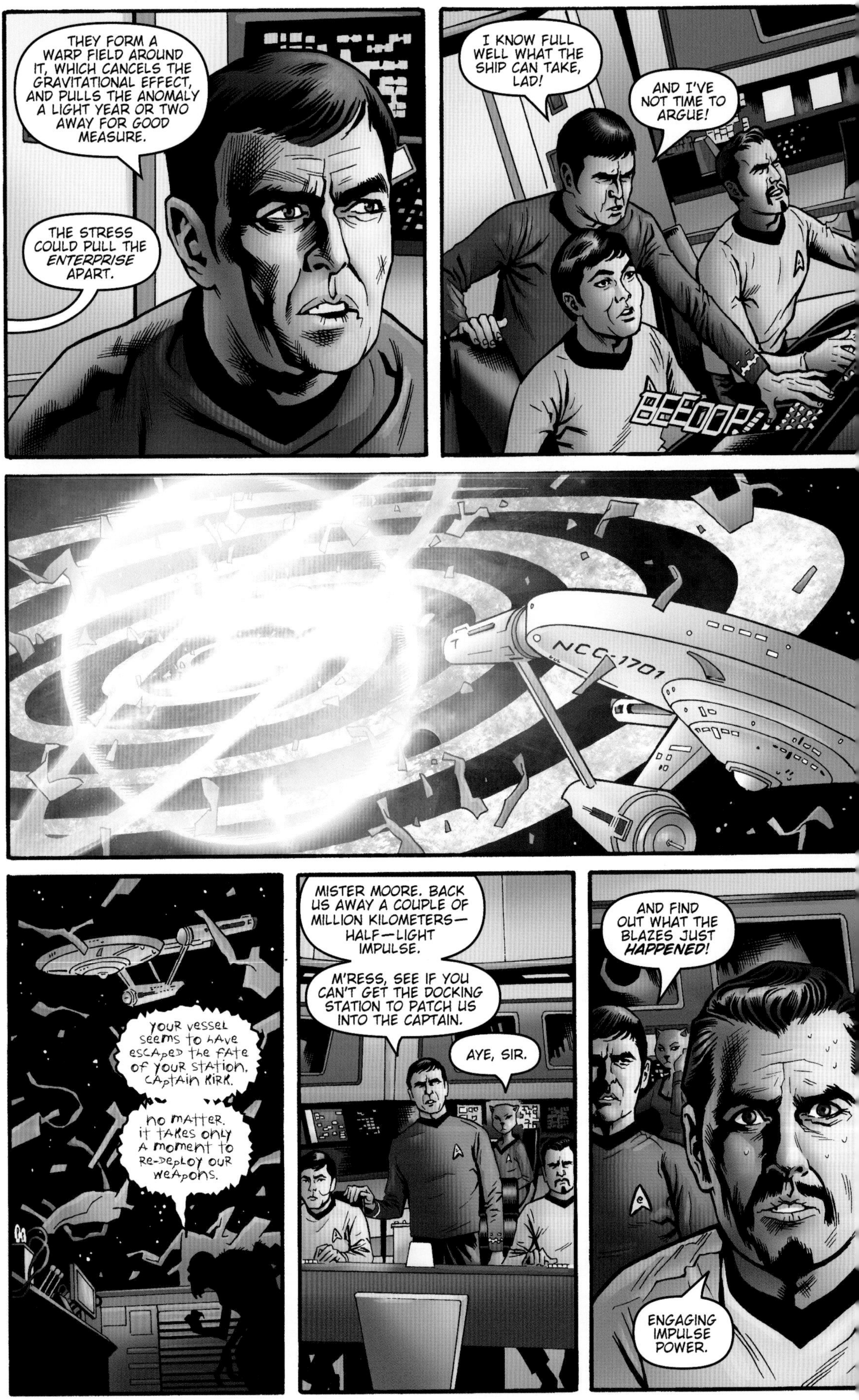
THEY FORM A WARP FIELD AROUND IT, WHICH CANCELS THE GRAVITATIONAL EFFECT, AND PULLS THE ANOMALY A LIGHT YEAR OR TWO AWAY FOR GOOD MEASURE.
THE STRESS COULD PULL THE *ENTERPRISE* APART.
I KNOW FULL WELL WHAT THE SHIP CAN TAKE, LAD!
AND I'VE NOT TIME TO ARGUE!
BEEOOP
NCC-1701
YOUR VESSEL SEEMS TO HAVE ESCAPED THE FATE OF YOUR STATION, CAPTAIN KIRK.
NO MATTER. IT TAKES ONLY A MOMENT TO RE-DEPLOY OUR WEAPONS.
MISTER MOORE. BACK US AWAY A COUPLE OF MILLION KILOMETERS— HALF—LIGHT IMPULSE.
M'RESS, SEE IF YOU CAN'T GET THE DOCKING STATION TO PATCH US INTO THE CAPTAIN.
AYE, SIR.
AND FIND OUT WHAT THE BLAZES JUST ***HAPPENED!***
ENGAGING IMPULSE POWER.

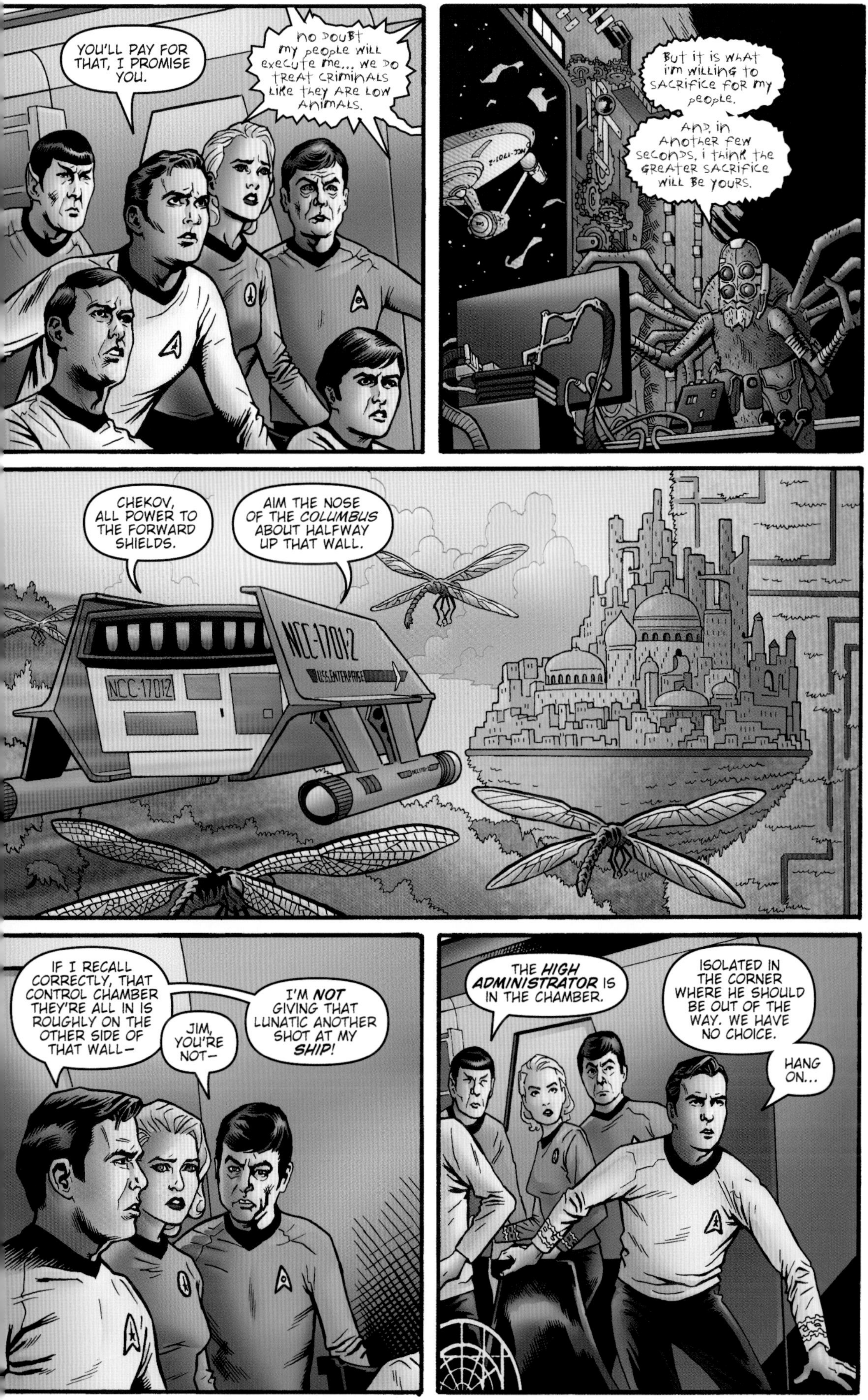
YOU'LL PAY FOR THAT, I PROMISE YOU.
no Doubt my people will execute me... we do treat criminals like they are low animals.
But it is what i'm willing to sacrifice for my people.
And, in another few seconds, i think the greater sacrifice will be yours.
CHEKOV, ALL POWER TO THE FORWARD SHIELDS.
AIM THE NOSE OF THE COLUMBUS ABOUT HALFWAY UP THAT WALL.
NCC-1701-2
U.S.S. ENTERPRISE
NCC-1701-2
IF I RECALL CORRECTLY, THAT CONTROL CHAMBER THEY'RE ALL IN IS ROUGHLY ON THE OTHER SIDE OF THAT WALL–
JIM, YOU'RE NOT–
I'M NOT GIVING THAT LUNATIC ANOTHER SHOT AT MY SHIP!
THE HIGH ADMINISTRATOR IS IN THE CHAMBER.
ISOLATED IN THE CORNER WHERE HE SHOULD BE OUT OF THE WAY. WE HAVE NO CHOICE.
HANG ON...

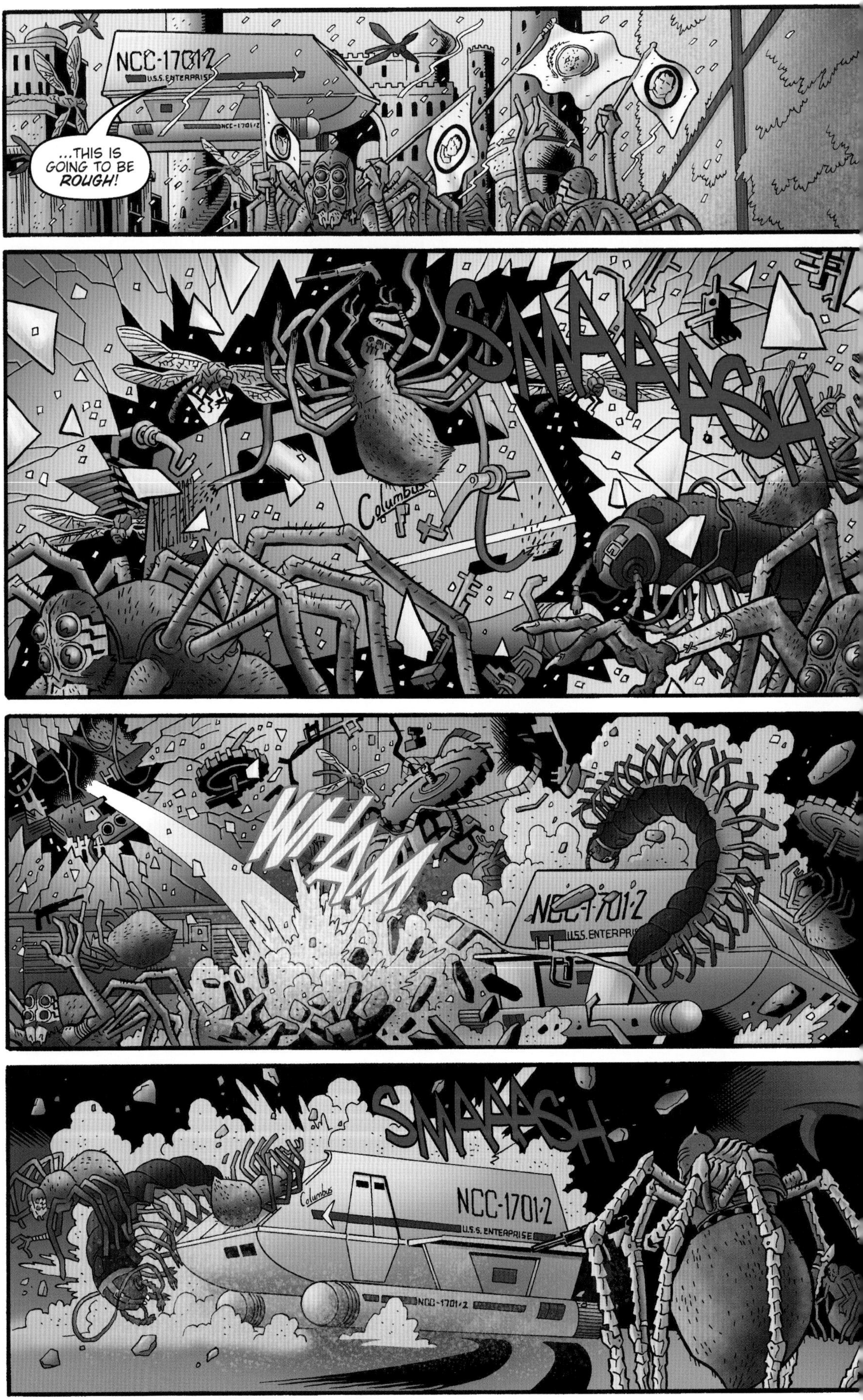
NCC-1701-2
U.S.S. ENTERPRISE
...THIS IS GOING TO BE *ROUGH!*
SMAAASH
Columbus
WHAM
NCC-1701-2
U.S.S. ENTERPRISE
SMAAASH
Columbus
NCC-1701-2
U.S.S. ENTERPRISE
NCC-1701-2

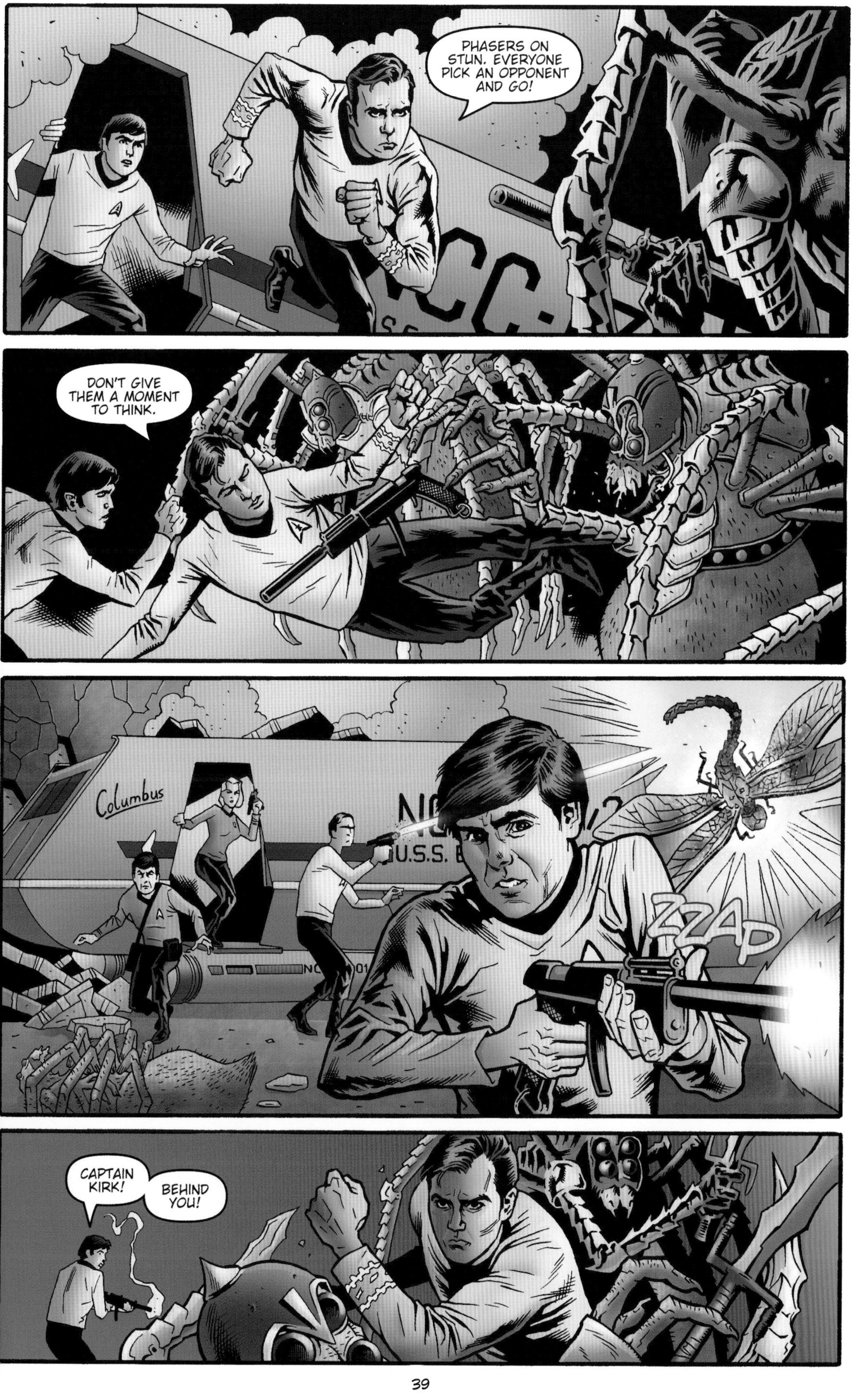
PHASERS ON STUN. EVERYONE PICK AN OPPONENT AND GO!
DON'T GIVE THEM A MOMENT TO THINK.
Columbus
U.S.S.
ZZAP
CAPTAIN KIRK!
BEHIND YOU!

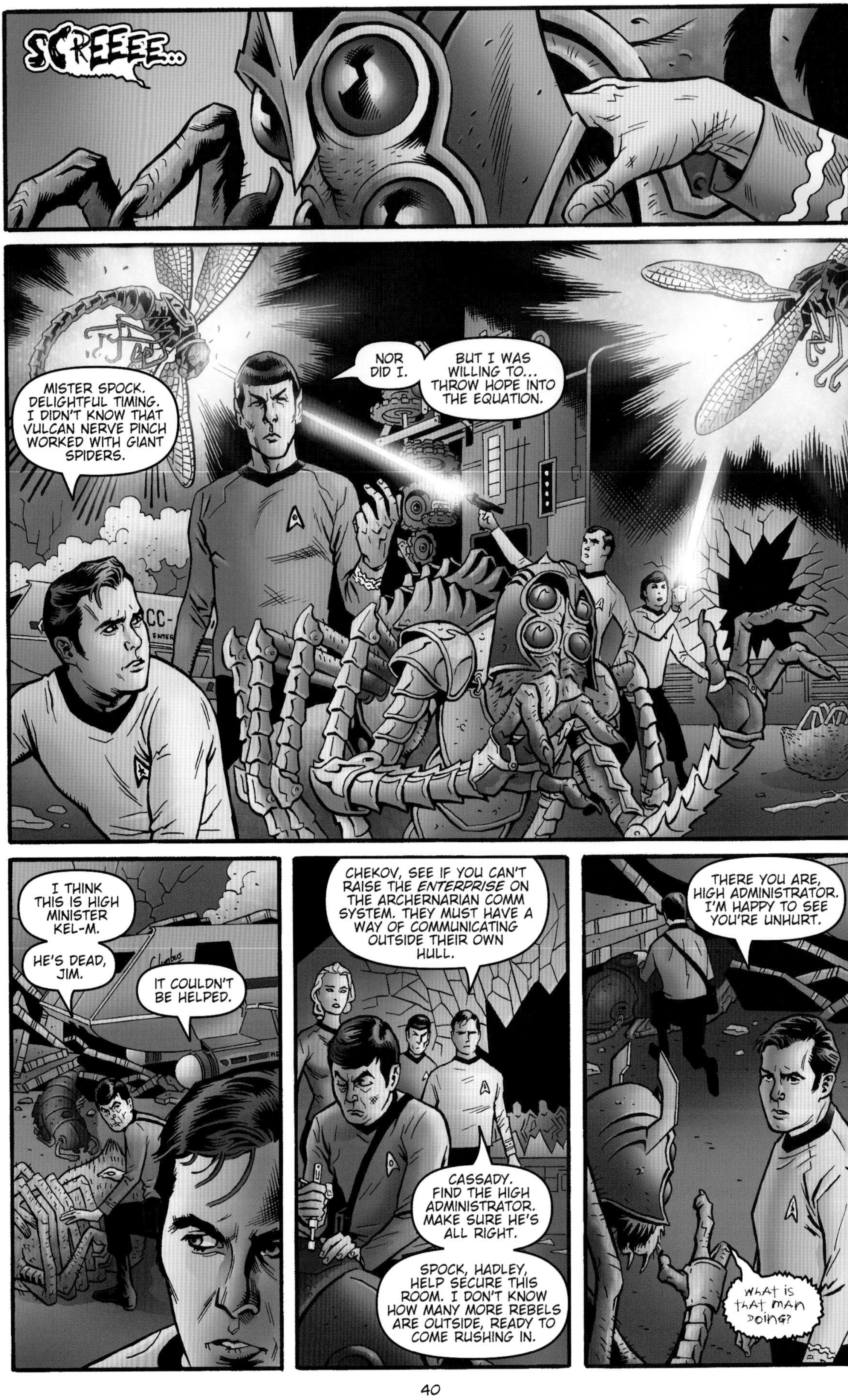
SCREEEE...
MISTER SPOCK. DELIGHTFUL TIMING. I DIDN'T KNOW THAT VULCAN NERVE PINCH WORKED WITH GIANT SPIDERS.
NOR DID I.
BUT I WAS WILLING TO... THROW HOPE INTO THE EQUATION.
I THINK THIS IS HIGH MINISTER KEL-M.
HE'S DEAD, JIM.
IT COULDN'T BE HELPED.
CHEKOV, SEE IF YOU CAN'T RAISE THE *ENTERPRISE* ON THE ARCHERNARIAN COMM SYSTEM. THEY MUST HAVE A WAY OF COMMUNICATING OUTSIDE THEIR OWN HULL.
CASSADY. FIND THE HIGH ADMINISTRATOR. MAKE SURE HE'S ALL RIGHT.
SPOCK, HADLEY, HELP SECURE THIS ROOM. I DON'T KNOW HOW MANY MORE REBELS ARE OUTSIDE, READY TO COME RUSHING IN.
THERE YOU ARE, HIGH ADMINISTRATOR. I'M HAPPY TO SEE YOU'RE UNHURT.
What is that man doing?

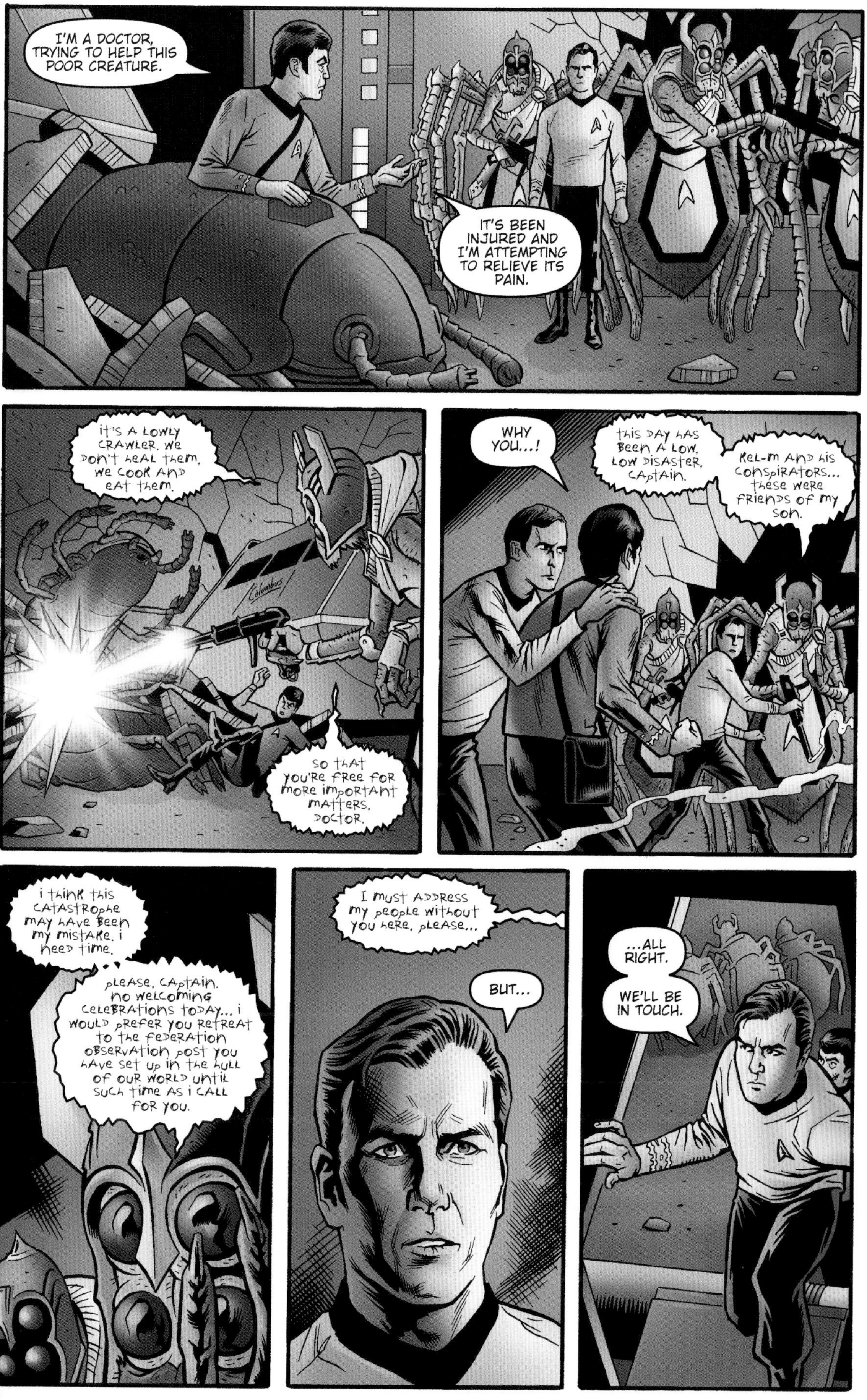
I'M A DOCTOR, TRYING TO HELP THIS POOR CREATURE.
IT'S BEEN INJURED AND I'M ATTEMPTING TO RELIEVE ITS PAIN.
IT'S A LOWLY CRAWLER. WE DON'T HEAL THEM, WE COOK AND EAT THEM.
Columbus
SO THAT YOU'RE FREE FOR MORE IMPORTANT MATTERS, DOCTOR.
WHY YOU...!
THIS DAY HAS BEEN A LOW, LOW DISASTER, CAPTAIN.
KEL-M AND HIS CONSPIRATORS... THESE WERE FRIENDS OF MY SON.
I THINK THIS CATASTROPHE MAY HAVE BEEN MY MISTAKE. I NEED TIME.
PLEASE, CAPTAIN. NO WELCOMING CELEBRATIONS TODAY... I WOULD PREFER YOU RETREAT TO THE FEDERATION OBSERVATION POST YOU HAVE SET UP IN THE HULL OF OUR WORLD UNTIL SUCH TIME AS I CALL FOR YOU.
I MUST ADDRESS MY PEOPLE WITHOUT YOU HERE, PLEASE...
BUT...
...ALL RIGHT.
WE'LL BE IN TOUCH.

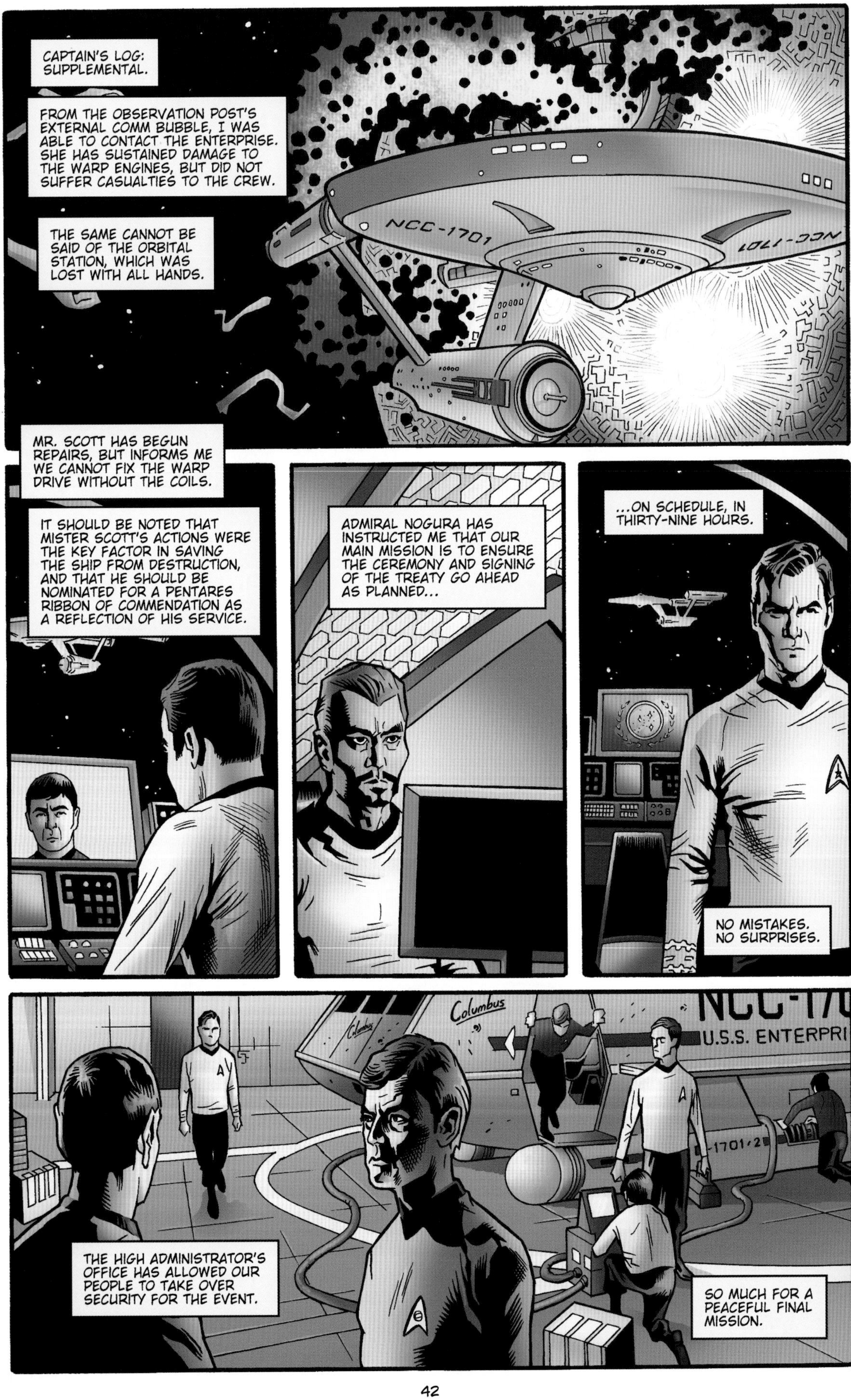
CAPTAIN'S LOG: SUPPLEMENTAL.
FROM THE OBSERVATION POST'S EXTERNAL COMM BUBBLE, I WAS ABLE TO CONTACT THE ENTERPRISE. SHE HAS SUSTAINED DAMAGE TO THE WARP ENGINES, BUT DID NOT SUFFER CASUALTIES TO THE CREW.
THE SAME CANNOT BE SAID OF THE ORBITAL STATION, WHICH WAS LOST WITH ALL HANDS.
NCC-1701
MR. SCOTT HAS BEGUN REPAIRS, BUT INFORMS ME WE CANNOT FIX THE WARP DRIVE WITHOUT THE COILS.
IT SHOULD BE NOTED THAT MISTER SCOTT'S ACTIONS WERE THE KEY FACTOR IN SAVING THE SHIP FROM DESTRUCTION, AND THAT HE SHOULD BE NOMINATED FOR A PENTARES RIBBON OF COMMENDATION AS A REFLECTION OF HIS SERVICE.
ADMIRAL NOGURA HAS INSTRUCTED ME THAT OUR MAIN MISSION IS TO ENSURE THE CEREMONY AND SIGNING OF THE TREATY GO AHEAD AS PLANNED...
...ON SCHEDULE, IN THIRTY-NINE HOURS.
NO MISTAKES. NO SURPRISES.
Columbus
U.S.S. ENTERPRI
1701/2
THE HIGH ADMINISTRATOR'S OFFICE HAS ALLOWED OUR PEOPLE TO TAKE OVER SECURITY FOR THE EVENT.
SO MUCH FOR A PEACEFUL FINAL MISSION.

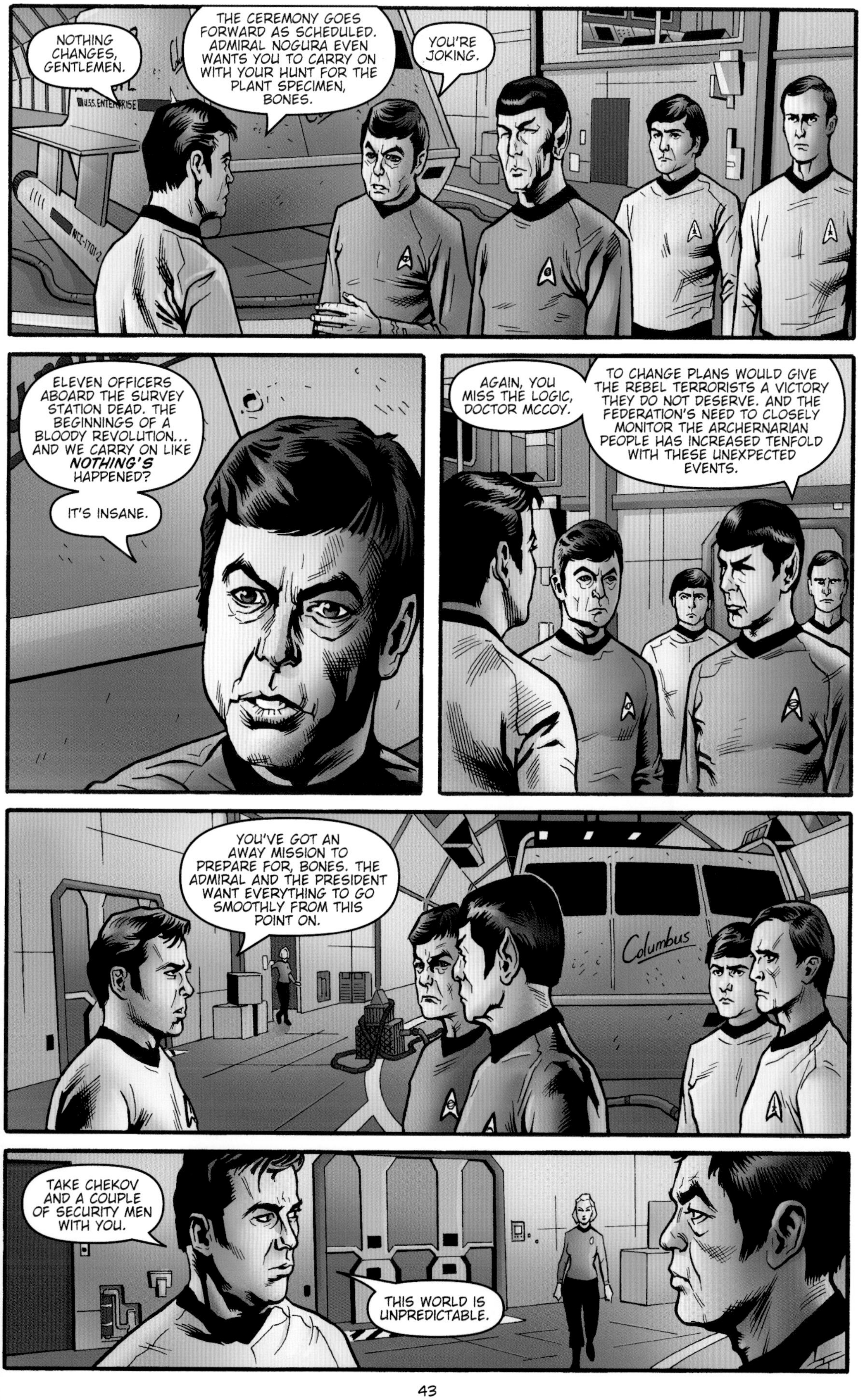
NOTHING CHANGES, GENTLEMEN.
THE CEREMONY GOES FORWARD AS SCHEDULED. ADMIRAL NOGURA EVEN WANTS YOU TO CARRY ON WITH YOUR HUNT FOR THE PLANT SPECIMEN, BONES.
YOU'RE JOKING.
U.S.S. ENTERPRISE
NCC-1701-2
ELEVEN OFFICERS ABOARD THE SURVEY STATION DEAD. THE BEGINNINGS OF A BLOODY REVOLUTION... AND WE CARRY ON LIKE *NOTHING'S* HAPPENED?
IT'S INSANE.
AGAIN, YOU MISS THE LOGIC, DOCTOR MCCOY.
TO CHANGE PLANS WOULD GIVE THE REBEL TERRORISTS A VICTORY THEY DO NOT DESERVE. AND THE FEDERATION'S NEED TO CLOSELY MONITOR THE ARCHERNARIAN PEOPLE HAS INCREASED TENFOLD WITH THESE UNEXPECTED EVENTS.
YOU'VE GOT AN AWAY MISSION TO PREPARE FOR, BONES. THE ADMIRAL AND THE PRESIDENT WANT EVERYTHING TO GO SMOOTHLY FROM THIS POINT ON.
Columbus
TAKE CHEKOV AND A COUPLE OF SECURITY MEN WITH YOU.
THIS WORLD IS UNPREDICTABLE.

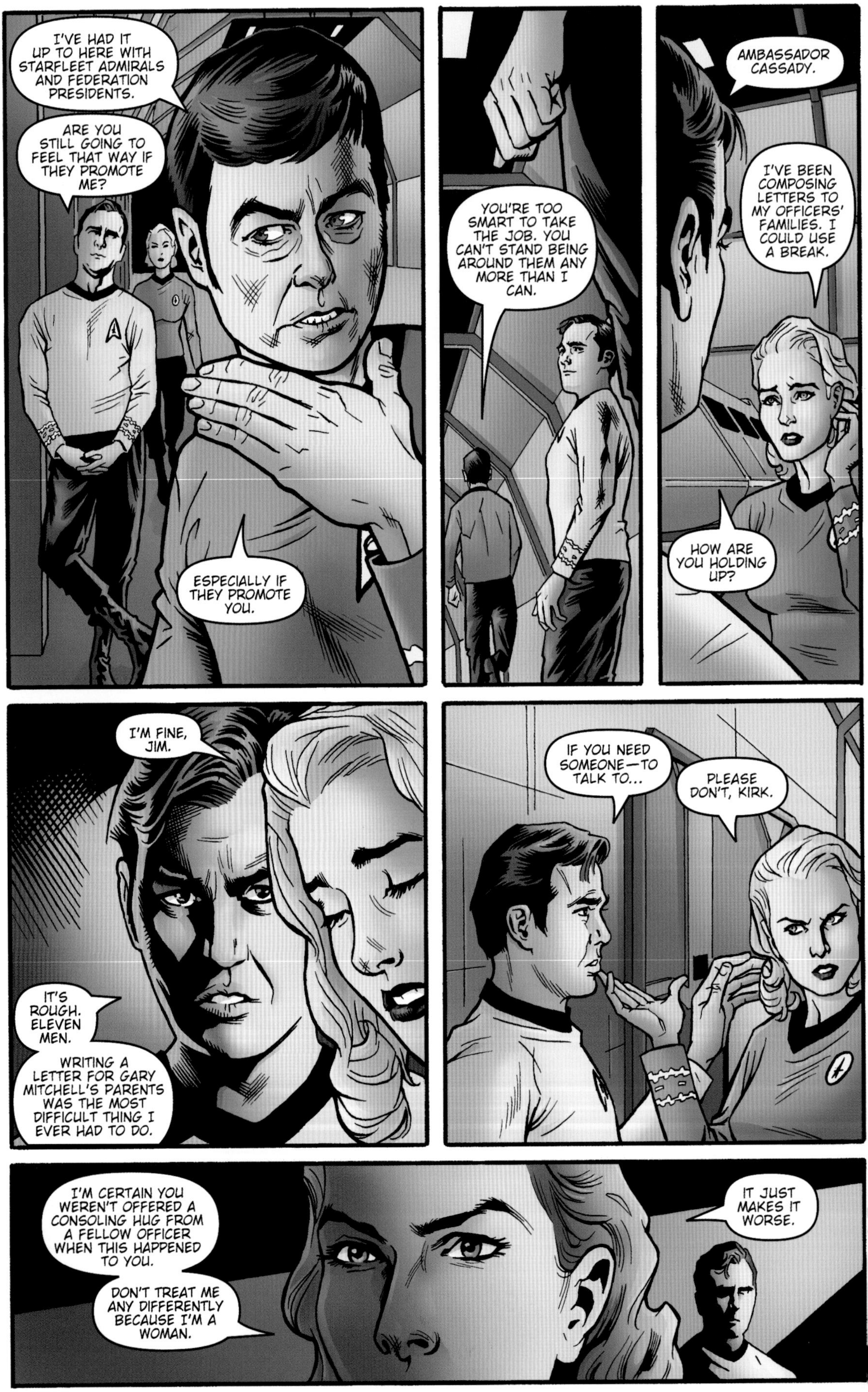
I'VE HAD IT UP TO HERE WITH STARFLEET ADMIRALS AND FEDERATION PRESIDENTS.
ARE YOU STILL GOING TO FEEL THAT WAY IF THEY PROMOTE ME?
ESPECIALLY IF THEY PROMOTE YOU.
YOU'RE TOO SMART TO TAKE THE JOB. YOU CAN'T STAND BEING AROUND THEM ANY MORE THAN I CAN.
AMBASSADOR CASSADY.
I'VE BEEN COMPOSING LETTERS TO MY OFFICERS' FAMILIES. I COULD USE A BREAK.
HOW ARE YOU HOLDING UP?
I'M FINE, JIM.
IT'S ROUGH. ELEVEN MEN.
WRITING A LETTER FOR GARY MITCHELL'S PARENTS WAS THE MOST DIFFICULT THING I EVER HAD TO DO.
IF YOU NEED SOMEONE—TO TALK TO...
PLEASE DON'T, KIRK.
I'M CERTAIN YOU WEREN'T OFFERED A CONSOLING HUG FROM A FELLOW OFFICER WHEN THIS HAPPENED TO YOU.
DON'T TREAT ME ANY DIFFERENTLY BECAUSE I'M A WOMAN.
IT JUST MAKES IT WORSE.

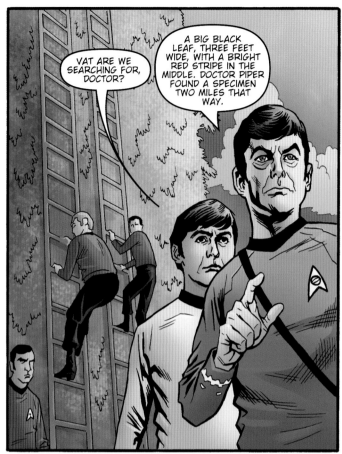

VAT ARE WE SEARCHING FOR, DOCTOR?

A BIG BLACK LEAF, THREE FEET WIDE, WITH A BRIGHT RED STRIPE IN THE MIDDLE. DOCTOR PIPER FOUND A SPECIMEN TWO MILES THAT WAY.

AND VY IS THIS LEAF SO SPECIAL?

IT WAS A THEORY PIPER HAD... A POSSIBLE CURE FOR BLAKE'S DISEASE HIDDEN IN THE PLANT'S PECULIAR DNA, BUT THE ONLY SAMPLES HE TOOK OFF-WORLD DIED.

OVER A BILLION PEOPLE IN THE ALPHA SECTOR SUFFER FROM THIS DISEASE, AND THE TRUTH IS, I COULD USE A PROJECT FOR THE NEXT YEAR.

OTHER THAN VISITING THE YONADA, I HAVE NO PLANS FOR THE FUTURE.

I GUESS I'M JUST WAITING TO SEE WHAT THE CAPTAIN DOES... BEFORE—

DOCTOR MCCOY. WE'VE GOT WILD CRAWLERS ALL AROUND US.

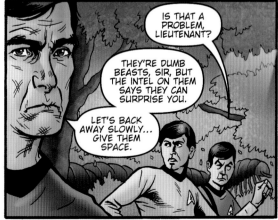

IS THAT A PROBLEM, LIEUTENANT?

THEY'RE DUMB BEASTS, SIR, BUT THE INTEL ON THEM SAYS THEY CAN SURPRISE YOU.

LET'S BACK AWAY SLOWLY... GIVE THEM SPACE.

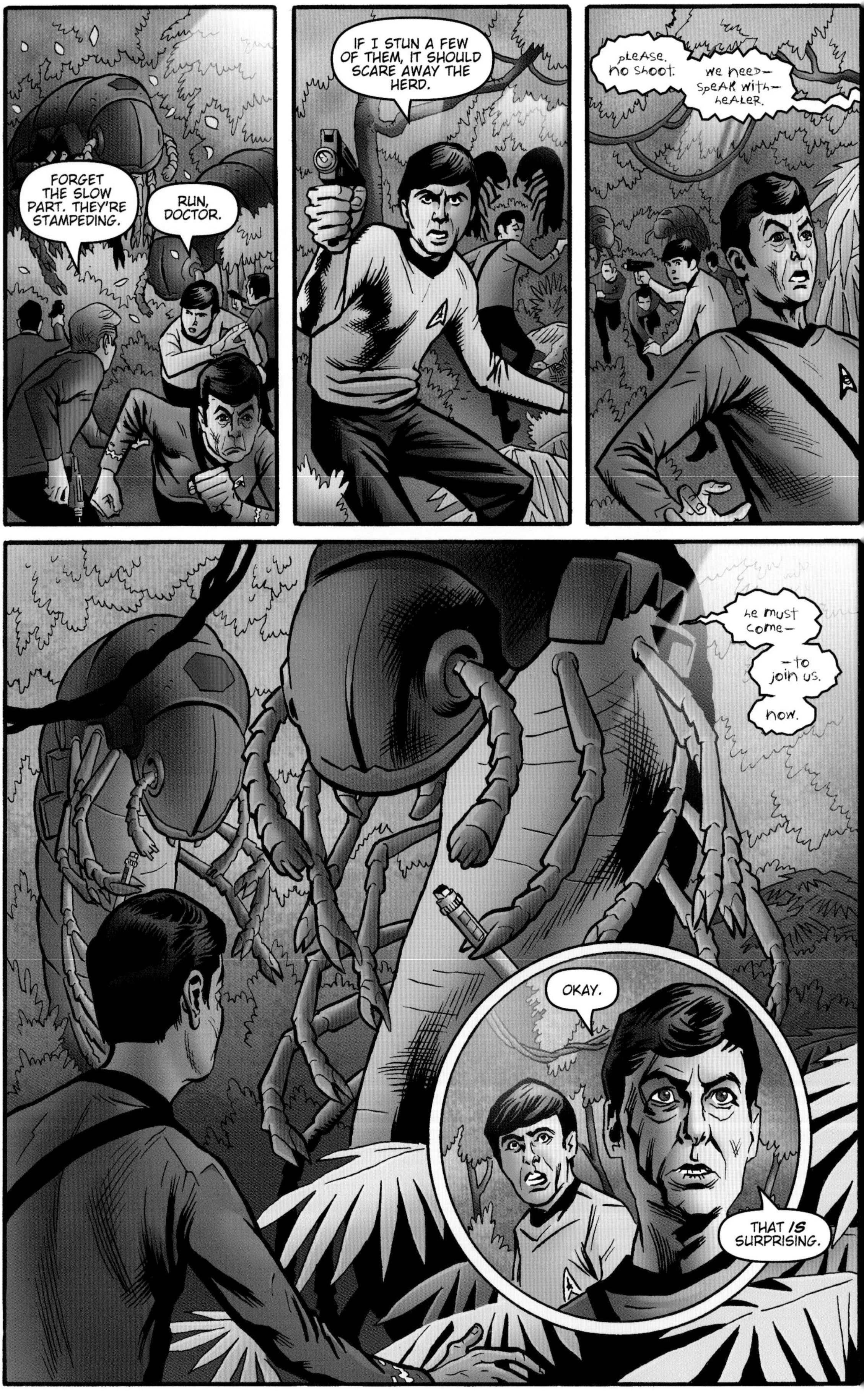
FORGET THE SLOW PART. THEY'RE STAMPEDING.
RUN, DOCTOR.
IF I STUN A FEW OF THEM, IT SHOULD SCARE AWAY THE HERD.
please. no shoot.
we need—speak with—healer.
he must come—
—to join us.
now.
OKAY.
THAT *IS* SURPRISING.

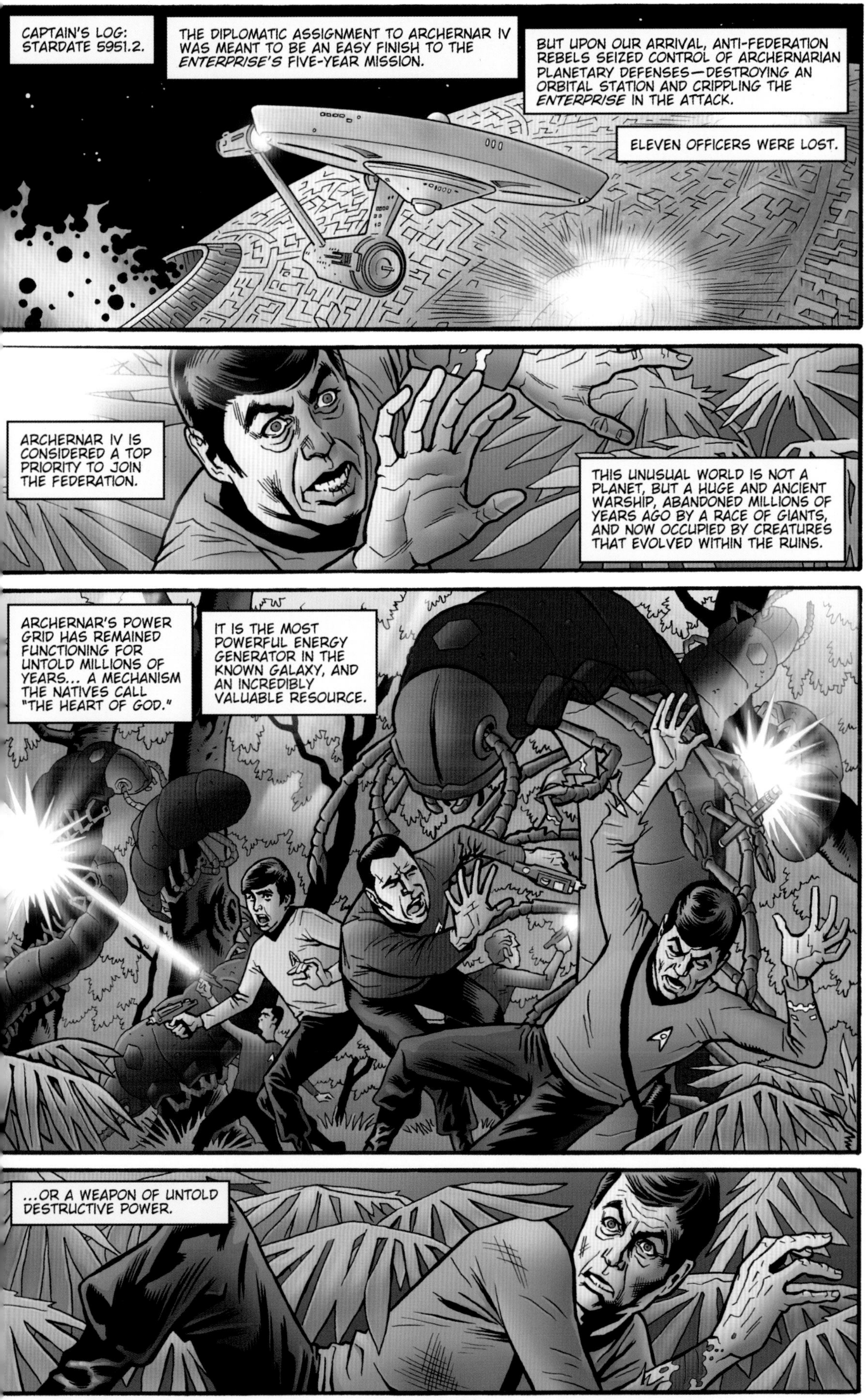
CAPTAIN'S LOG: STARDATE 5951.2.
THE DIPLOMATIC ASSIGNMENT TO ARCHERNAR IV WAS MEANT TO BE AN EASY FINISH TO THE *ENTERPRISE'S* FIVE-YEAR MISSION.
BUT UPON OUR ARRIVAL, ANTI-FEDERATION REBELS SEIZED CONTROL OF ARCHERNARIAN PLANETARY DEFENSES—DESTROYING AN ORBITAL STATION AND CRIPPLING THE *ENTERPRISE* IN THE ATTACK.
ELEVEN OFFICERS WERE LOST.
ARCHERNAR IV IS CONSIDERED A TOP PRIORITY TO JOIN THE FEDERATION.
THIS UNUSUAL WORLD IS NOT A PLANET, BUT A HUGE AND ANCIENT WARSHIP, ABANDONED MILLIONS OF YEARS AGO BY A RACE OF GIANTS, AND NOW OCCUPIED BY CREATURES THAT EVOLVED WITHIN THE RUINS.
ARCHERNAR'S POWER GRID HAS REMAINED FUNCTIONING FOR UNTOLD MILLIONS OF YEARS... A MECHANISM THE NATIVES CALL "THE HEART OF GOD."
IT IS THE MOST POWERFUL ENERGY GENERATOR IN THE KNOWN GALAXY, AND AN INCREDIBLY VALUABLE RESOURCE.
...OR A WEAPON OF UNTOLD DESTRUCTIVE POWER.

TO ADD TO MY WORRIES, THE CHIEF MEDICAL OFFICER IS TEN MINUTES LATE CHECKING IN WITH HIS AWAY TEAM.

DOCTOR MCCOY IS HUNTING DOWN A CURE FOR *BLAKE'S DISEASE.*

HE THINKS IT CAN BE FOUND IN SOME LOCAL FLORA DR. PIPER NOTED WHEN WE FIRST VISITED THIS WORLD.

no... fear... no harm... four legs safe

GET OFF ME!

I HOPE THAT CURE IS OUT THERE.

WITH ELEVEN DEAD, IT WOULD OFFER SOME BALANCE, IF THIS MISSION ENDS UP SAVING LIVES IN THE LONG RUN.

four legs... safe... no harm...

GAAAH!

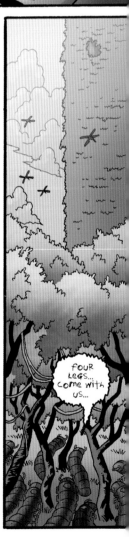

four legs... come with us...

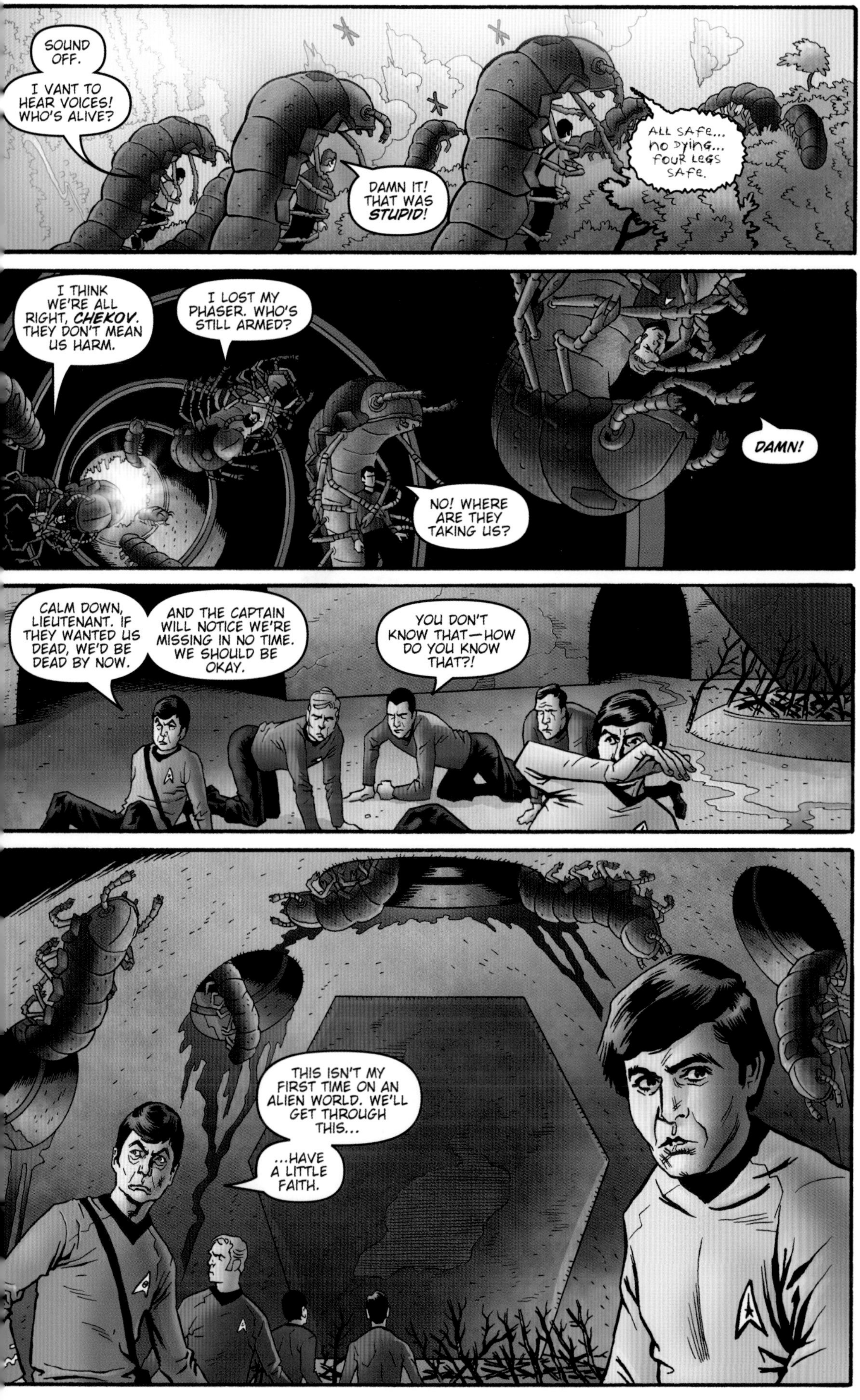
SOUND OFF.
I VANT TO HEAR VOICES! WHO'S ALIVE?
DAMN IT! THAT WAS **STUPID**!
All safe... no dying... four legs safe.
I THINK WE'RE ALL RIGHT, **CHEKOV**. THEY DON'T MEAN US HARM.
I LOST MY PHASER. WHO'S STILL ARMED?
NO! WHERE ARE THEY TAKING US?
DAMN!
CALM DOWN, LIEUTENANT. IF THEY WANTED US DEAD, WE'D BE DEAD BY NOW.
AND THE CAPTAIN WILL NOTICE WE'RE MISSING IN NO TIME. WE SHOULD BE OKAY.
YOU DON'T KNOW THAT—HOW DO YOU KNOW THAT?!
THIS ISN'T MY FIRST TIME ON AN ALIEN WORLD. WE'LL GET THROUGH THIS...
...HAVE A LITTLE FAITH.

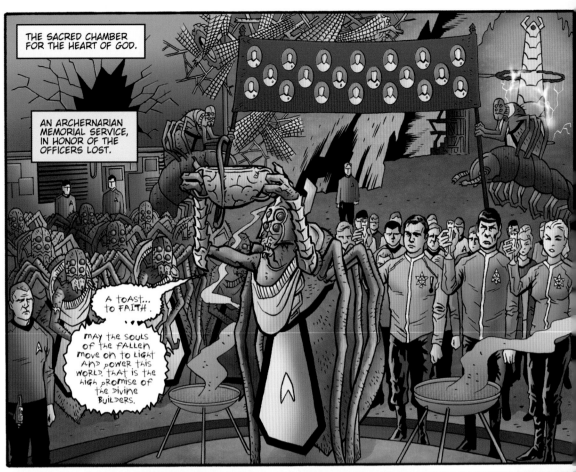

THE SACRED CHAMBER FOR THE HEART OF GOD.

AN ARCHERNARIAN MEMORIAL SERVICE, IN HONOR OF THE OFFICERS LOST.

A TOAST... TO FAITH.

MAY THE SOULS OF THE FALLEN MOVE ON TO LIGHT AND POWER THIS WORLD. THAT IS THE HIGH PROMISE OF THE DIVINE BUILDERS.

I HOPE I DID THAT CORRECTLY. I NEED TO UNDERSTAND YOUR TRADITIONS IF MY WORLD IS TO BECOME A PART OF YOUR FEDERATION.

THE TOAST WAS APPROPRIATE, HIGH ADMINISTRATOR.

AMBASSADOR CASSADY...

...MY PERSONAL APOLOGY FOR YOUR LOST CREW. THE TRAITORS ARE AS LOW AS CRAWLERS. THOSE RESPONSIBLE ARE DEAD OR AWAITING TRIAL.

SO MANY OF THEM... MY HIGH TRUSTED MINISTERS AND ADVISORS.

FOR THOUSANDS OF GENERATIONS, MY FAMILY MADE THE DECISIONS FOR MY PEOPLE. WE ARE THE CARETAKERS FOR THESE THINGS LEFT BY THE DIVINE BUILDERS.

UNTIL I DECIDED WE SHOULD JOIN YOUR FEDERATION... NO ONE QUESTIONED MY FAMILY.

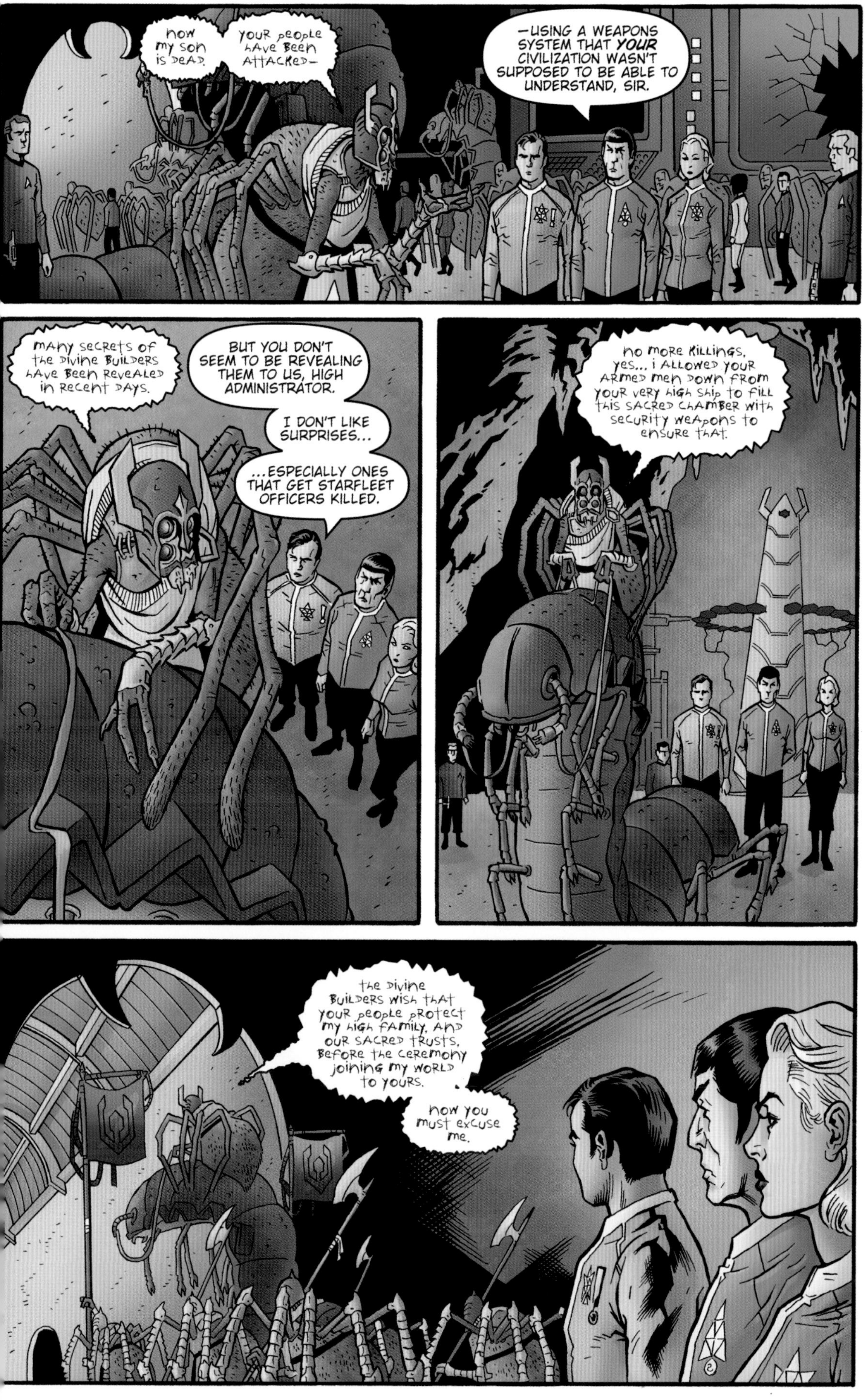
now my son is DEAD.
YOUR people have Been Attacked—
—USING A WEAPONS SYSTEM THAT *YOUR* CIVILIZATION WASN'T SUPPOSED TO BE ABLE TO UNDERSTAND, SIR.
many secrets of the Divine Builders have Been Revealed in Recent Days.
BUT YOU DON'T SEEM TO BE REVEALING THEM TO US, HIGH ADMINISTRATOR.
I DON'T LIKE SURPRISES...
...ESPECIALLY ONES THAT GET STARFLEET OFFICERS KILLED.
no more Killings, yes... i Allowed your Armed men Down from your very high ship to fill this SACRED Chamber with security weapons to ensure that.
the Divine Builders wish that your people protect my high family, And our SACRED trusts, Before the ceremony joining my world to yours.
now you must excuse me.

HE IS STILL RELUCTANT TO SPEAK OF THE STRANGE INTELLECTUAL ADVANCEMENTS HIS PEOPLE HAVE RECENTLY MADE.

HE'S RELUCTANT ABOUT EVERYTHING.

HESITANT. UNSURE.

IT'S NOT WHAT THIS SITUATION NEEDS—

HIS FAITH IN HIS POSITION OF POWER IS UNWAVERING.

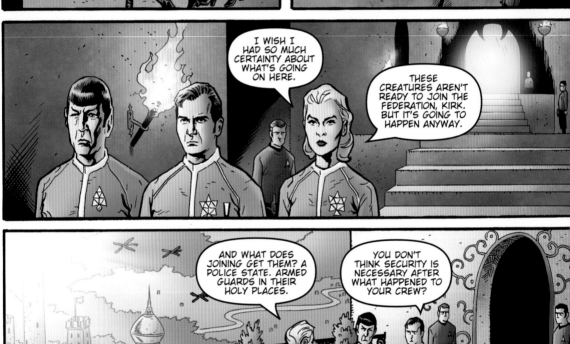

I WISH I HAD SO MUCH CERTAINTY ABOUT WHAT'S GOING ON HERE.

THESE CREATURES AREN'T READY TO JOIN THE FEDERATION, KIRK. BUT IT'S GOING TO HAPPEN ANYWAY.

AND WHAT DOES JOINING GET THEM? A POLICE STATE. ARMED GUARDS IN THEIR HOLY PLACES.

YOU DON'T THINK SECURITY IS NECESSARY AFTER WHAT HAPPENED TO YOUR CREW?

OF COURSE IT IS. BUT THIS WORLD WAS A PARADISE WHEN WE FIRST FOUND IT.

YOUR CONTINUED COMPARISON TO BIBLICAL EDEN IS FLAWED, AMBASSADOR. ARCHERNAR IV IS POTENTIALLY THE MOST POWERFUL WEAPONS SYSTEM EVER DEVISED.

EDEN WAS NOT.

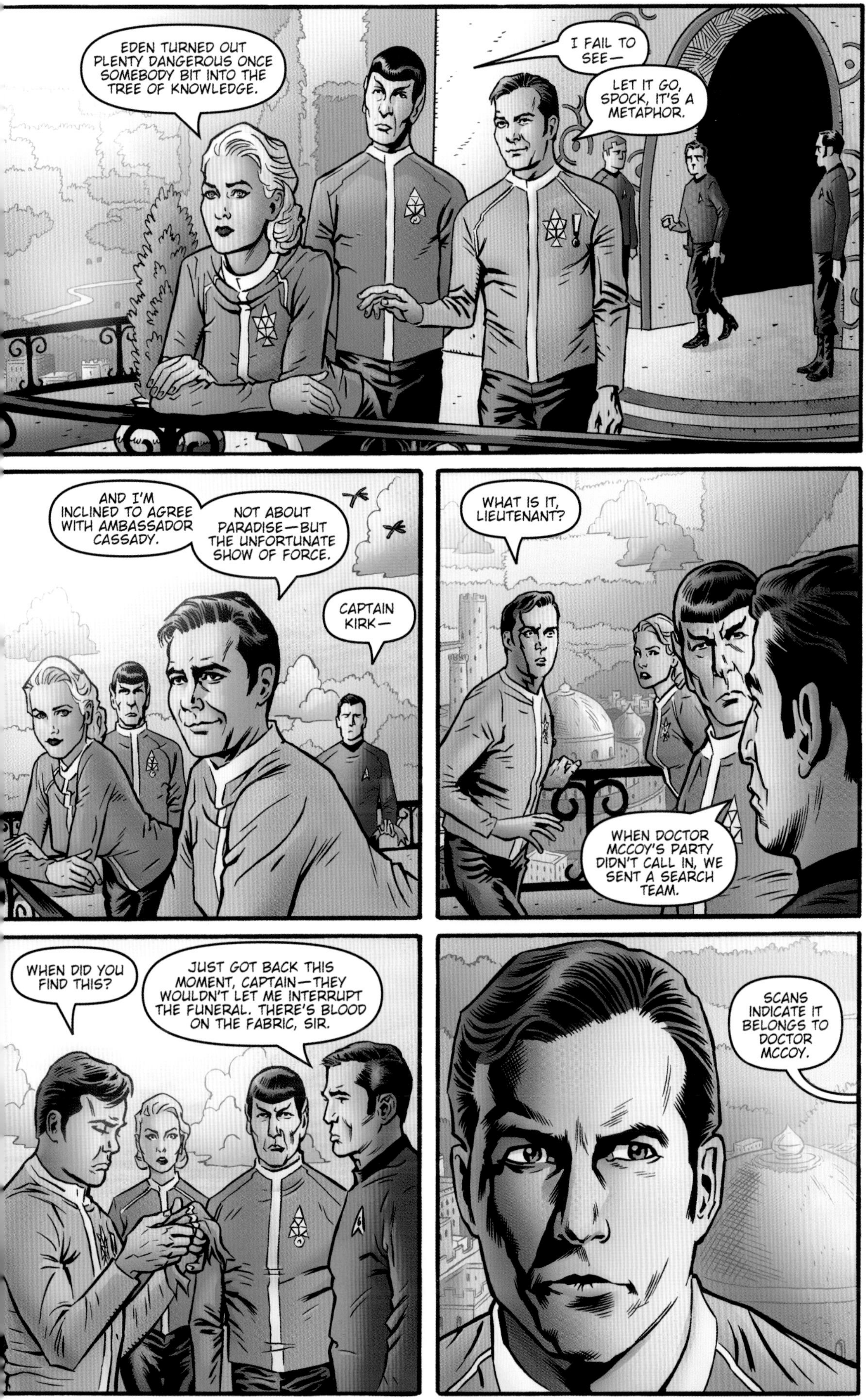
EDEN TURNED OUT PLENTY DANGEROUS ONCE SOMEBODY BIT INTO THE TREE OF KNOWLEDGE.
I FAIL TO SEE—
LET IT GO, SPOCK, IT'S A METAPHOR.
AND I'M INCLINED TO AGREE WITH AMBASSADOR CASSADY.
NOT ABOUT PARADISE—BUT THE UNFORTUNATE SHOW OF FORCE.
CAPTAIN KIRK—
WHAT IS IT, LIEUTENANT?
WHEN DOCTOR MCCOY'S PARTY DIDN'T CALL IN, WE SENT A SEARCH TEAM.
WHEN DID YOU FIND THIS?
JUST GOT BACK THIS MOMENT, CAPTAIN—THEY WOULDN'T LET ME INTERRUPT THE FUNERAL. THERE'S BLOOD ON THE FABRIC, SIR.
SCANS INDICATE IT BELONGS TO DOCTOR MCCOY.

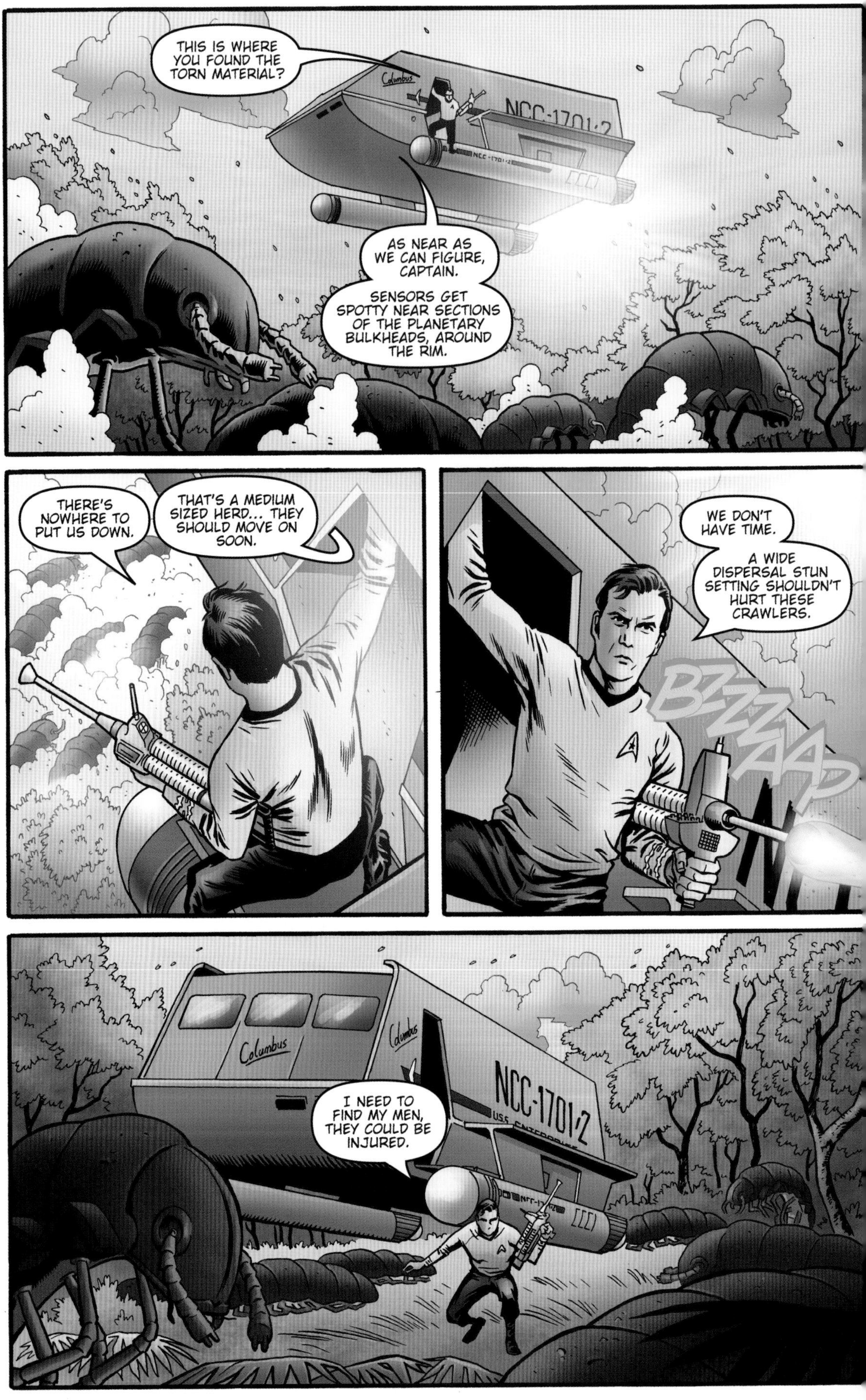

THIS IS WHERE YOU FOUND THE TORN MATERIAL?
NCC-1701-2
AS NEAR AS WE CAN FIGURE, CAPTAIN.
SENSORS GET SPOTTY NEAR SECTIONS OF THE PLANETARY BULKHEADS, AROUND THE RIM.
THERE'S NOWHERE TO PUT US DOWN.
THAT'S A MEDIUM SIZED HERD... THEY SHOULD MOVE ON SOON.
WE DON'T HAVE TIME.
A WIDE DISPERSAL STUN SETTING SHOULDN'T HURT THESE CRAWLERS.
BZZZAAP
Columbus
NCC-1701-2
I NEED TO FIND MY MEN, THEY COULD BE INJURED.

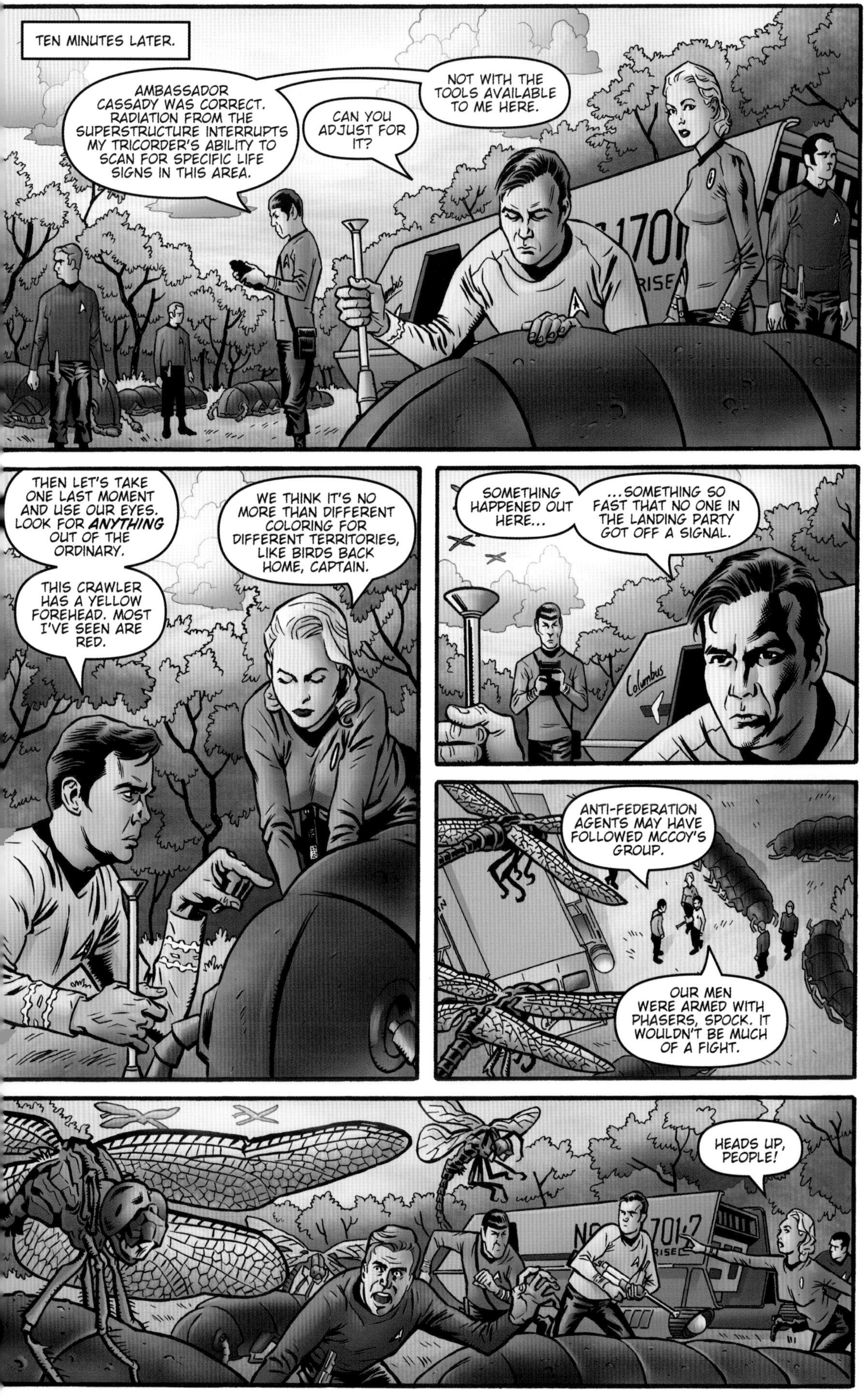
TEN MINUTES LATER.
AMBASSADOR CASSADY WAS CORRECT. RADIATION FROM THE SUPERSTRUCTURE INTERRUPTS MY TRICORDER'S ABILITY TO SCAN FOR SPECIFIC LIFE SIGNS IN THIS AREA.
CAN YOU ADJUST FOR IT?
NOT WITH THE TOOLS AVAILABLE TO ME HERE.
1701
RISE
THEN LET'S TAKE ONE LAST MOMENT AND USE OUR EYES. LOOK FOR ANYTHING OUT OF THE ORDINARY.
THIS CRAWLER HAS A YELLOW FOREHEAD. MOST I'VE SEEN ARE RED.
WE THINK IT'S NO MORE THAN DIFFERENT COLORING FOR DIFFERENT TERRITORIES, LIKE BIRDS BACK HOME, CAPTAIN.
SOMETHING HAPPENED OUT HERE...
...SOMETHING SO FAST THAT NO ONE IN THE LANDING PARTY GOT OFF A SIGNAL.
Columbus
ANTI-FEDERATION AGENTS MAY HAVE FOLLOWED MCCOY'S GROUP.
OUR MEN WERE ARMED WITH PHASERS, SPOCK. IT WOULDN'T BE MUCH OF A FIGHT.
HEADS UP, PEOPLE!
701-7
RISE

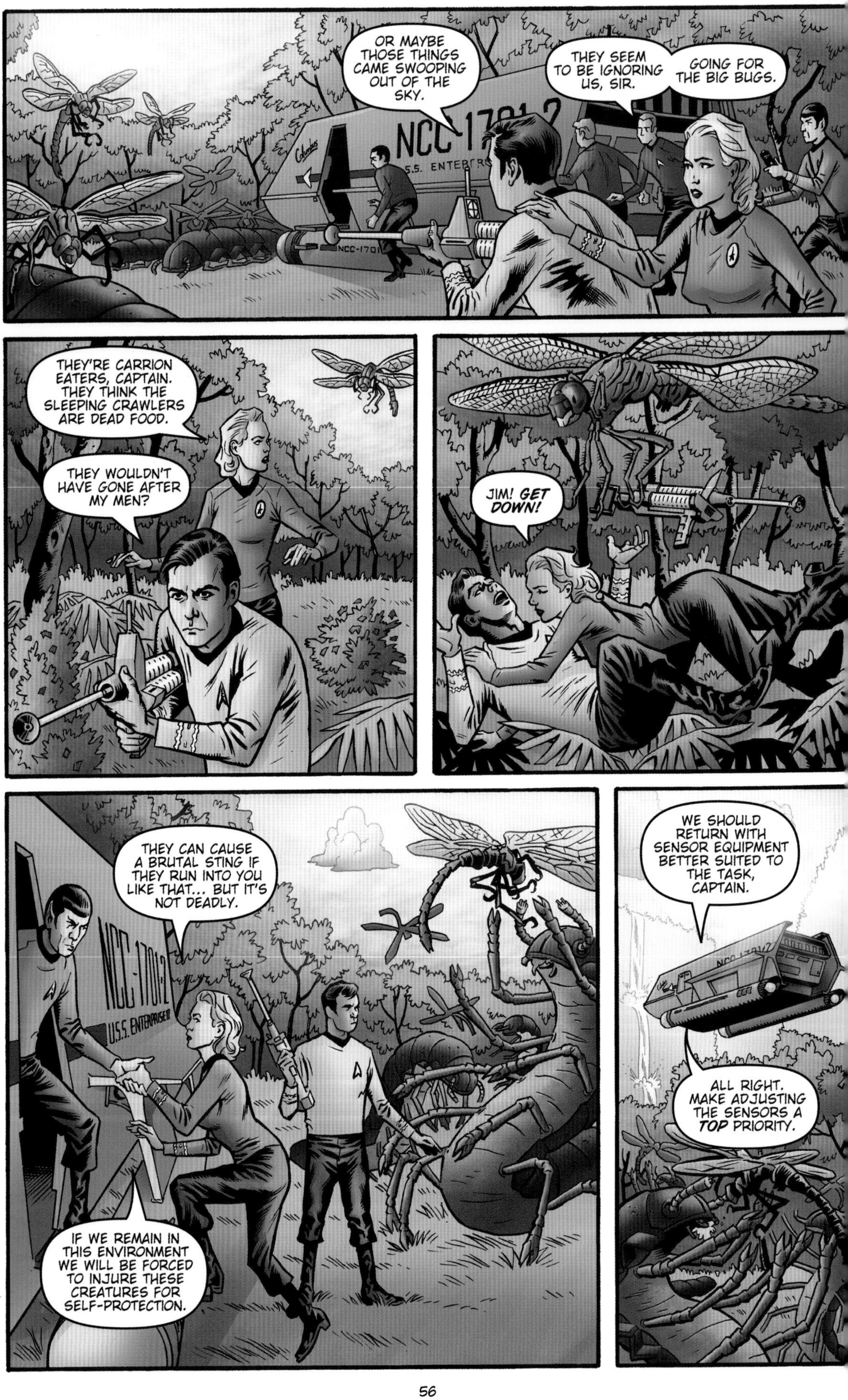
OR MAYBE THOSE THINGS CAME SWOOPING OUT OF THE SKY.
THEY SEEM TO BE IGNORING US, SIR.
GOING FOR THE BIG BUGS.
THEY'RE CARRION EATERS, CAPTAIN. THEY THINK THE SLEEPING CRAWLERS ARE DEAD FOOD.
THEY WOULDN'T HAVE GONE AFTER MY MEN?
JIM! **GET DOWN!**
THEY CAN CAUSE A BRUTAL STING IF THEY RUN INTO YOU LIKE THAT... BUT IT'S NOT DEADLY.
IF WE REMAIN IN THIS ENVIRONMENT WE WILL BE FORCED TO INJURE THESE CREATURES FOR SELF-PROTECTION.
WE SHOULD RETURN WITH SENSOR EQUIPMENT BETTER SUITED TO THE TASK, CAPTAIN.
ALL RIGHT. MAKE ADJUSTING THE SENSORS A **TOP** PRIORITY.

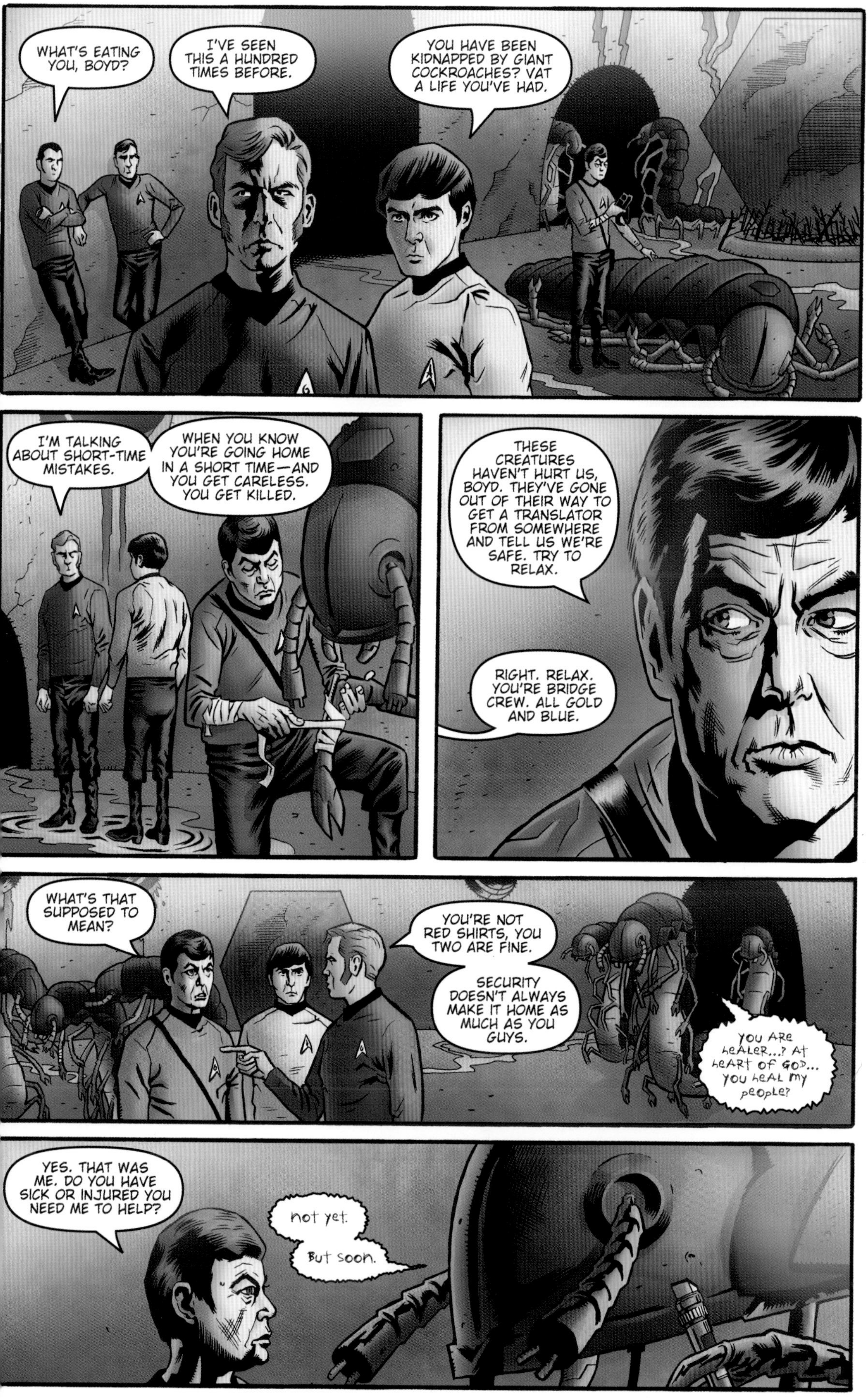
WHAT'S EATING YOU, BOYD?
I'VE SEEN THIS A HUNDRED TIMES BEFORE.
YOU HAVE BEEN KIDNAPPED BY GIANT COCKROACHES? VAT A LIFE YOU'VE HAD.
I'M TALKING ABOUT SHORT-TIME MISTAKES.
WHEN YOU KNOW YOU'RE GOING HOME IN A SHORT TIME—AND YOU GET CARELESS. YOU GET KILLED.
THESE CREATURES HAVEN'T HURT US, BOYD. THEY'VE GONE OUT OF THEIR WAY TO GET A TRANSLATOR FROM SOMEWHERE AND TELL US WE'RE SAFE. TRY TO RELAX.
RIGHT. RELAX. YOU'RE BRIDGE CREW. ALL GOLD AND BLUE.
WHAT'S THAT SUPPOSED TO MEAN?
YOU'RE NOT RED SHIRTS, YOU TWO ARE FINE.
SECURITY DOESN'T ALWAYS MAKE IT HOME AS MUCH AS YOU GUYS.
YOU ARE HEALER...? AT HEART OF GOD... YOU HEAL MY PEOPLE?
YES. THAT WAS ME. DO YOU HAVE SICK OR INJURED YOU NEED ME TO HELP?
not yet.
But soon.

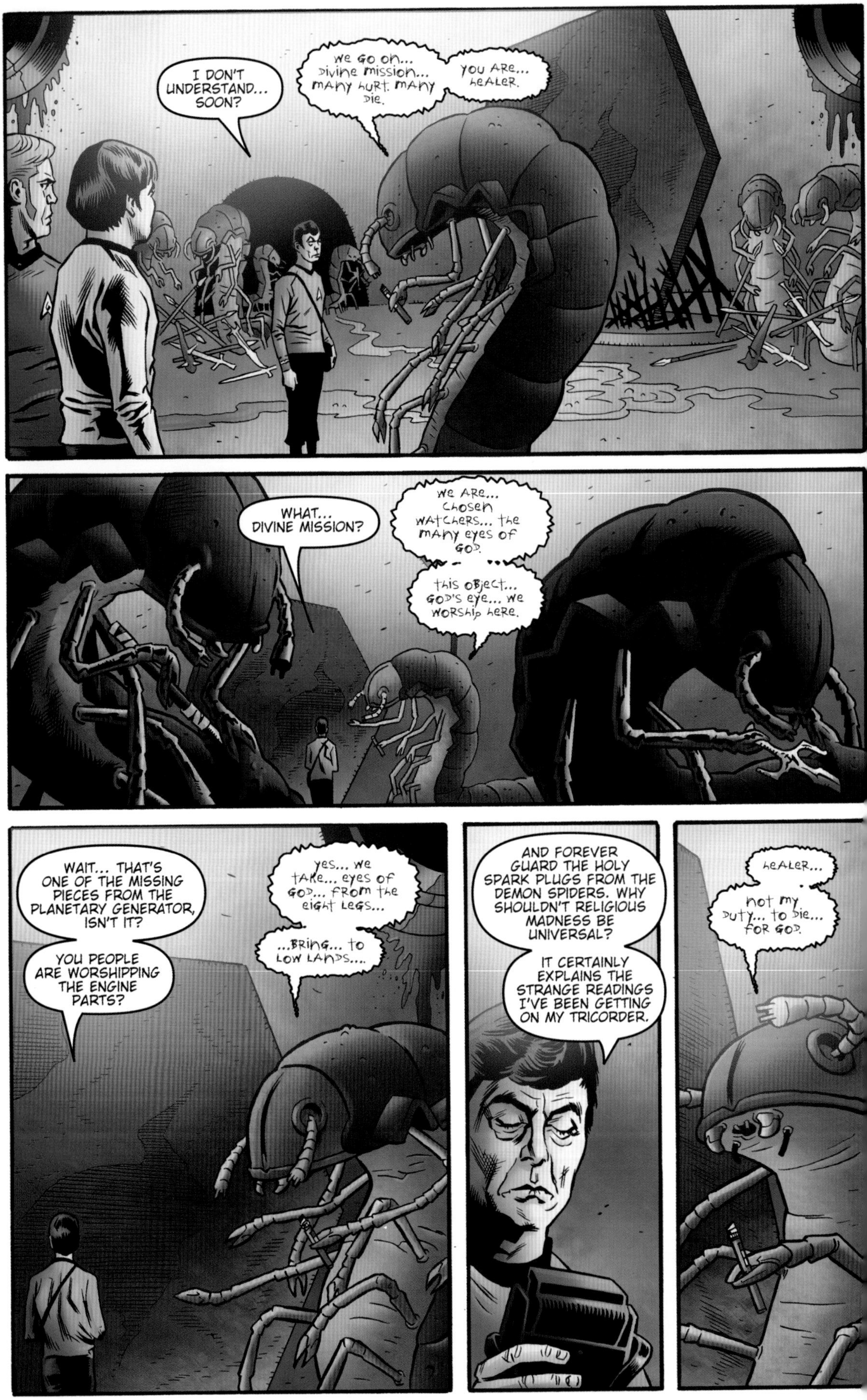
I DON'T UNDERSTAND... SOON?
WE GO ON... DIVINE MISSION... MANY HURT. MANY DIE.
YOU ARE... HEALER.
WHAT... DIVINE MISSION?
WE ARE... CHOSEN WATCHERS... THE MANY EYES OF GOD.
THIS OBJECT... GOD'S EYE... WE WORSHIP HERE.
WAIT... THAT'S ONE OF THE MISSING PIECES FROM THE PLANETARY GENERATOR, ISN'T IT?
YOU PEOPLE ARE WORSHIPPING THE ENGINE PARTS?
YES... WE TAKE... EYES OF GOD... FROM THE EIGHT LEGS...
...BRING... TO LOW LANDS....
AND FOREVER GUARD THE HOLY SPARK PLUGS FROM THE DEMON SPIDERS. WHY SHOULDN'T RELIGIOUS MADNESS BE UNIVERSAL?
IT CERTAINLY EXPLAINS THE STRANGE READINGS I'VE BEEN GETTING ON MY TRICORDER.
HEALER...
NOT MY DUTY... TO DIE... FOR GOD.

PARDON ME? HAS SOMEONE SAID YOU HAVE TO DIE?
DUTY TO FAMILY AND GOD...
THE EIGHT LEGS... STEAL EYES OF GOD... WE GET EYES OF GOD BACK... IN WAR...
NOW FOUR LEGS COME... YOU...
...YOU FOUR LEGS... WILL TAKE... TAKE THE EYES OF GOD?
NO WE WON'T. I MEAN...
...I DON'T THINK THAT'S GOING TO HAPPEN.
WAR... FOR GOD... TAKE EYES BACK FROM THE EIGHT LEGS... RETURN HERE.
BUT... NOT DUTY... TO DIE... FOR GOD...
...I RETURN... FROM WAR... WITH EYES OF GOD... AND I AM HURT...?
YOU WILL HEAL ME?
I WILL DO MY BEST.
DUTY OF WAR... FOR GOD.
NOT DUTY... TO DIE... FOR GOD.

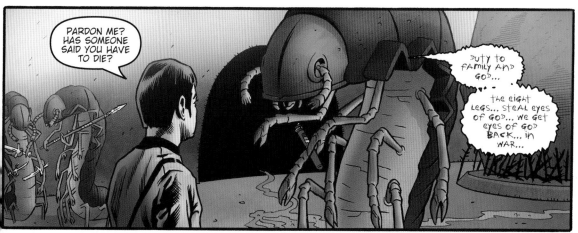

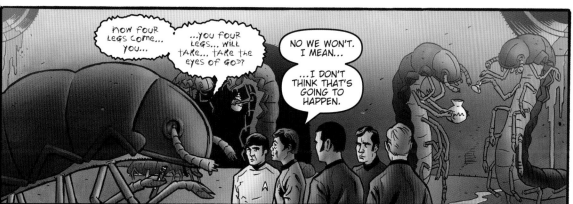

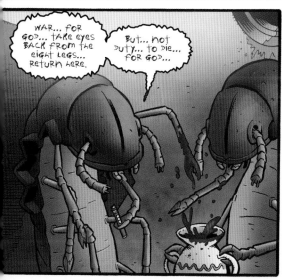

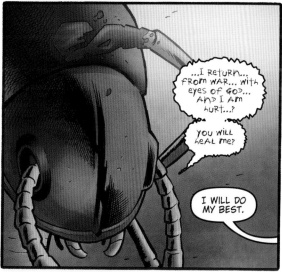

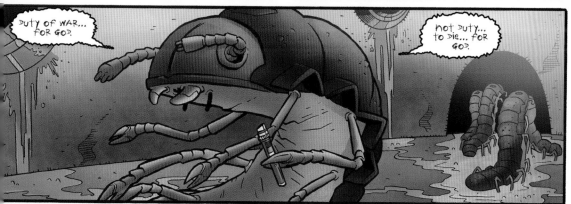

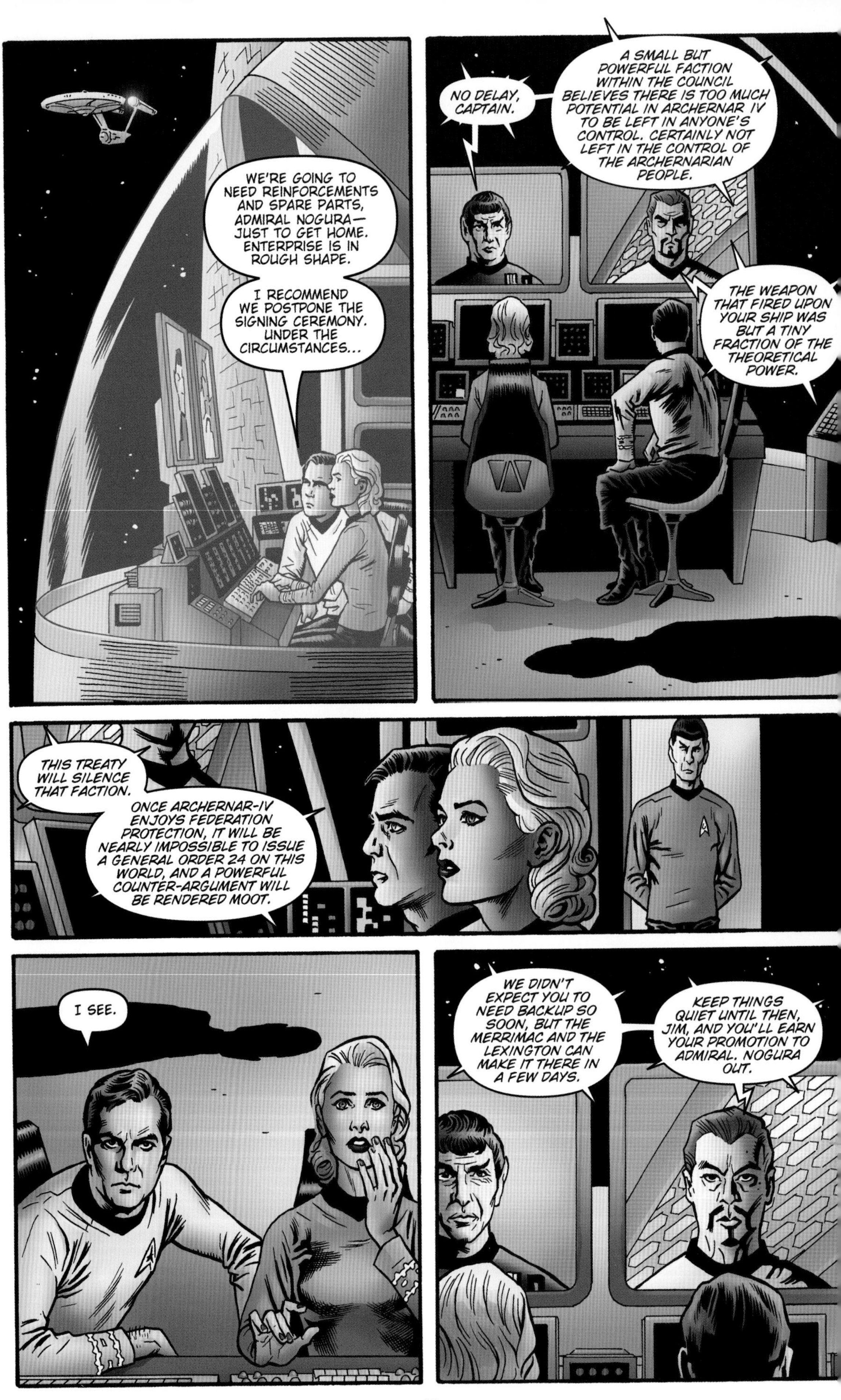
WE'RE GOING TO NEED REINFORCEMENTS AND SPARE PARTS, ADMIRAL NOGURA— JUST TO GET HOME. ENTERPRISE IS IN ROUGH SHAPE.
I RECOMMEND WE POSTPONE THE SIGNING CEREMONY. UNDER THE CIRCUMSTANCES...
NO DELAY, CAPTAIN.
A SMALL BUT POWERFUL FACTION WITHIN THE COUNCIL BELIEVES THERE IS TOO MUCH POTENTIAL IN ARCHERNAR IV TO BE LEFT IN ANYONE'S CONTROL. CERTAINLY NOT LEFT IN THE CONTROL OF THE ARCHERNARIAN PEOPLE.
THE WEAPON THAT FIRED UPON YOUR SHIP WAS BUT A TINY FRACTION OF THE THEORETICAL POWER.
THIS TREATY WILL SILENCE THAT FACTION.
ONCE ARCHERNAR-IV ENJOYS FEDERATION PROTECTION, IT WILL BE NEARLY IMPOSSIBLE TO ISSUE A GENERAL ORDER 24 ON THIS WORLD, AND A POWERFUL COUNTER-ARGUMENT WILL BE RENDERED MOOT.
I SEE.
WE DIDN'T EXPECT YOU TO NEED BACKUP SO SOON, BUT THE MERRIMAC AND THE LEXINGTON CAN MAKE IT THERE IN A FEW DAYS.
KEEP THINGS QUIET UNTIL THEN, JIM, AND YOU'LL EARN YOUR PROMOTION TO ADMIRAL. NOGURA OUT.

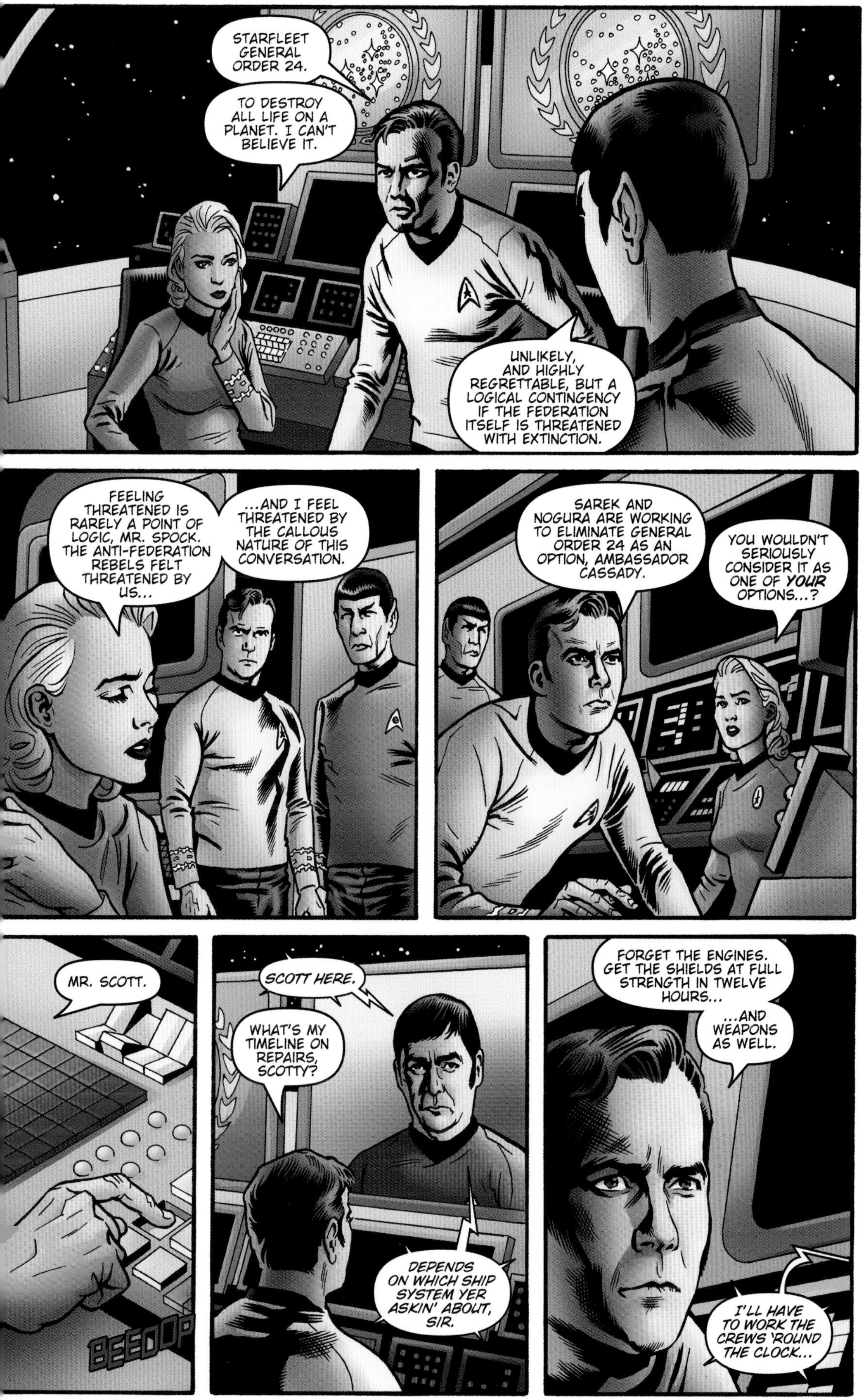
STARFLEET GENERAL ORDER 24.
TO DESTROY ALL LIFE ON A PLANET. I CAN'T BELIEVE IT.
UNLIKELY, AND HIGHLY REGRETTABLE, BUT A LOGICAL CONTINGENCY IF THE FEDERATION ITSELF IS THREATENED WITH EXTINCTION.
FEELING THREATENED IS RARELY A POINT OF LOGIC, MR. SPOCK. THE ANTI-FEDERATION REBELS FELT THREATENED BY US...
...AND I FEEL THREATENED BY THE CALLOUS NATURE OF THIS CONVERSATION.
SAREK AND NOGURA ARE WORKING TO ELIMINATE GENERAL ORDER 24 AS AN OPTION, AMBASSADOR CASSADY.
YOU WOULDN'T SERIOUSLY CONSIDER IT AS ONE OF *YOUR* OPTIONS...?
MR. SCOTT.
BEEDOP
SCOTT HERE.
WHAT'S MY TIMELINE ON REPAIRS, SCOTTY?
DEPENDS ON WHICH SHIP SYSTEM YER ASKIN' ABOUT, SIR.
FORGET THE ENGINES. GET THE SHIELDS AT FULL STRENGTH IN TWELVE HOURS...
...AND WEAPONS AS WELL.
I'LL HAVE TO WORK THE CREWS 'ROUND THE CLOCK...

"...BUT IT'S NOT LIKE THE WEE LADS WERE GOING TO SLEEP ANYWAY."

YOU'RE HEADING TO YOUR QUARTERS, MOORE? THE WHOLE SHIP IS ON A DOUBLE SHIFT.

I KNOW. JUST GRABBING A QUICK SHOWER BEFORE I HEAD BACK ON DUTY.

BLEEP

MARIKK BOTAR RECEIVES YOUR MESSAGE.

ARE YOU IN POSITION?

I'VE MADE IT.

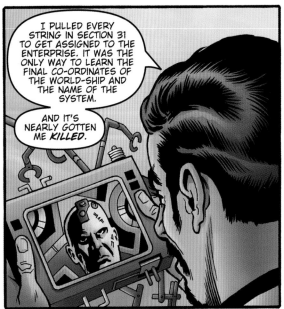

I PULLED EVERY STRING IN SECTION 31 TO GET ASSIGNED TO THE ENTERPRISE. IT WAS THE ONLY WAY TO LEARN THE FINAL CO-ORDINATES OF THE WORLD-SHIP AND THE NAME OF THE SYSTEM.

AND IT'S NEARLY GOTTEN ME KILLED.

I AM UNINTERESTED IN YOUR WELL BEING. ONLY THAT YOU TRANSMIT THE CO-ORDINATES OF THIS OMEGA-WEAPON TO THE ORION SYNDICATE SO WE CAN COMPLETE OUR BUSINESS.

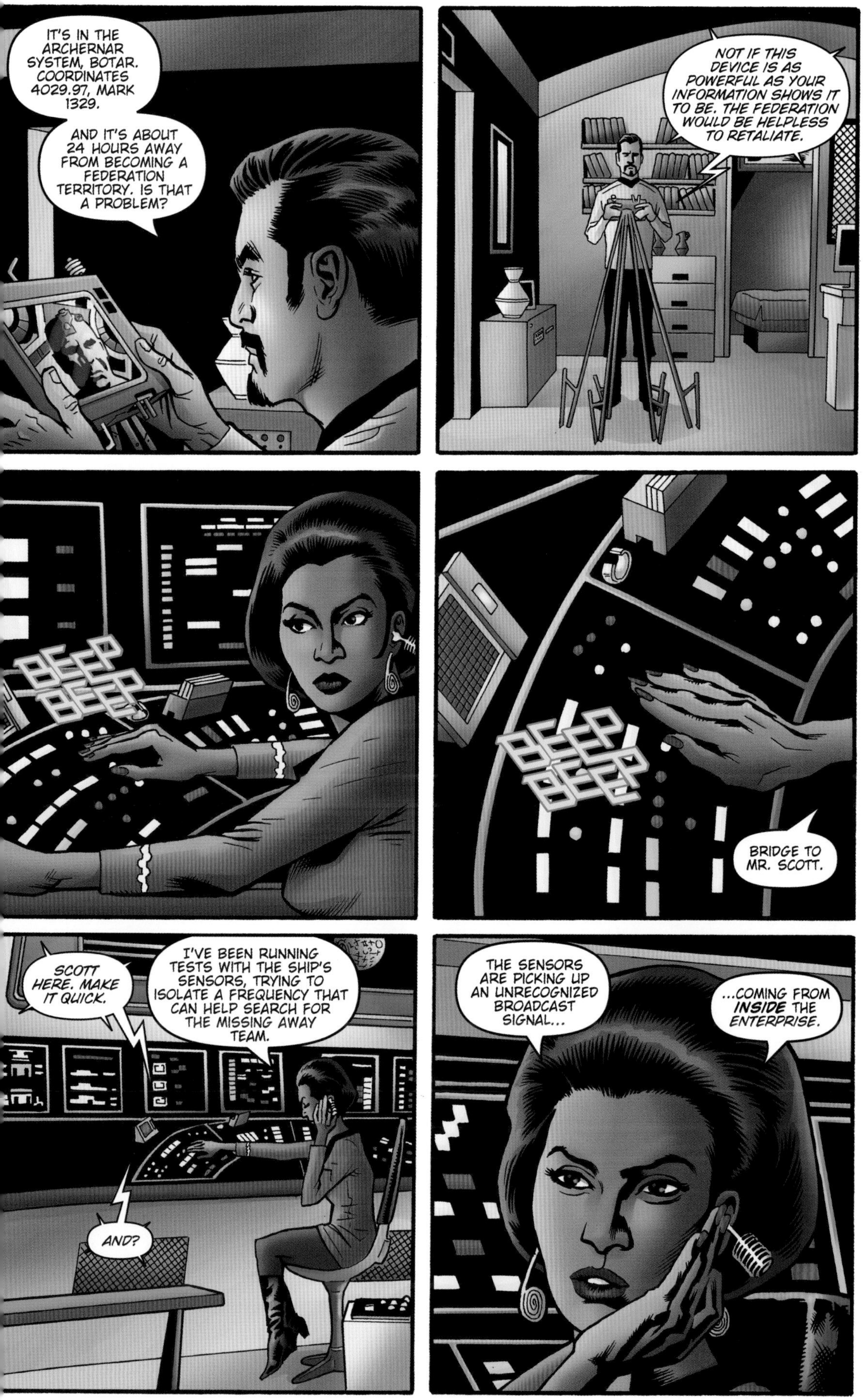
IT'S IN THE ARCHERNAR SYSTEM, BOTAR. COORDINATES 4029.97, MARK 1329.
AND IT'S ABOUT 24 HOURS AWAY FROM BECOMING A FEDERATION TERRITORY. IS THAT A PROBLEM?
NOT IF THIS DEVICE IS AS POWERFUL AS YOUR INFORMATION SHOWS IT TO BE. THE FEDERATION WOULD BE HELPLESS TO RETALIATE.
BEEP BEEP
BEEP BEEP
BRIDGE TO MR. SCOTT.
SCOTT HERE. MAKE IT QUICK.
I'VE BEEN RUNNING TESTS WITH THE SHIP'S SENSORS, TRYING TO ISOLATE A FREQUENCY THAT CAN HELP SEARCH FOR THE MISSING AWAY TEAM.
AND?
THE SENSORS ARE PICKING UP AN UNRECOGNIZED BROADCAST SIGNAL...
...COMING FROM *INSIDE* THE ENTERPRISE.

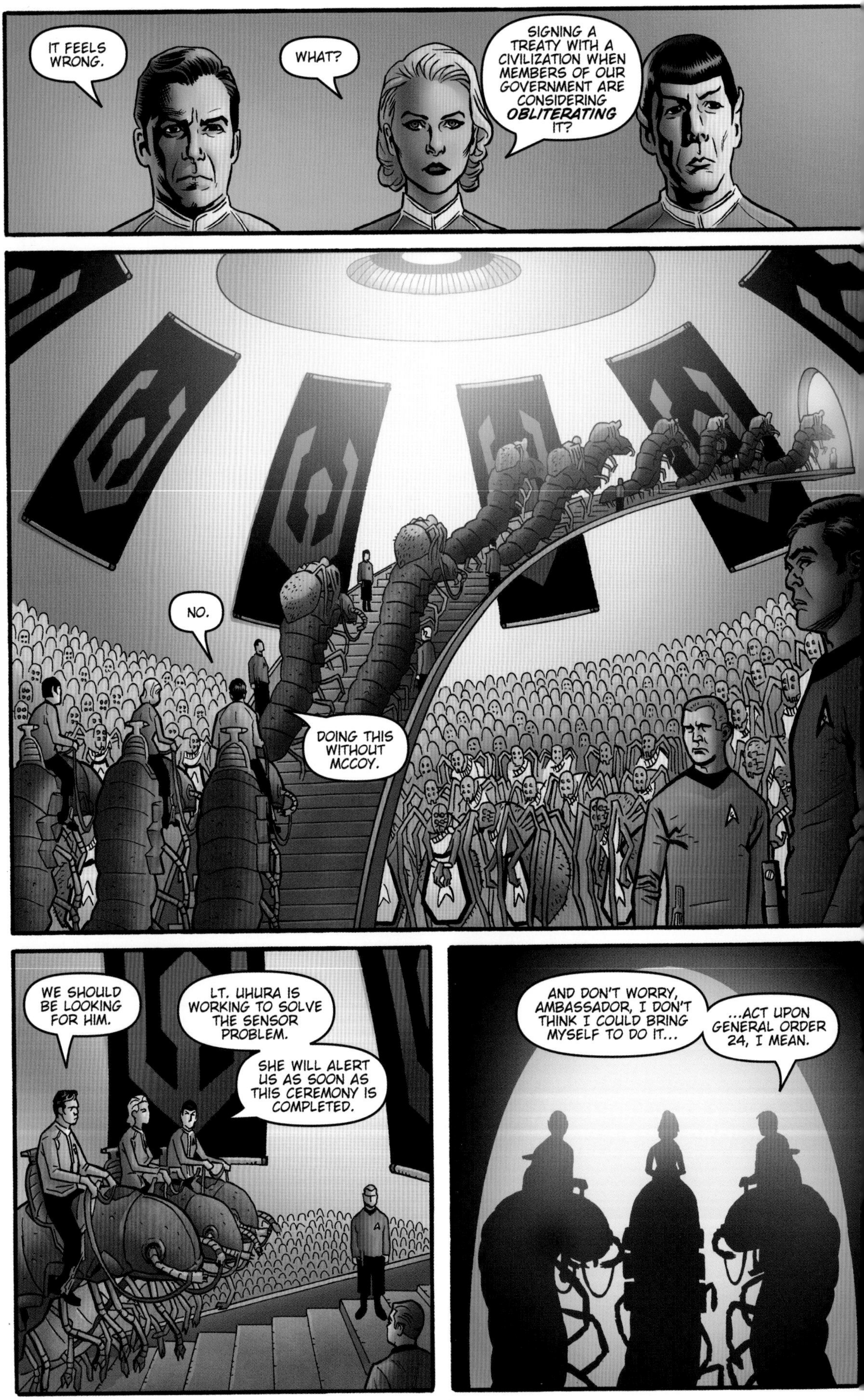

IT FEELS WRONG.
WHAT?
SIGNING A TREATY WITH A CIVILIZATION WHEN MEMBERS OF OUR GOVERNMENT ARE CONSIDERING *OBLITERATING* IT?
NO.
DOING THIS WITHOUT MCCOY.
WE SHOULD BE LOOKING FOR HIM.
LT. UHURA IS WORKING TO SOLVE THE SENSOR PROBLEM.
SHE WILL ALERT US AS SOON AS THIS CEREMONY IS COMPLETED.
AND DON'T WORRY, AMBASSADOR, I DON'T THINK I COULD BRING MYSELF TO DO IT...
...ACT UPON GENERAL ORDER 24, I MEAN.

NOT EVEN IF YOU WERE DIRECTLY COMMANDED TO?

IT WOULDN'T COME TO THAT. WE'D FIGURE SOMETHING OUT.

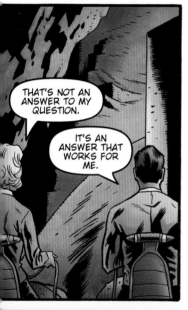

THAT'S NOT AN ANSWER TO MY QUESTION.

IT'S AN ANSWER THAT WORKS FOR ME.

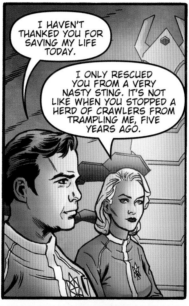

I HAVEN'T THANKED YOU FOR SAVING MY LIFE TODAY.

I ONLY RESCUED YOU FROM A VERY NASTY STING. IT'S NOT LIKE WHEN YOU STOPPED A HERD OF CRAWLERS FROM TRAMPLING ME, FIVE YEARS AGO.

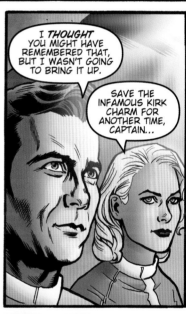

I *THOUGHT* YOU MIGHT HAVE REMEMBERED THAT, BUT I WASN'T GOING TO BRING IT UP.

SAVE THE INFAMOUS KIRK CHARM FOR ANOTHER TIME, CAPTAIN...

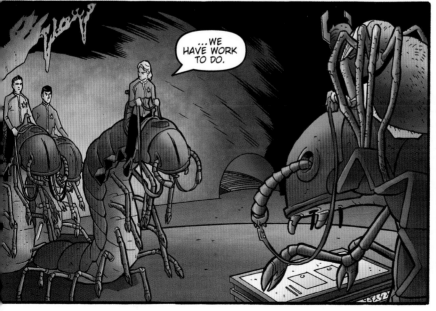

...WE HAVE WORK TO DO.

LET US BEGIN.

BENEATH THE GLORIOUS POWER OF THE HEART OF GOD ITSELF...

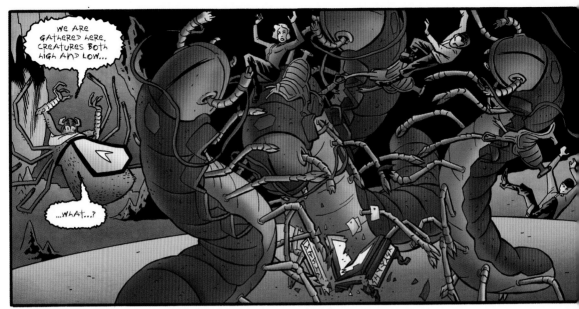

WE ARE GATHERED HERE, CREATURES BOTH HIGH AND LOW...

...WHAT...?

SOMETHING HAS SPOOKED THE CRAWLERS!

IT'S AN ATTACK!

THEY'RE ONLY ATTACKING THE SPIDER-PEOPLE.

OVER THERE! THEY'RE HEADING UP THE WALL.

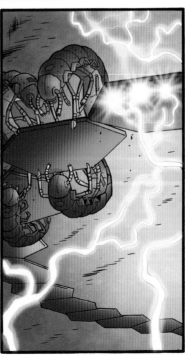

I BELIEVE THE CRAWLERS ARE ATTEMPTING TO DAMAGE THE STRUCTURE OF THE HEART OF GOD, CAPTAIN.

SPOCK! ARE YOU ALL RIGHT?

IT IS DIFFICULT TO FIND A PATH TO SAFETY.

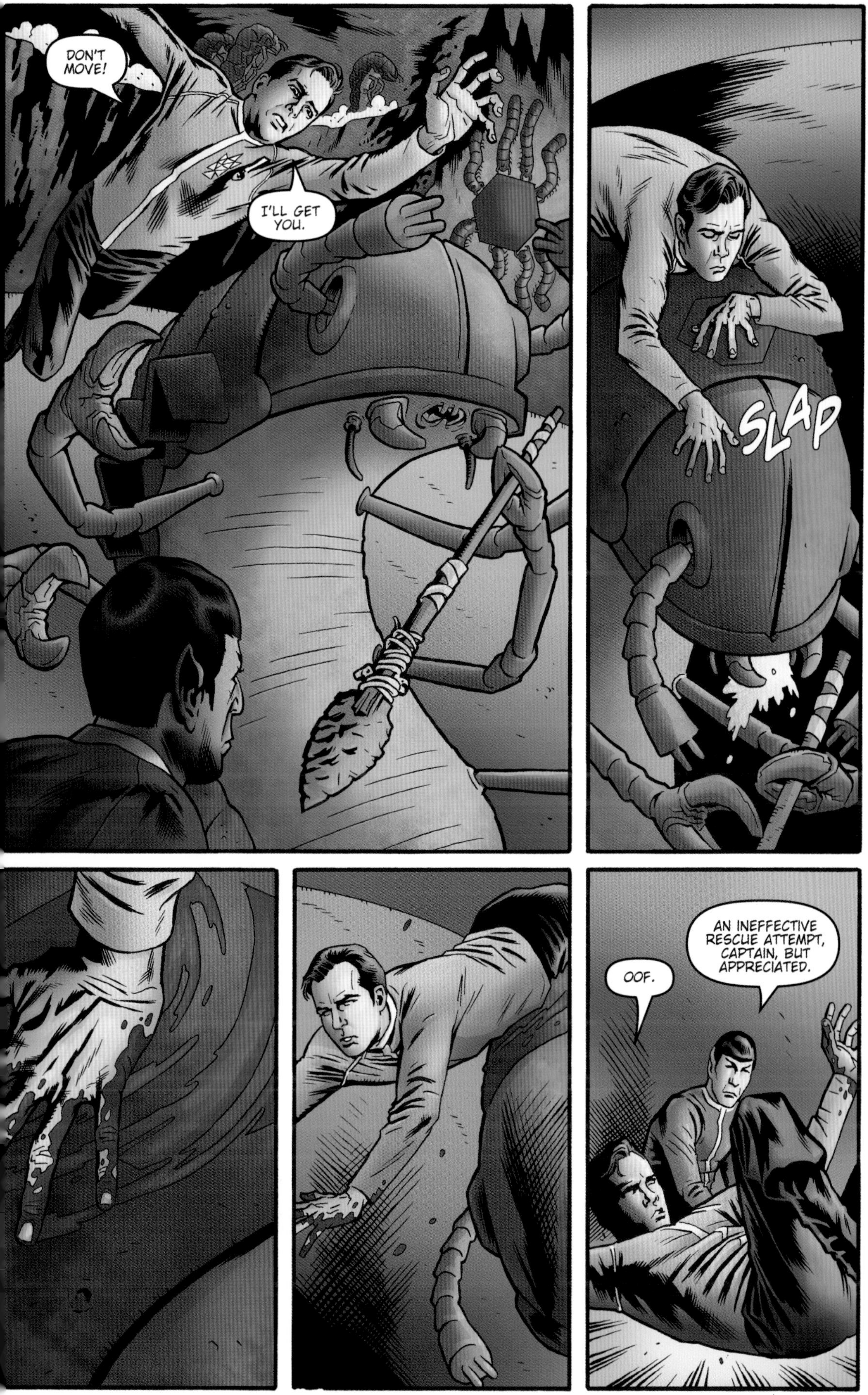
DON'T MOVE!
I'LL GET YOU.
SLAP
OOF.
AN INEFFECTIVE RESCUE ATTEMPT, CAPTAIN, BUT APPRECIATED.

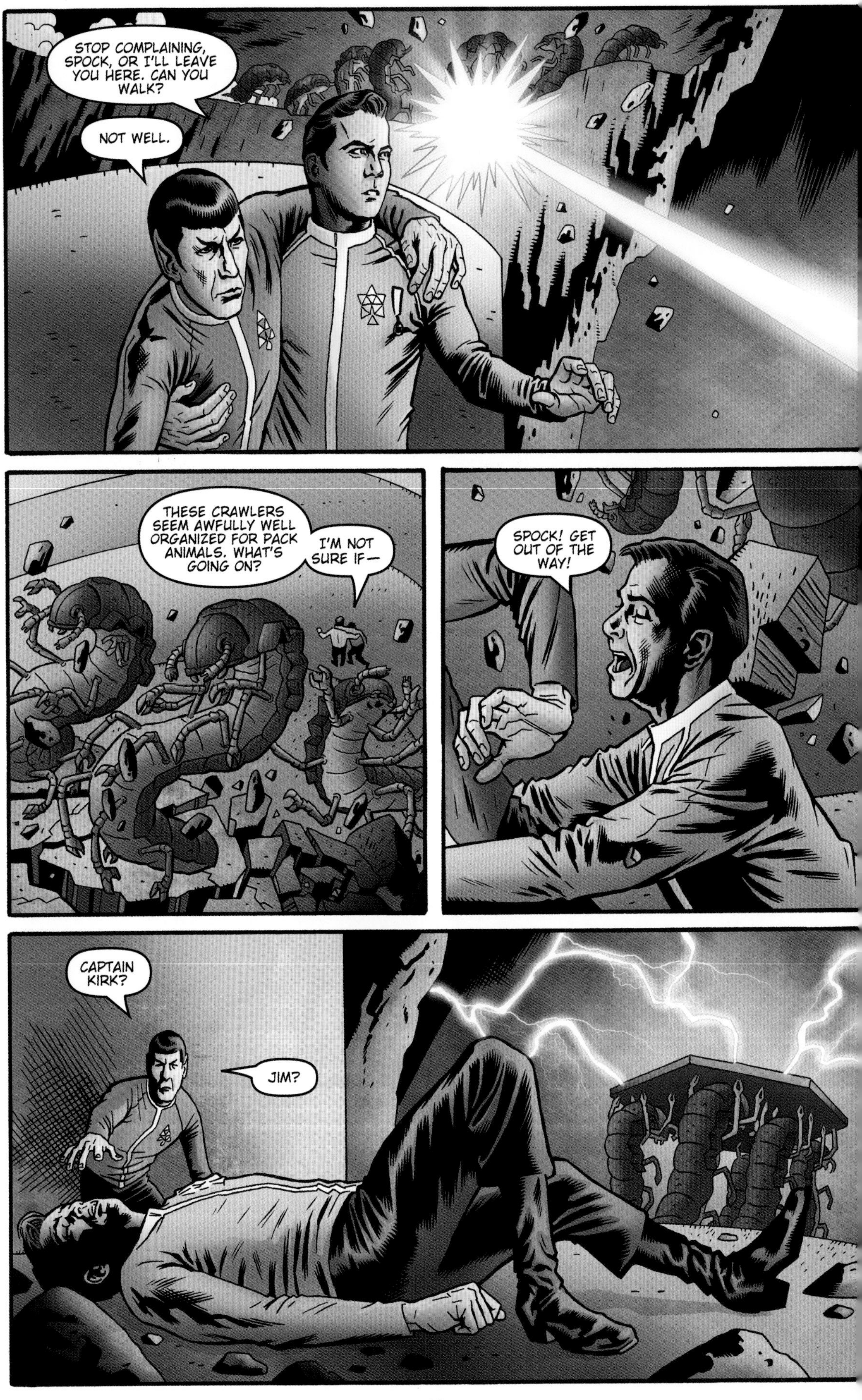
STOP COMPLAINING, SPOCK, OR I'LL LEAVE YOU HERE. CAN YOU WALK?
NOT WELL.
THESE CRAWLERS SEEM AWFULLY WELL ORGANIZED FOR PACK ANIMALS. WHAT'S GOING ON?
I'M NOT SURE IF—
SPOCK! GET OUT OF THE WAY!
CAPTAIN KIRK?
JIM?

CHAPTER FOUR

FIRST OFFICER'S LOG, STARDATE 5958.4.

ARCHERNAR IV IS AN ANCIENT WORLDSHIP, WHOSE ENGINES SEEM CAPABLE OF PRODUCING NEAR LIMITLESS POWER. THE CURRENT OCCUPIERS OF THIS WORLD, A SPIDER-LIKE SPECIES WHO EVOLVED ON THE LONG ABANDONED SHIP, NOW LAY CLAIM TO THE ALIEN TECHNOLOGY THAT THEY CALL THE "HEART OF GOD."

THE *ENTERPRISE'S* MISSION TO WELCOME ARCHERNAR IV INTO THE FEDERATION HAS MET WITH SEVERAL SETBACKS.

SINCE OUR ARRIVAL, TWELVE MEMBERS OF THE STARFLEET DIPLOMATIC CORPS HAVE BEEN KILLED, AND THE *ENTERPRISE* HAS BEEN DAMAGED IN ATTACKS BY ANTI-GOVERNMENT FORCES FROM WITHIN THE NATIVE POPULATION.

DOCTOR MCCOY'S LANDING PARTY HAS BEEN MISSING FOR OVER TWENTY-FOUR HOURS, LOST ON AN EXPEDITION TO RETRIEVE BIOLOGICAL SAMPLES OF LOCAL FLORA.

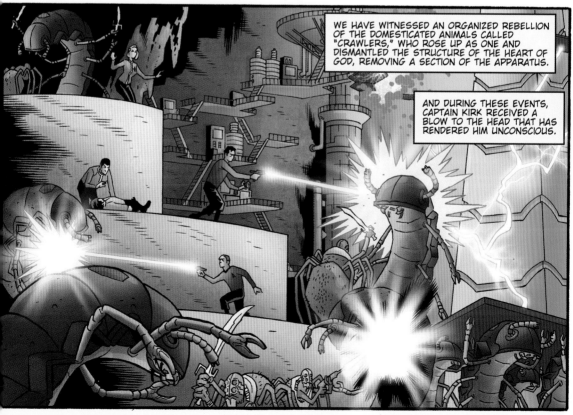

WE HAVE WITNESSED AN ORGANIZED REBELLION OF THE DOMESTICATED ANIMALS CALLED "CRAWLERS," WHO ROSE UP AS ONE AND DISMANTLED THE STRUCTURE OF THE HEART OF GOD, REMOVING A SECTION OF THE APPARATUS.

AND DURING THESE EVENTS, CAPTAIN KIRK RECEIVED A BLOW TO THE HEAD THAT HAS RENDERED HIM UNCONSCIOUS.

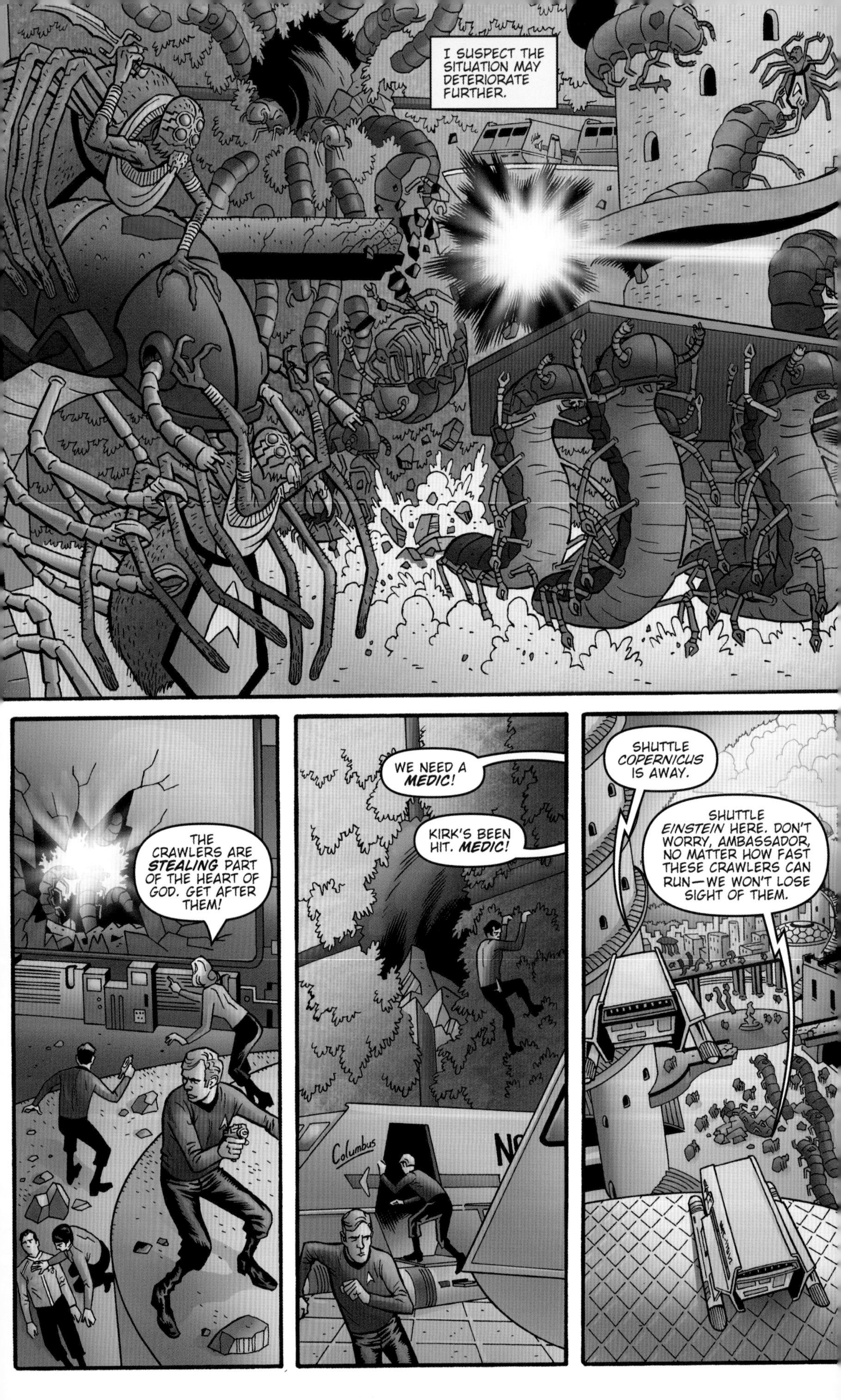
I SUSPECT THE SITUATION MAY DETERIORATE FURTHER.
THE CRAWLERS ARE *STEALING* PART OF THE HEART OF GOD. GET AFTER THEM!
WE NEED A *MEDIC!*
KIRK'S BEEN HIT. *MEDIC!*
Columbus
SHUTTLE *COPERNICUS* IS AWAY.
SHUTTLE *EINSTEIN* HERE. DON'T WORRY, AMBASSADOR, NO MATTER HOW FAST THESE CRAWLERS CAN RUN—WE WON'T LOSE SIGHT OF THEM.

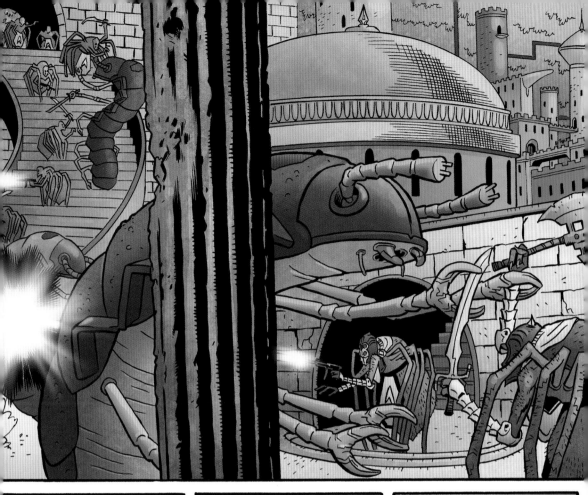

WAIT A MOMENT. LOOK AT THAT...

IT'S LIKE THEY'RE DELIBERATELY HIDING IT FROM US.

IF I HADN'T SEEN IT WITH MY OWN EYES—

—THESE INSECT CREATURES KNOW WE'RE CHASING THEM. THEY'RE COVERING THE BIG RED PLATFORM WITH THEIR OWN BODIES. SMART LITTLE THINGS—

DON'T LOSE SIGHT OF THE HERD. IF WE LOSE THAT ENGINE PART...

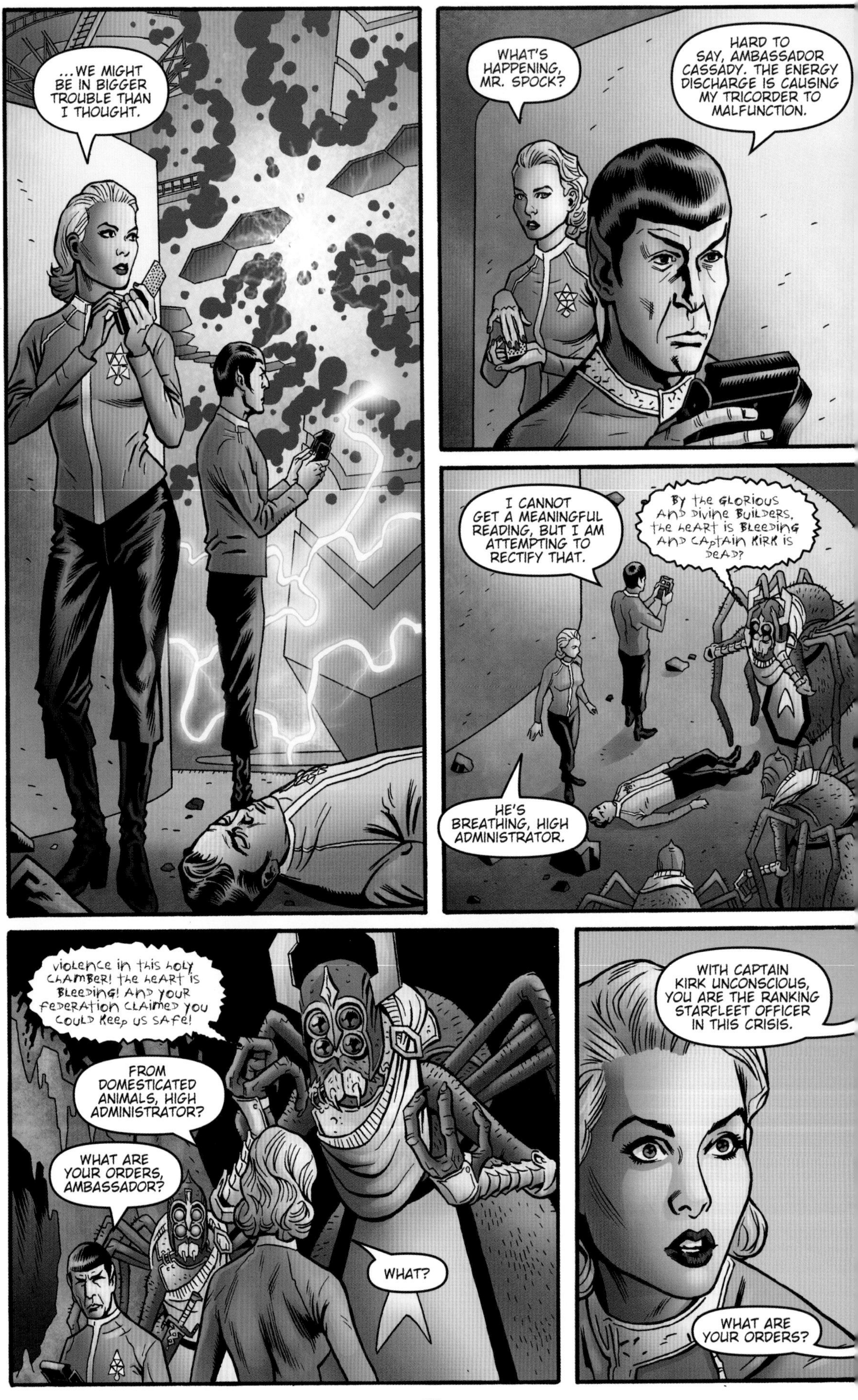
...WE MIGHT BE IN BIGGER TROUBLE THAN I THOUGHT.
WHAT'S HAPPENING, MR. SPOCK?
HARD TO SAY, AMBASSADOR CASSADY. THE ENERGY DISCHARGE IS CAUSING MY TRICORDER TO MALFUNCTION.
I CANNOT GET A MEANINGFUL READING, BUT I AM ATTEMPTING TO RECTIFY THAT.
By the GLORIOUS AND DIVINE BUILDERS, the HEART is BLEEDING AND CAPTAIN KIRK is DEAD?
HE'S BREATHING, HIGH ADMINISTRATOR.
violence in this holy chamber! the heart is bleeding! and your federation claimed you could keep us safe!
FROM DOMESTICATED ANIMALS, HIGH ADMINISTRATOR?
WHAT ARE YOUR ORDERS, AMBASSADOR?
WHAT?
WITH CAPTAIN KIRK UNCONSCIOUS, YOU ARE THE RANKING STARFLEET OFFICER IN THIS CRISIS.
WHAT ARE YOUR ORDERS?

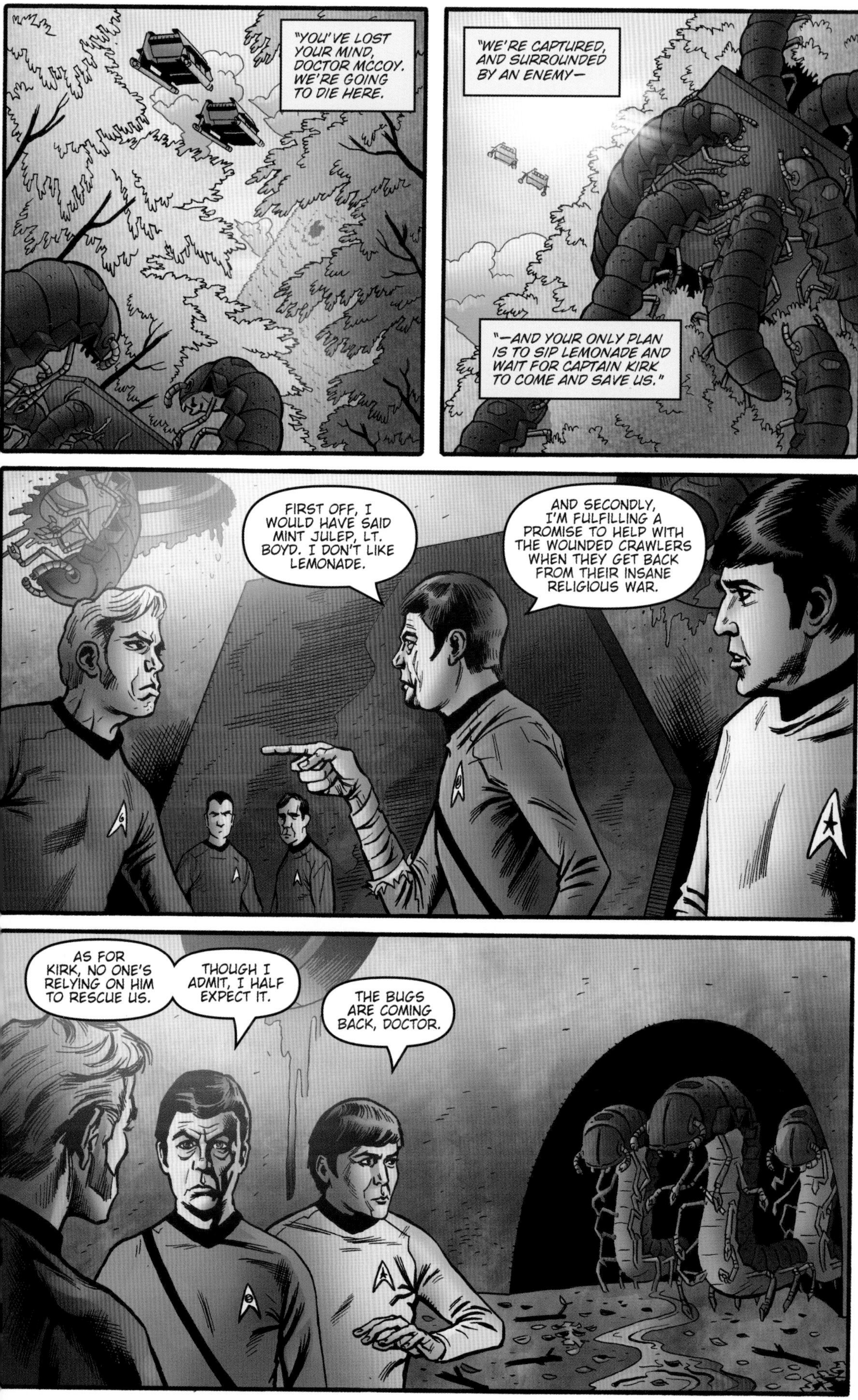
"YOU'VE LOST YOUR MIND, DOCTOR MCCOY. WE'RE GOING TO DIE HERE.
"WE'RE CAPTURED, AND SURROUNDED BY AN ENEMY—
"—AND YOUR ONLY PLAN IS TO SIP LEMONADE AND WAIT FOR CAPTAIN KIRK TO COME AND SAVE US."
FIRST OFF, I WOULD HAVE SAID MINT JULEP, LT. BOYD. I DON'T LIKE LEMONADE.
AND SECONDLY, I'M FULFILLING A PROMISE TO HELP WITH THE WOUNDED CRAWLERS WHEN THEY GET BACK FROM THEIR INSANE RELIGIOUS WAR.
AS FOR KIRK, NO ONE'S RELYING ON HIM TO RESCUE US.
THOUGH I ADMIT, I HALF EXPECT IT.
THE BUGS ARE COMING BACK, DOCTOR.

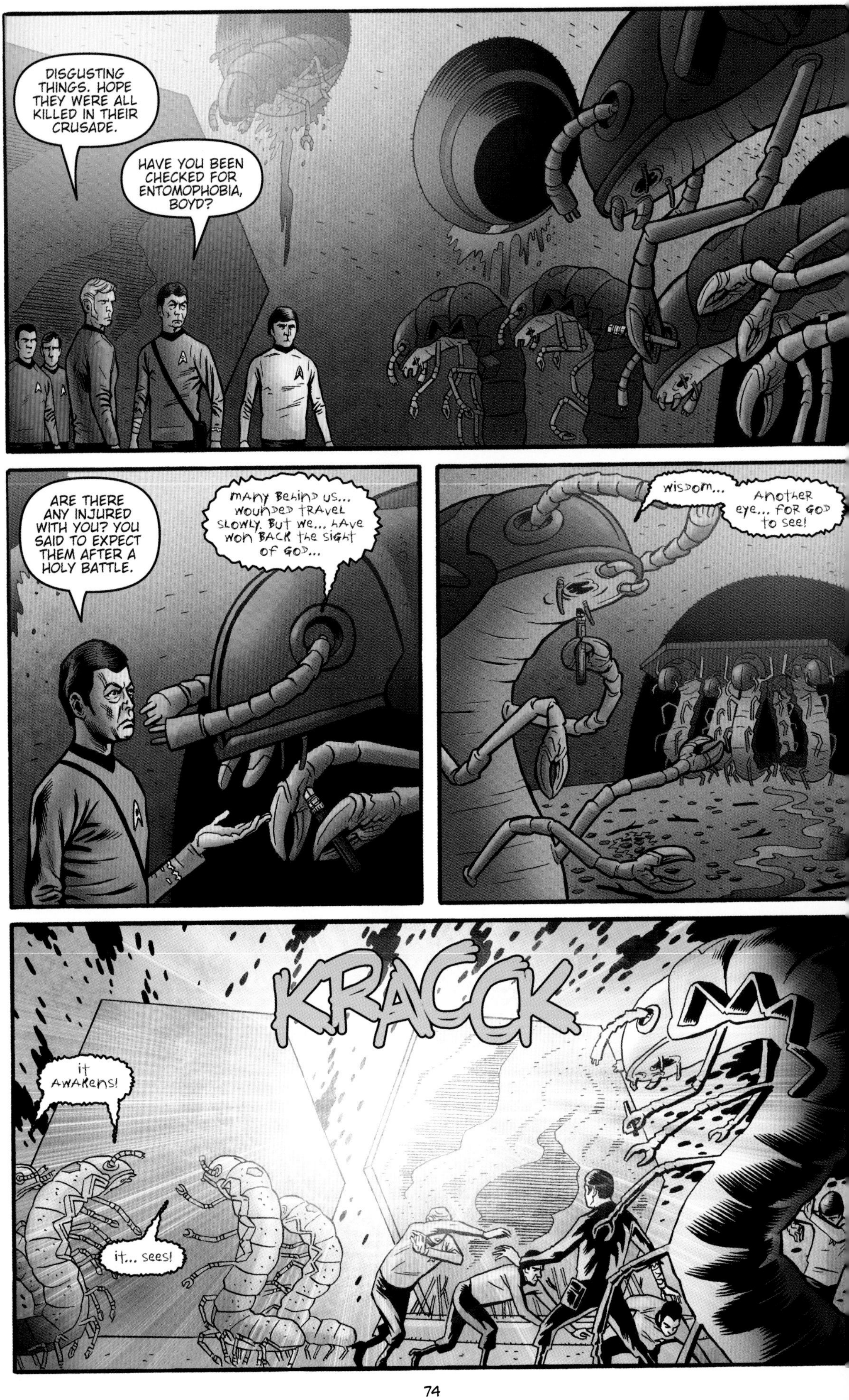

DISGUSTING THINGS. HOPE THEY WERE ALL KILLED IN THEIR CRUSADE.
HAVE YOU BEEN CHECKED FOR ENTOMOPHOBIA, BOYD?
ARE THERE ANY INJURED WITH YOU? YOU SAID TO EXPECT THEM AFTER A HOLY BATTLE.
many behind us... wounded travel slowly. But we... have won back the sight of God...
wisdom...
Another eye... for God to see!
KRACCK
it awakens!
it... sees!

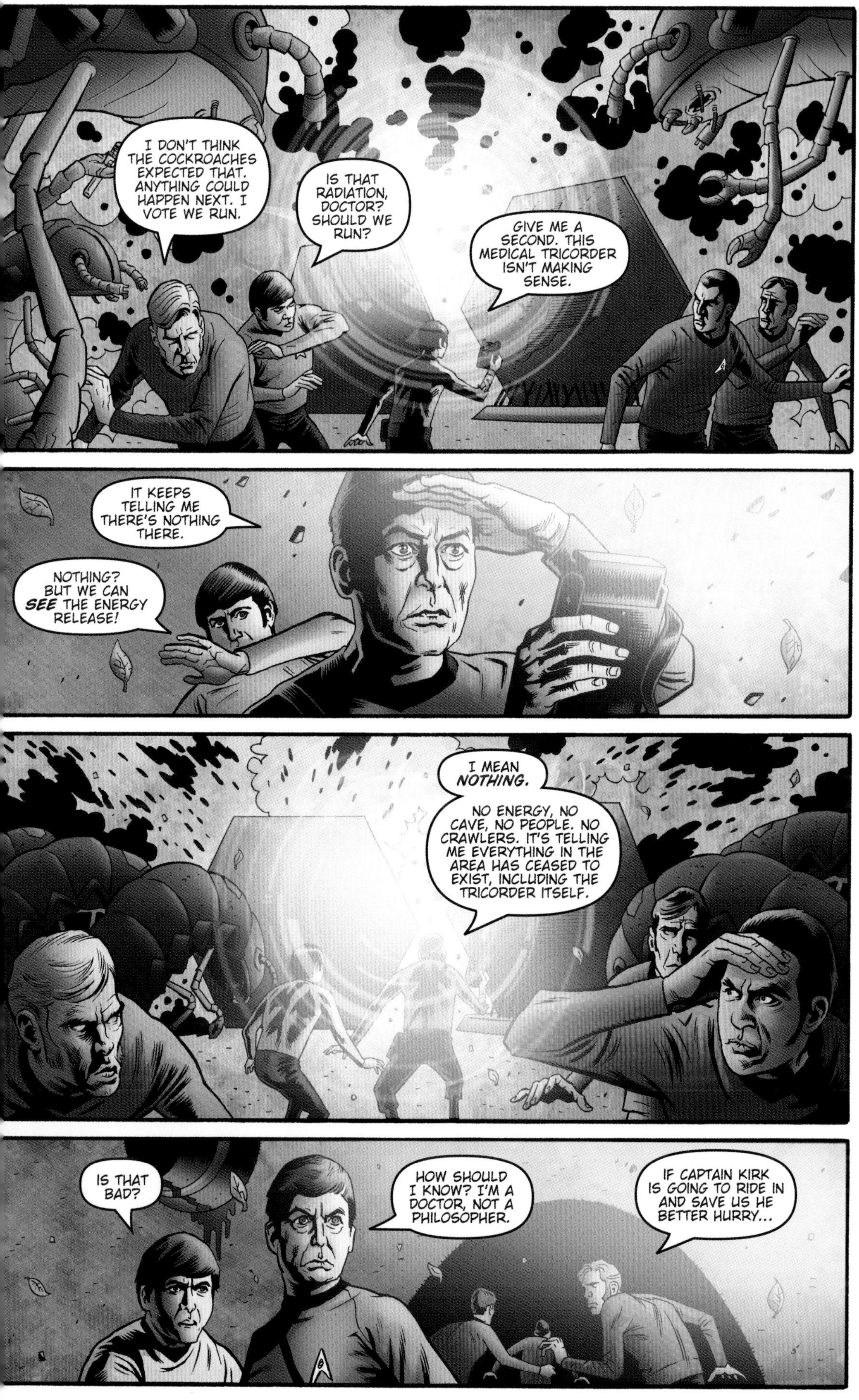
I DON'T THINK THE COCKROACHES EXPECTED THAT. ANYTHING COULD HAPPEN NEXT. I VOTE WE RUN.
IS THAT RADIATION, DOCTOR? SHOULD WE RUN?
GIVE ME A SECOND. THIS MEDICAL TRICORDER ISN'T MAKING SENSE.
IT KEEPS TELLING ME THERE'S NOTHING THERE.
NOTHING? BUT WE CAN *SEE* THE ENERGY RELEASE!
I MEAN *NOTHING.*
NO ENERGY, NO CAVE, NO PEOPLE. NO CRAWLERS. IT'S TELLING ME EVERYTHING IN THE AREA HAS CEASED TO EXIST, INCLUDING THE TRICORDER ITSELF.
IS THAT BAD?
HOW SHOULD I KNOW? I'M A DOCTOR, NOT A PHILOSOPHER.
IF CAPTAIN KIRK IS GOING TO RIDE IN AND SAVE US HE BETTER HURRY...

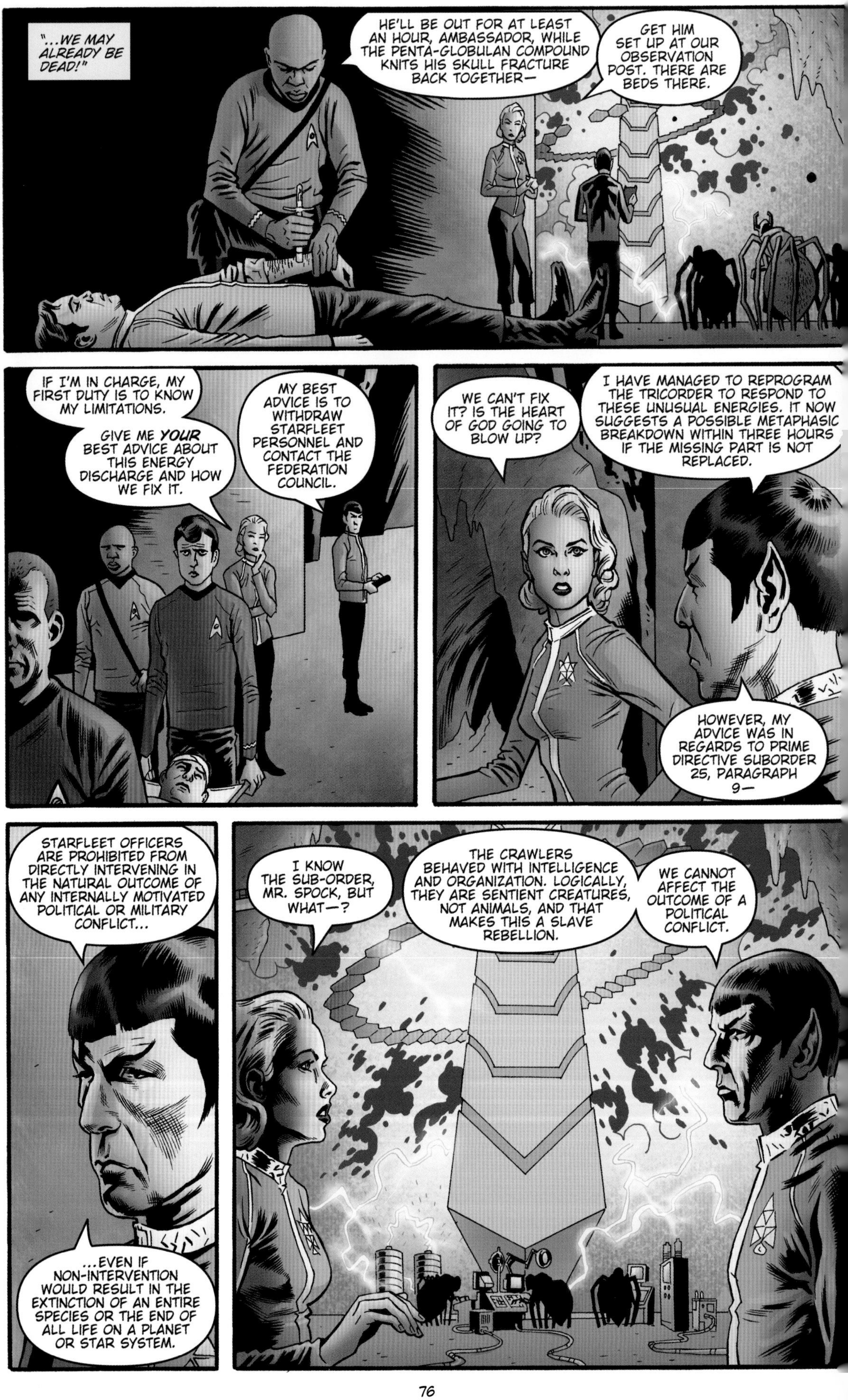
"...WE MAY ALREADY BE DEAD!"
HE'LL BE OUT FOR AT LEAST AN HOUR, AMBASSADOR, WHILE THE PENTA-GLOBULAN COMPOUND KNITS HIS SKULL FRACTURE BACK TOGETHER—
GET HIM SET UP AT OUR OBSERVATION POST. THERE ARE BEDS THERE.
IF I'M IN CHARGE, MY FIRST DUTY IS TO KNOW MY LIMITATIONS.
GIVE ME YOUR BEST ADVICE ABOUT THIS ENERGY DISCHARGE AND HOW WE FIX IT.
MY BEST ADVICE IS TO WITHDRAW STARFLEET PERSONNEL AND CONTACT THE FEDERATION COUNCIL.
WE CAN'T FIX IT? IS THE HEART OF GOD GOING TO BLOW UP?
I HAVE MANAGED TO REPROGRAM THE TRICORDER TO RESPOND TO THESE UNUSUAL ENERGIES. IT NOW SUGGESTS A POSSIBLE METAPHASIC BREAKDOWN WITHIN THREE HOURS IF THE MISSING PART IS NOT REPLACED.
HOWEVER, MY ADVICE WAS IN REGARDS TO PRIME DIRECTIVE SUBORDER 25, PARAGRAPH 9—
STARFLEET OFFICERS ARE PROHIBITED FROM DIRECTLY INTERVENING IN THE NATURAL OUTCOME OF ANY INTERNALLY MOTIVATED POLITICAL OR MILITARY CONFLICT...
...EVEN IF NON-INTERVENTION WOULD RESULT IN THE EXTINCTION OF AN ENTIRE SPECIES OR THE END OF ALL LIFE ON A PLANET OR STAR SYSTEM.
I KNOW THE SUB-ORDER, MR. SPOCK, BUT WHAT—?
THE CRAWLERS BEHAVED WITH INTELLIGENCE AND ORGANIZATION. LOGICALLY, THEY ARE SENTIENT CREATURES, NOT ANIMALS, AND THAT MAKES THIS A SLAVE REBELLION.
WE CANNOT AFFECT THE OUTCOME OF A POLITICAL CONFLICT.

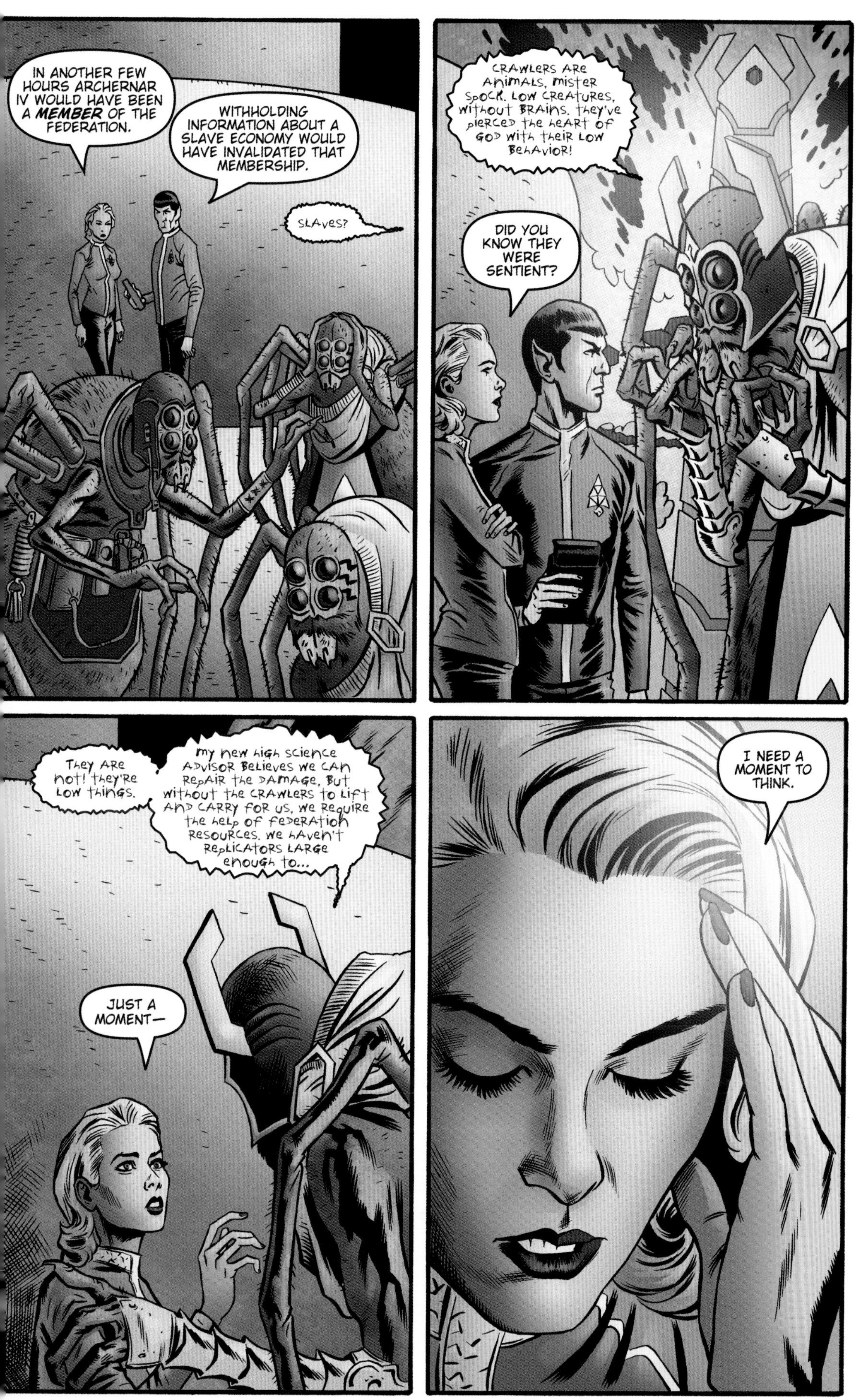
IN ANOTHER FEW HOURS ARCHERNAR IV WOULD HAVE BEEN A **MEMBER** OF THE FEDERATION.
WITHHOLDING INFORMATION ABOUT A SLAVE ECONOMY WOULD HAVE INVALIDATED THAT MEMBERSHIP.
SLAVES?
CRAWLERS ARE ANIMALS, MISTER SPOCK. LOW CREATURES, WITHOUT BRAINS. THEY'VE PIERCED THE HEART OF GOD WITH THEIR LOW BEHAVIOR!
DID YOU KNOW THEY WERE SENTIENT?
THEY ARE NOT! THEY'RE LOW THINGS.
MY NEW HIGH SCIENCE ADVISOR BELIEVES WE CAN REPAIR THE DAMAGE, BUT WITHOUT THE CRAWLERS TO LIFT AND CARRY FOR US, WE REQUIRE THE HELP OF FEDERATION RESOURCES. WE HAVEN'T REPLICATORS LARGE ENOUGH TO...
JUST A MOMENT—
I NEED A MOMENT TO THINK.

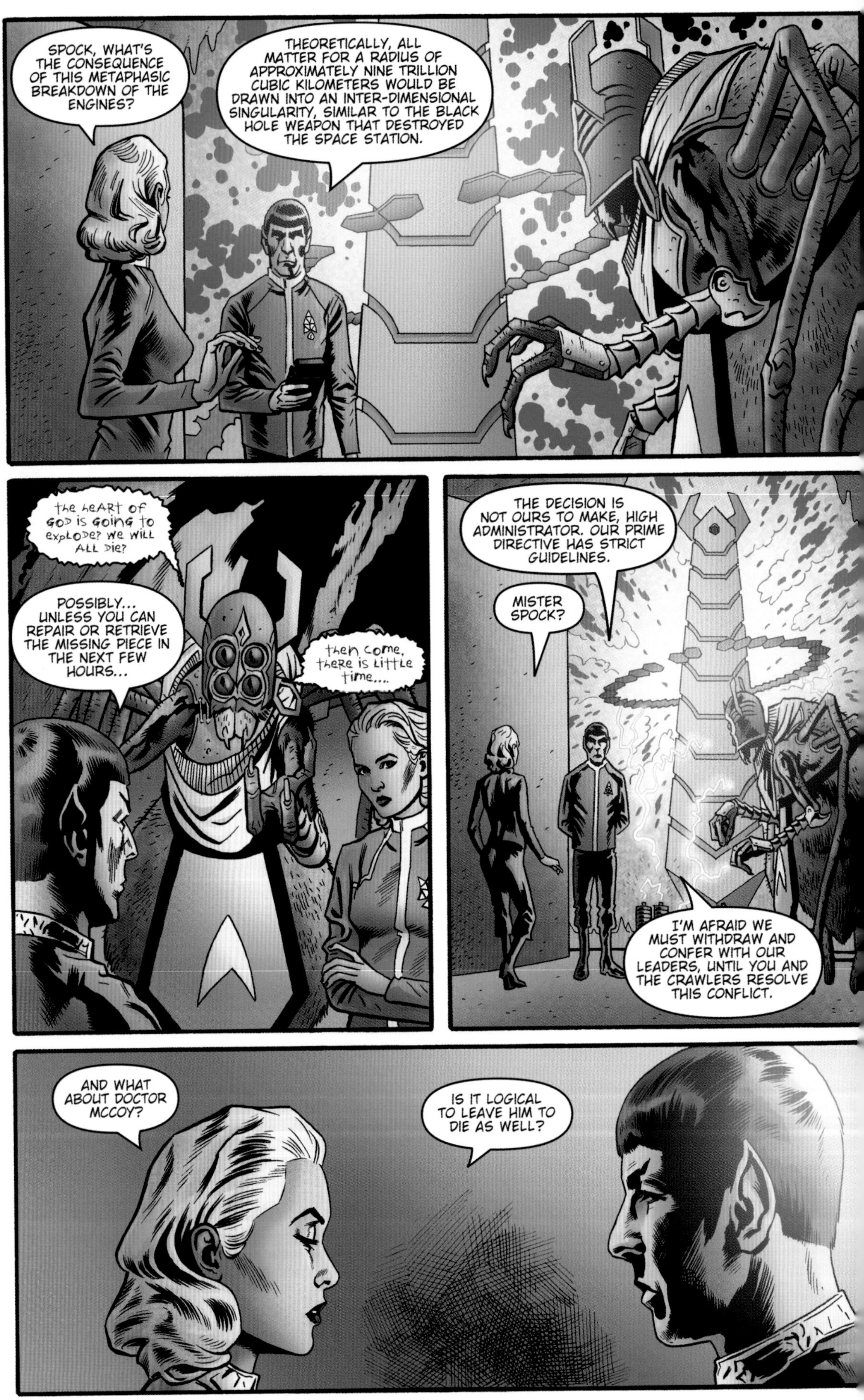
SPOCK, WHAT'S THE CONSEQUENCE OF THIS METAPHASIC BREAKDOWN OF THE ENGINES?
THEORETICALLY, ALL MATTER FOR A RADIUS OF APPROXIMATELY NINE TRILLION CUBIC KILOMETERS WOULD BE DRAWN INTO AN INTER-DIMENSIONAL SINGULARITY, SIMILAR TO THE BLACK HOLE WEAPON THAT DESTROYED THE SPACE STATION.
the heart of God is going to explode? we will all die?
POSSIBLY... UNLESS YOU CAN REPAIR OR RETRIEVE THE MISSING PIECE IN THE NEXT FEW HOURS...
then come. there is little time....
THE DECISION IS NOT OURS TO MAKE, HIGH ADMINISTRATOR. OUR PRIME DIRECTIVE HAS STRICT GUIDELINES.
MISTER SPOCK?
I'M AFRAID WE MUST WITHDRAW AND CONFER WITH OUR LEADERS, UNTIL YOU AND THE CRAWLERS RESOLVE THIS CONFLICT.
AND WHAT ABOUT DOCTOR MCCOY?
IS IT LOGICAL TO LEAVE HIM TO DIE AS WELL?

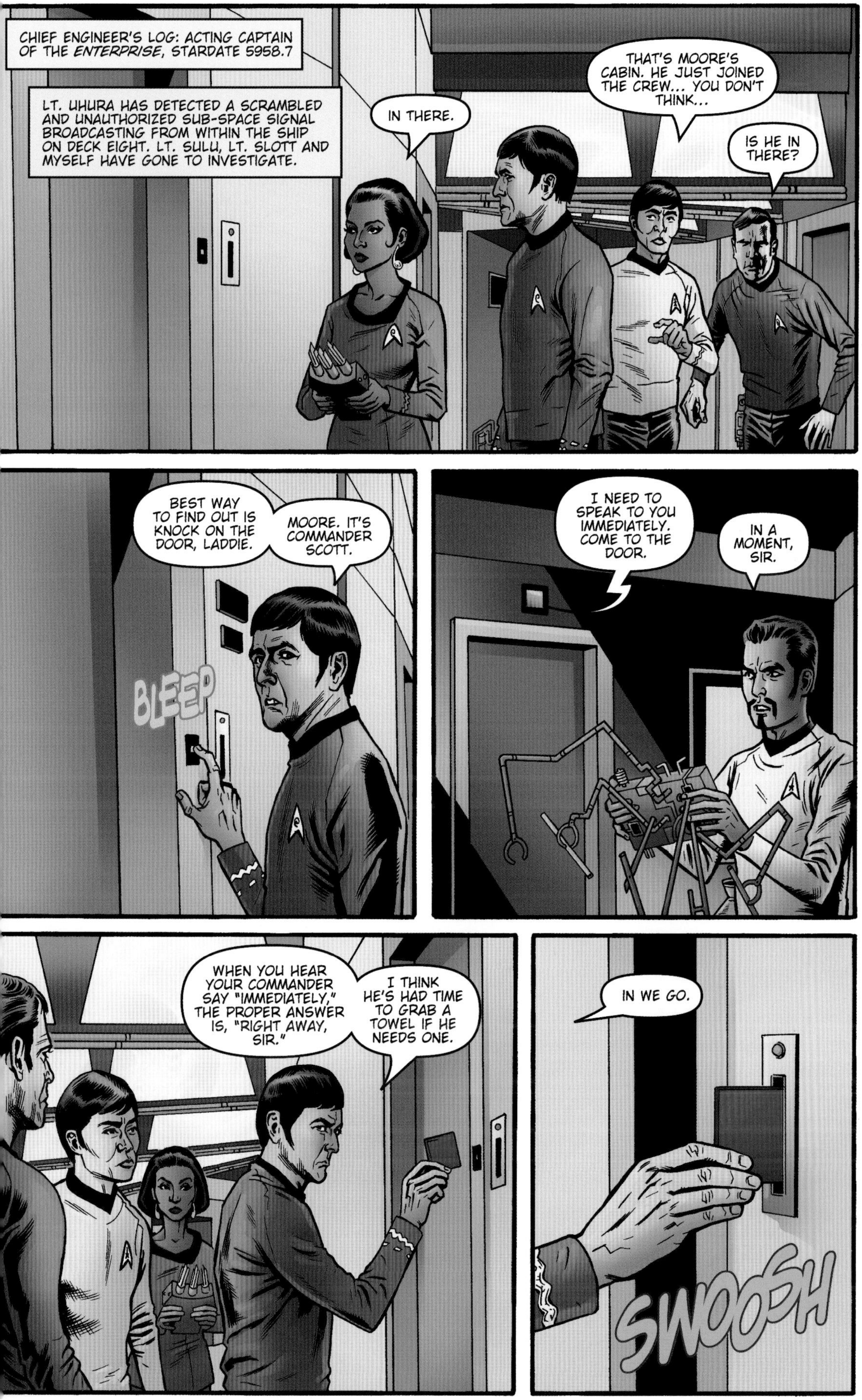

CHIEF ENGINEER'S LOG: ACTING CAPTAIN OF THE *ENTERPRISE*, STARDATE 5958.7
LT. UHURA HAS DETECTED A SCRAMBLED AND UNAUTHORIZED SUB-SPACE SIGNAL BROADCASTING FROM WITHIN THE SHIP ON DECK EIGHT. LT. SULU, LT. SLOTT AND MYSELF HAVE GONE TO INVESTIGATE.
IN THERE.
THAT'S MOORE'S CABIN. HE JUST JOINED THE CREW... YOU DON'T THINK...
IS HE IN THERE?
BEST WAY TO FIND OUT IS KNOCK ON THE DOOR, LADDIE.
MOORE. IT'S COMMANDER SCOTT.
BLEEP
I NEED TO SPEAK TO YOU IMMEDIATELY. COME TO THE DOOR.
IN A MOMENT, SIR.
WHEN YOU HEAR YOUR COMMANDER SAY "IMMEDIATELY," THE PROPER ANSWER IS, "RIGHT AWAY, SIR."
I THINK HE'S HAD TIME TO GRAB A TOWEL IF HE NEEDS ONE.
IN WE GO.
SWOOSH

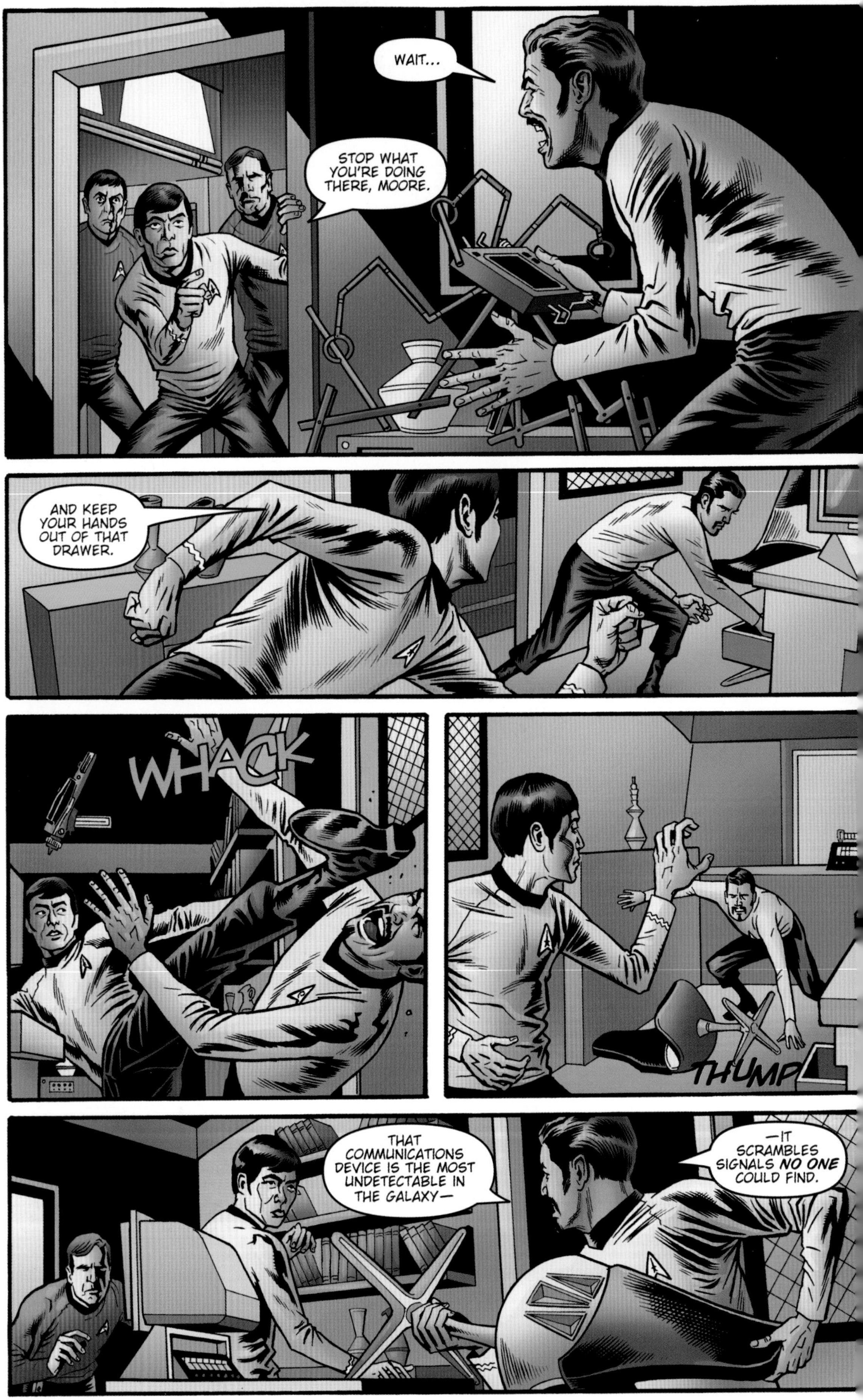
WAIT...
STOP WHAT YOU'RE DOING THERE, MOORE.
AND KEEP YOUR HANDS OUT OF THAT DRAWER.
WHACK
THUMP
THAT COMMUNICATIONS DEVICE IS THE MOST UNDETECTABLE IN THE GALAXY—
—IT SCRAMBLES SIGNALS **NO ONE** COULD FIND.

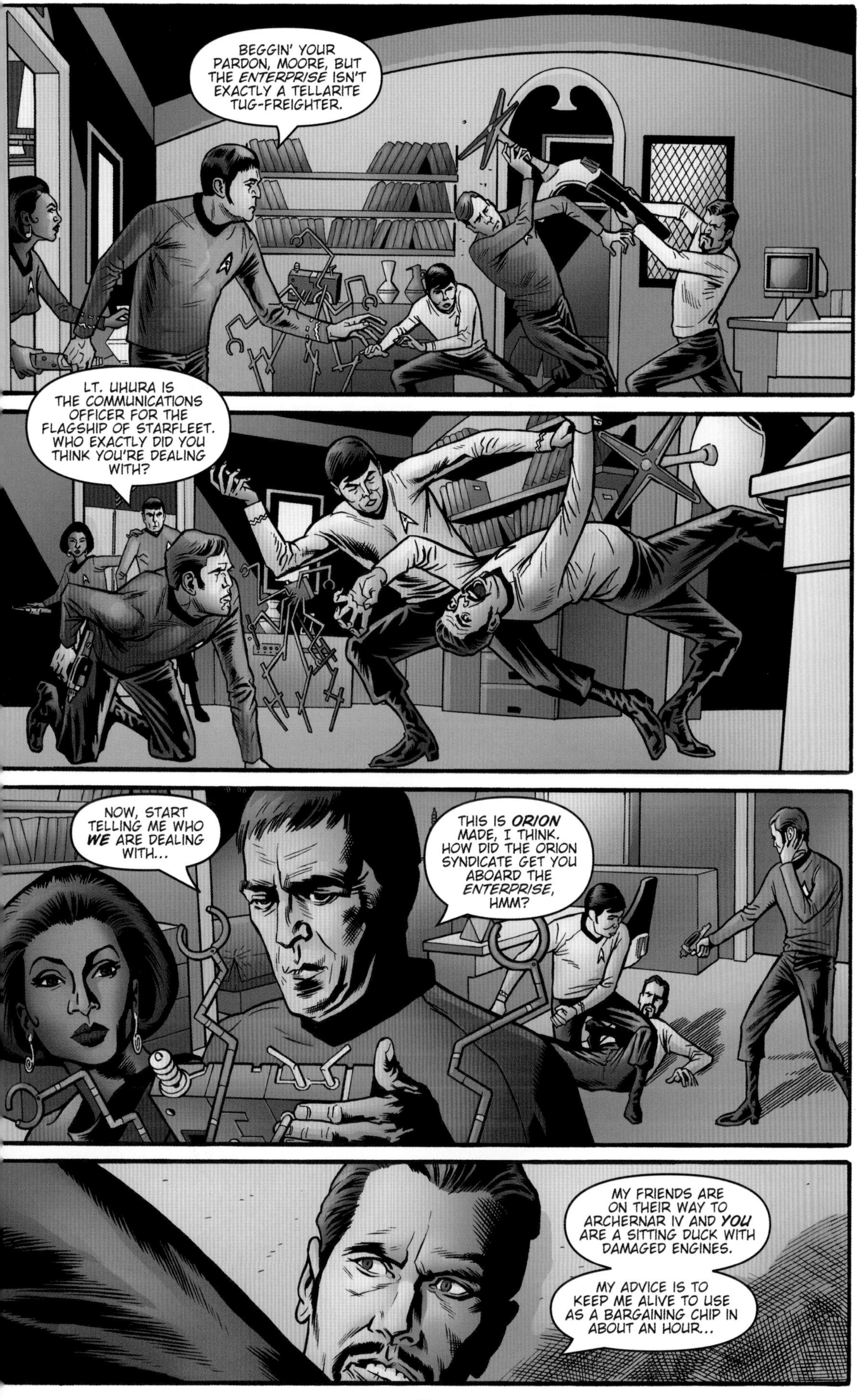
BEGGIN' YOUR PARDON, MOORE, BUT THE *ENTERPRISE* ISN'T EXACTLY A TELLARITE TUG-FREIGHTER.
LT. UHURA IS THE COMMUNICATIONS OFFICER FOR THE FLAGSHIP OF STARFLEET. WHO EXACTLY DID YOU THINK YOU'RE DEALING WITH?
NOW, START TELLING ME WHO ***WE*** ARE DEALING WITH...
THIS IS ***ORION*** MADE, I THINK. HOW DID THE ORION SYNDICATE GET YOU ABOARD THE *ENTERPRISE*, HMM?
MY FRIENDS ARE ON THEIR WAY TO ARCHERNAR IV AND ***YOU*** ARE A SITTING DUCK WITH DAMAGED ENGINES.
MY ADVICE IS TO KEEP ME ALIVE TO USE AS A BARGAINING CHIP IN ABOUT AN HOUR...

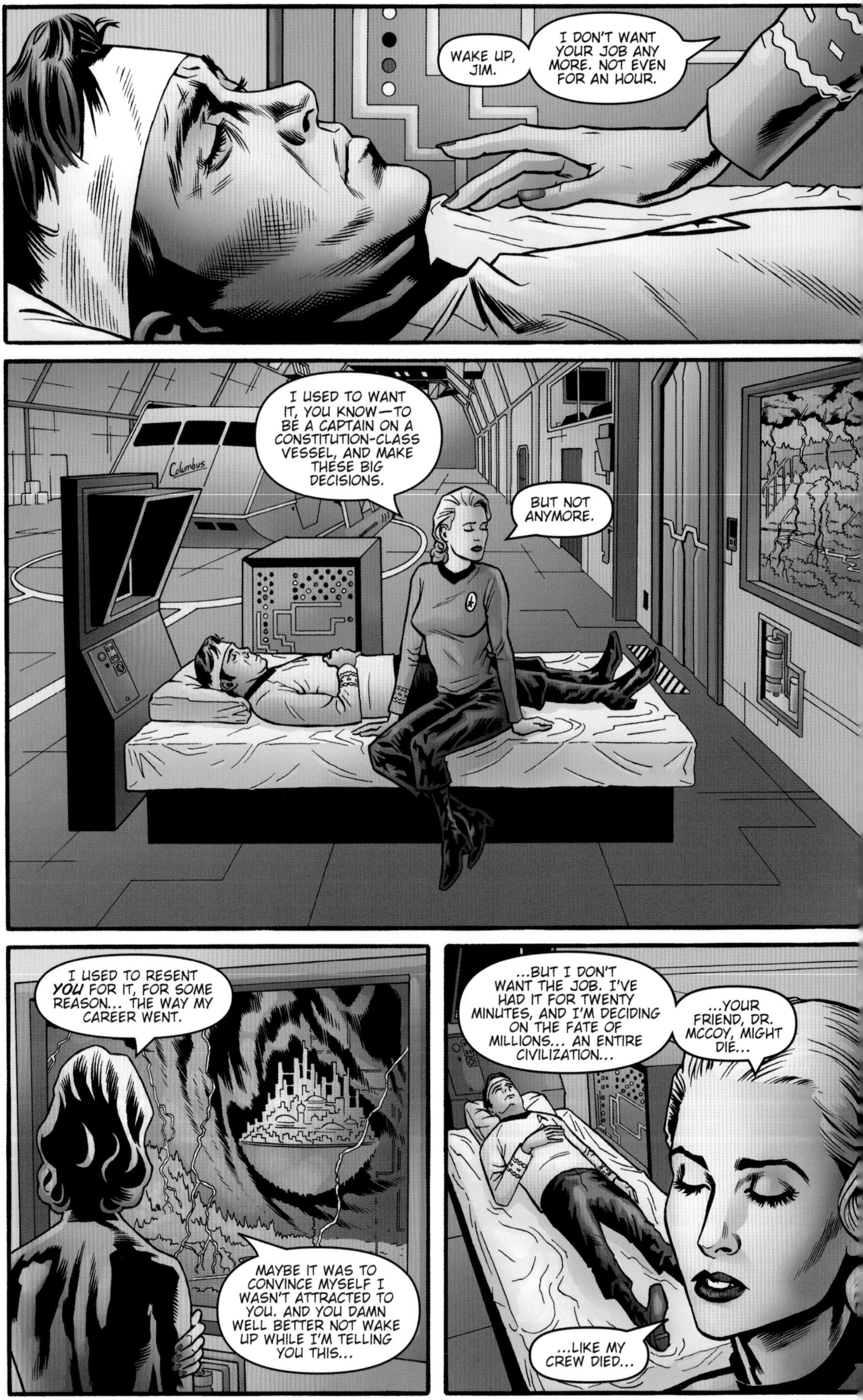
WAKE UP, JIM.
I DON'T WANT YOUR JOB ANY MORE. NOT EVEN FOR AN HOUR.
Columbus
I USED TO WANT IT, YOU KNOW—TO BE A CAPTAIN ON A CONSTITUTION-CLASS VESSEL, AND MAKE THESE BIG DECISIONS.
BUT NOT ANYMORE.
I USED TO RESENT **YOU** FOR IT, FOR SOME REASON... THE WAY MY CAREER WENT.
MAYBE IT WAS TO CONVINCE MYSELF I WASN'T ATTRACTED TO YOU. AND YOU DAMN WELL BETTER NOT WAKE UP WHILE I'M TELLING YOU THIS...
...BUT I DON'T WANT THE JOB. I'VE HAD IT FOR TWENTY MINUTES, AND I'M DECIDING ON THE FATE OF MILLIONS... AN ENTIRE CIVILIZATION...
...YOUR FRIEND, DR. MCCOY, MIGHT DIE...
...LIKE MY CREW DIED...

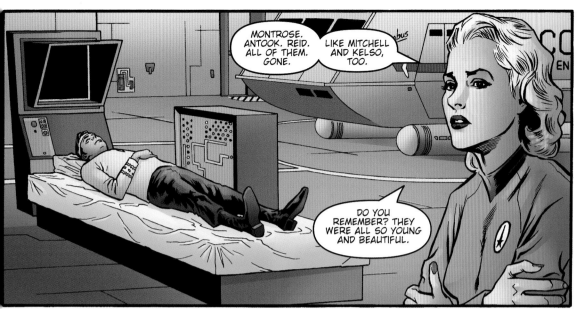

MONTROSE. ANTOOK. REID. ALL OF THEM. GONE.

LIKE MITCHELL AND KELSO, TOO.

DO YOU REMEMBER? THEY WERE ALL SO YOUNG AND BEAUTIFUL.

I ORDERED THE EVACUATION AND I'M WAITING FOR A MESSAGE BACK FROM STARFLEET. YOU'RE OUT LAST, JIM... SO YOU CAN KNIT TOGETHER BEFORE WE MOVE YOU.

BUT THE DECISION TO EVACUATE IS KILLING ME.

MCCOY SAID THERE WAS TOO MUCH POWER IN THE HEART OF GOD, TOO MUCH GREED AND TROUBLE... THAT THIS WORLD SHOULD NEVER HAVE EXISTED.

I THINK WE SHOULD HAVE QUARANTINED IT LIKE TALOS 4.

MAYBE SPOCK'S RIGHT. MAYBE THE LOGICAL SOLUTION IS TO QUOTE THE PRIME DIRECTIVE, AND DO NOTHING WHILE THIS ACCIDENT OF THE UNIVERSE CORRECTS ITSELF.

AND WE JUST WALK AWAY.

I DON'T KNOW.

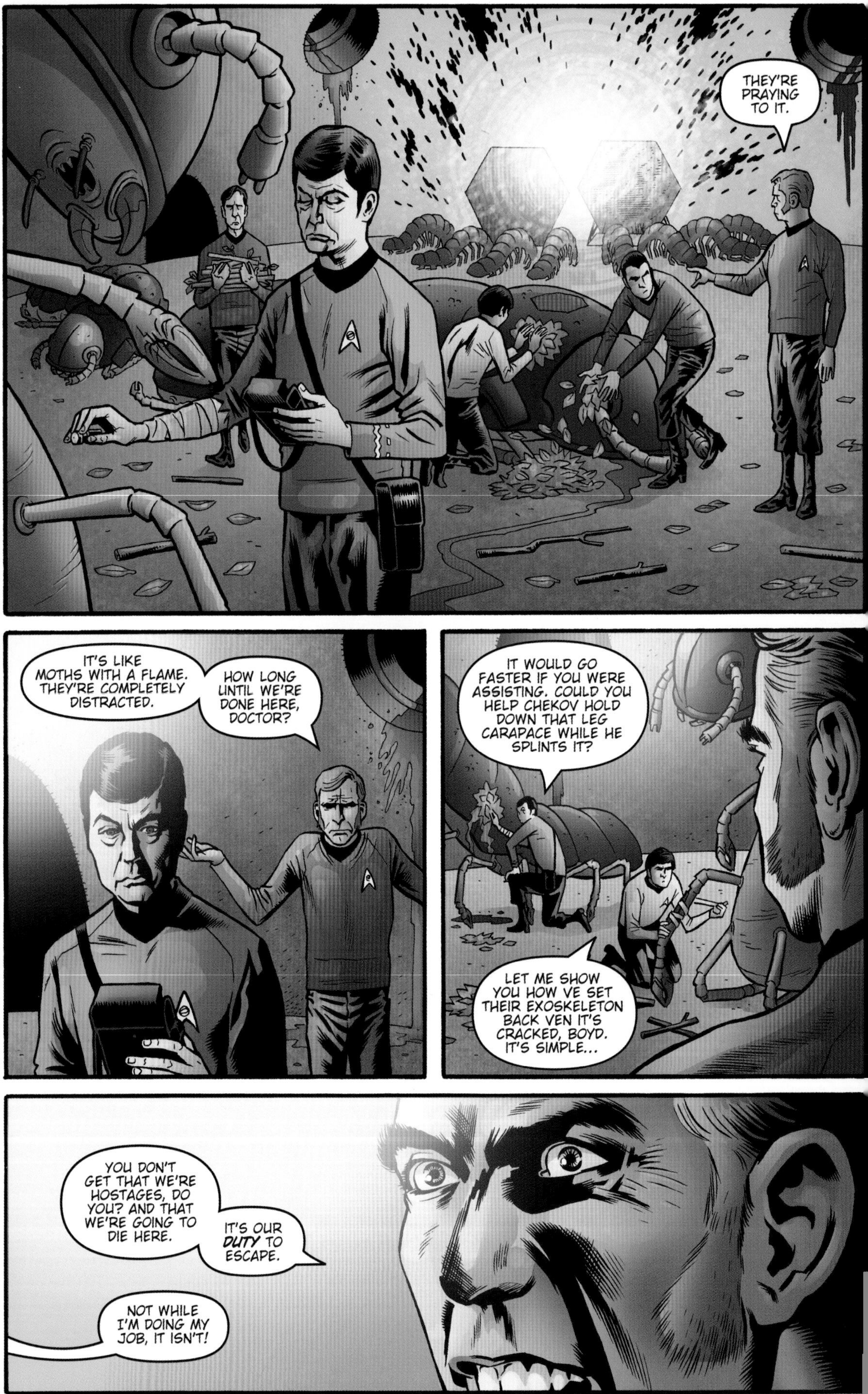
THEY'RE PRAYING TO IT.
IT'S LIKE MOTHS WITH A FLAME. THEY'RE COMPLETELY DISTRACTED.
HOW LONG UNTIL WE'RE DONE HERE, DOCTOR?
IT WOULD GO FASTER IF YOU WERE ASSISTING. COULD YOU HELP CHEKOV HOLD DOWN THAT LEG CARAPACE WHILE HE SPLINTS IT?
LET ME SHOW YOU HOW VE SET THEIR EXOSKELETON BACK VEN IT'S CRACKED, BOYD. IT'S SIMPLE...
YOU DON'T GET THAT WE'RE HOSTAGES, DO YOU? AND THAT WE'RE GOING TO DIE HERE.
IT'S OUR DUTY TO ESCAPE.
NOT WHILE I'M DOING MY JOB, IT ISN'T!

SUIT YOURSELF, DOCTOR. BUT I'M NOT GIVING THESE ROACHES THE CHANCE TO SNAP OUT OF THIS CRAZY RELIGIOUS TRANCE THEY'RE IN.

IT MAY BE OUR ONLY OPPORTUNITY. I'LL SEE YOU BACK ON THE *ENTERPRISE*. DON'T WORRY, I'LL SEND BACK HELP.

NO.

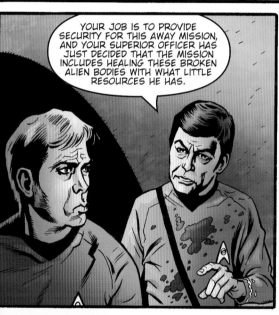

YOUR JOB IS TO PROVIDE SECURITY FOR THIS AWAY MISSION, AND YOUR SUPERIOR OFFICER HAS JUST DECIDED THAT THE MISSION INCLUDES HEALING THESE BROKEN ALIEN BODIES WITH WHAT LITTLE RESOURCES HE HAS.

YOU WILL NOT ABANDON YOUR POST.

IS THAT *CLEAR*?

YES, SIR.

NOW GO FIND ME SOME MORE TWIGS AND BRANCHES FOR SPLINTS.

MAKE YOURSELF USEFUL.

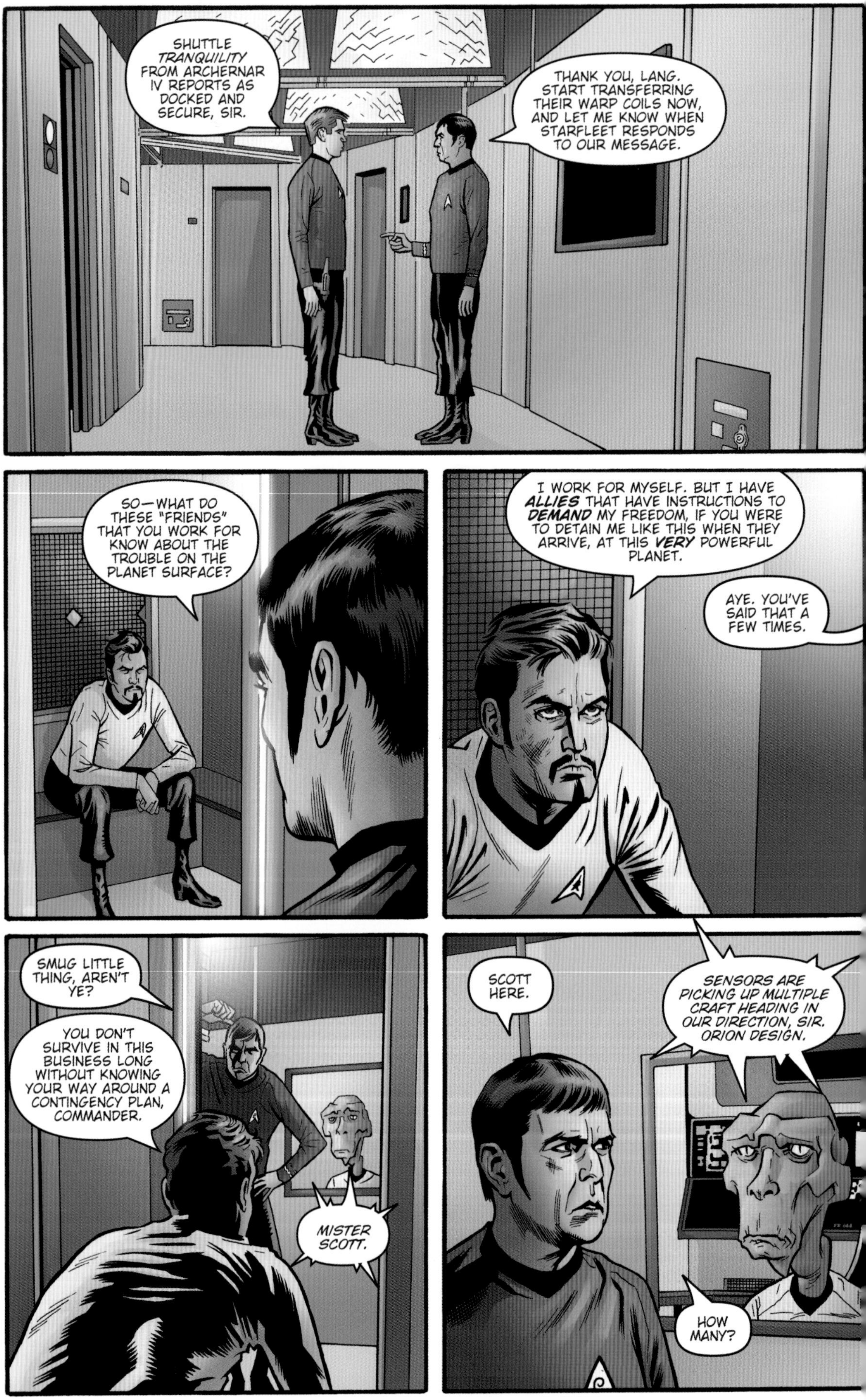

SHUTTLE TRANQUILITY FROM ARCHERNAR IV REPORTS AS DOCKED AND SECURE, SIR.
THANK YOU, LANG. START TRANSFERRING THEIR WARP COILS NOW, AND LET ME KNOW WHEN STARFLEET RESPONDS TO OUR MESSAGE.
SO—WHAT DO THESE "FRIENDS" THAT YOU WORK FOR KNOW ABOUT THE TROUBLE ON THE PLANET SURFACE?
I WORK FOR MYSELF. BUT I HAVE ALLIES THAT HAVE INSTRUCTIONS TO DEMAND MY FREEDOM, IF YOU WERE TO DETAIN ME LIKE THIS WHEN THEY ARRIVE, AT THIS VERY POWERFUL PLANET.
AYE. YOU'VE SAID THAT A FEW TIMES.
SMUG LITTLE THING, AREN'T YE?
YOU DON'T SURVIVE IN THIS BUSINESS LONG WITHOUT KNOWING YOUR WAY AROUND A CONTINGENCY PLAN, COMMANDER.
MISTER SCOTT.
SCOTT HERE.
SENSORS ARE PICKING UP MULTIPLE CRAFT HEADING IN OUR DIRECTION, SIR. ORION DESIGN.
HOW MANY?

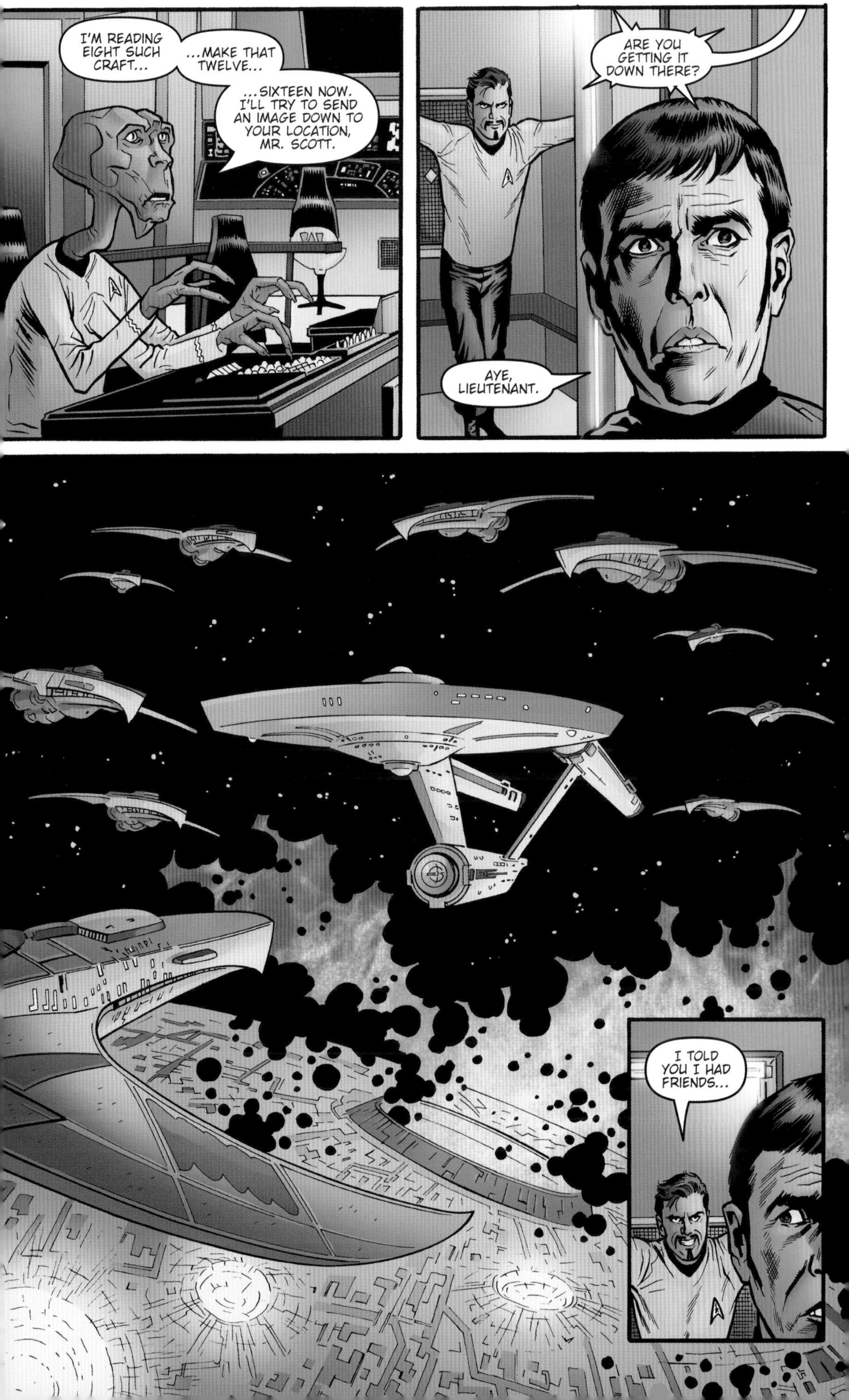
I'M READING EIGHT SUCH CRAFT...
...MAKE THAT TWELVE...
...SIXTEEN NOW. I'LL TRY TO SEND AN IMAGE DOWN TO YOUR LOCATION, MR. SCOTT.
ARE YOU GETTING IT DOWN THERE?
AYE, LIEUTENANT.
I TOLD YOU I HAD FRIENDS...

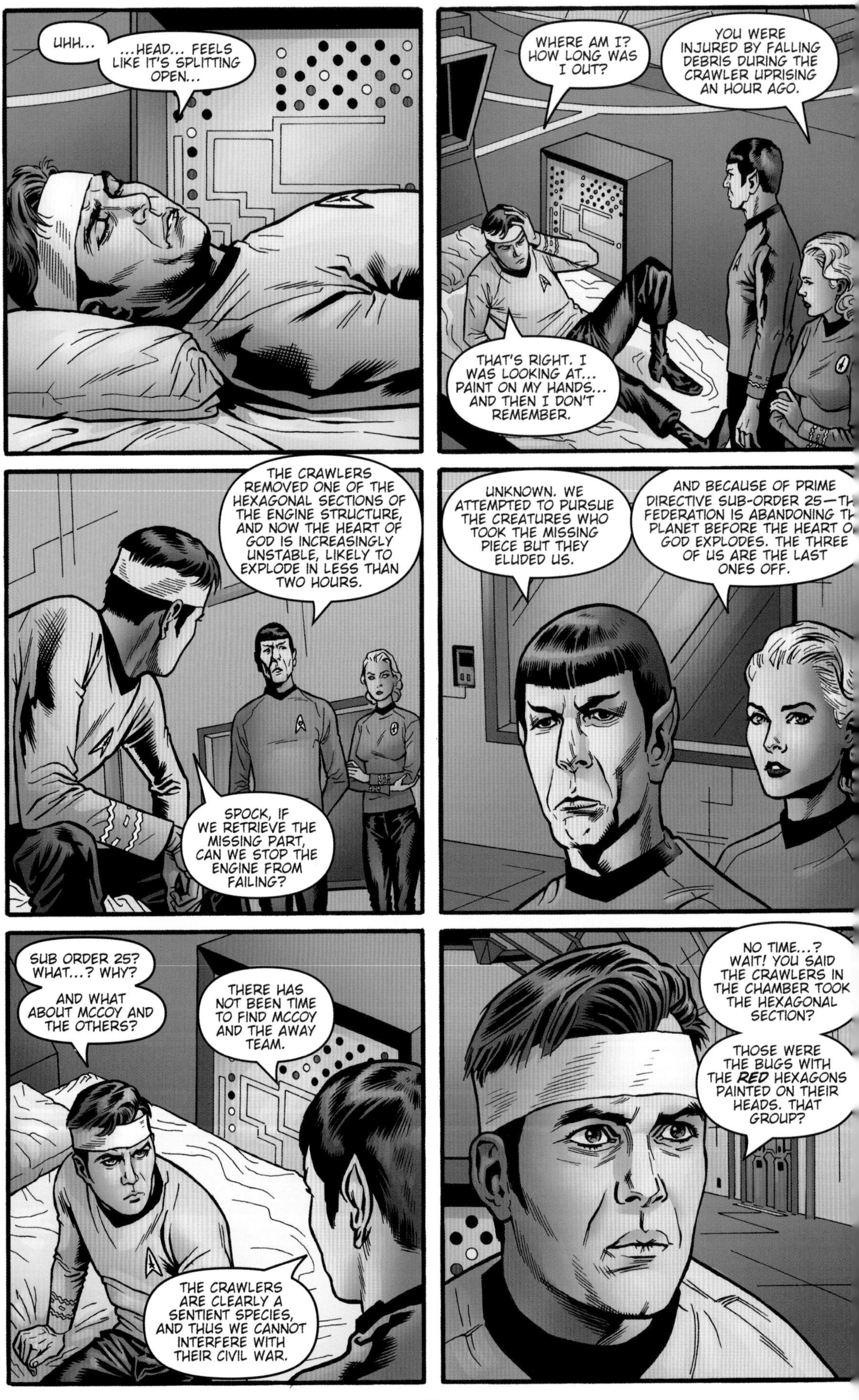
UHH...
...HEAD... FEELS LIKE IT'S SPLITTING OPEN...
WHERE AM I? HOW LONG WAS I OUT?
YOU WERE INJURED BY FALLING DEBRIS DURING THE CRAWLER UPRISING AN HOUR AGO.
THAT'S RIGHT. I WAS LOOKING AT... PAINT ON MY HANDS... AND THEN I DON'T REMEMBER.
THE CRAWLERS REMOVED ONE OF THE HEXAGONAL SECTIONS OF THE ENGINE STRUCTURE, AND NOW THE HEART OF GOD IS INCREASINGLY UNSTABLE, LIKELY TO EXPLODE IN LESS THAN TWO HOURS.
SPOCK, IF WE RETRIEVE THE MISSING PART, CAN WE STOP THE ENGINE FROM FAILING?
UNKNOWN. WE ATTEMPTED TO PURSUE THE CREATURES WHO TOOK THE MISSING PIECE BUT THEY ELUDED US.
AND BECAUSE OF PRIME DIRECTIVE SUB-ORDER 25—TH FEDERATION IS ABANDONING TH PLANET BEFORE THE HEART O GOD EXPLODES. THE THREE OF US ARE THE LAST ONES OFF.
SUB ORDER 25? WHAT...? WHY?
AND WHAT ABOUT MCCOY AND THE OTHERS?
THERE HAS NOT BEEN TIME TO FIND MCCOY AND THE AWAY TEAM.
THE CRAWLERS ARE CLEARLY A SENTIENT SPECIES, AND THUS WE CANNOT INTERFERE WITH THEIR CIVIL WAR.
NO TIME...? WAIT! YOU SAID THE CRAWLERS IN THE CHAMBER TOOK THE HEXAGONAL SECTION?
THOSE WERE THE BUGS WITH THE ***RED*** HEXAGONS PAINTED ON THEIR HEADS. THAT GROUP?

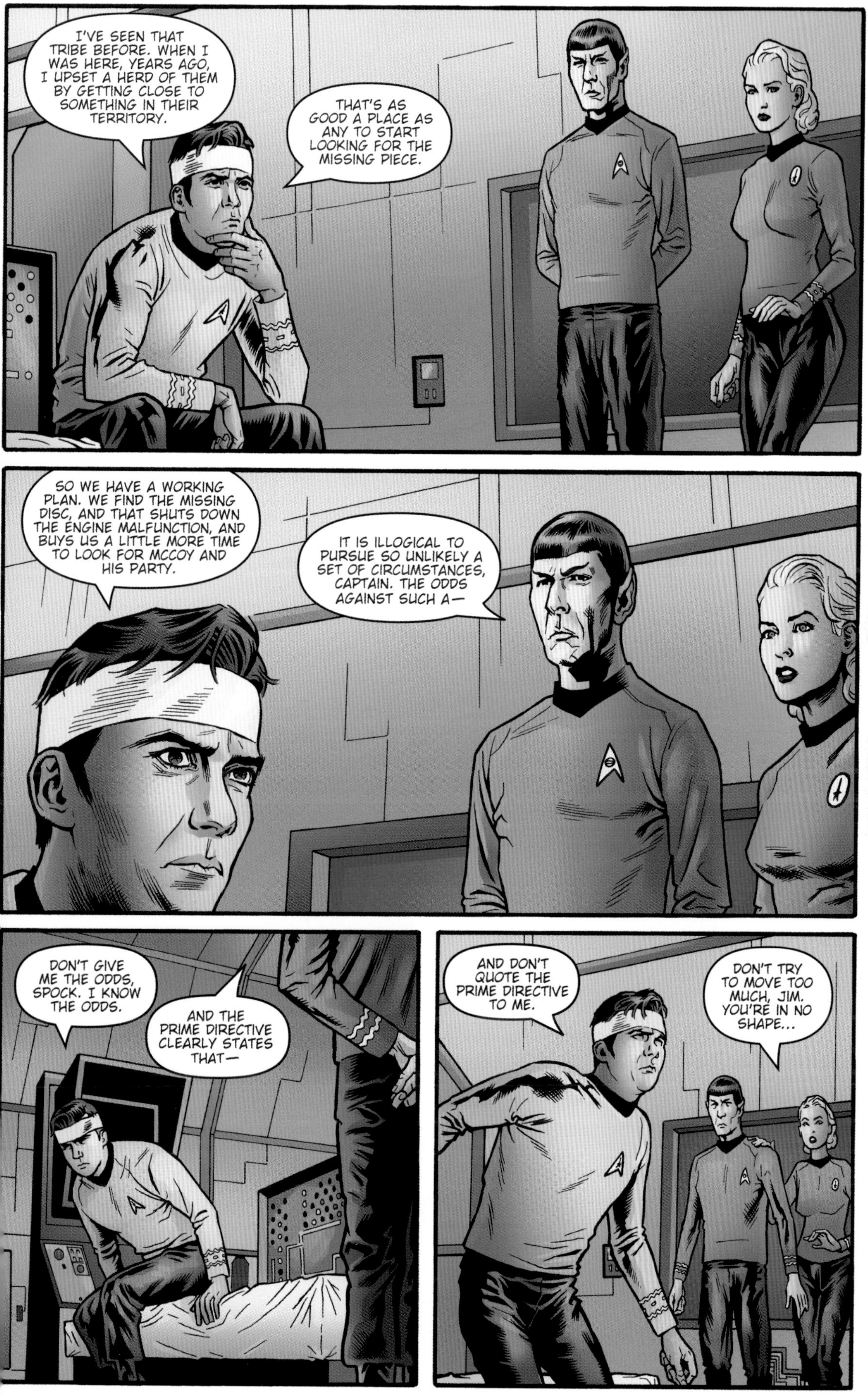
I'VE SEEN THAT TRIBE BEFORE. WHEN I WAS HERE, YEARS AGO, I UPSET A HERD OF THEM BY GETTING CLOSE TO SOMETHING IN THEIR TERRITORY.
THAT'S AS GOOD A PLACE AS ANY TO START LOOKING FOR THE MISSING PIECE.
SO WE HAVE A WORKING PLAN. WE FIND THE MISSING DISC, AND THAT SHUTS DOWN THE ENGINE MALFUNCTION, AND BUYS US A LITTLE MORE TIME TO LOOK FOR MCCOY AND HIS PARTY.
IT IS ILLOGICAL TO PURSUE SO UNLIKELY A SET OF CIRCUMSTANCES, CAPTAIN. THE ODDS AGAINST SUCH A—
DON'T GIVE ME THE ODDS, SPOCK. I KNOW THE ODDS.
AND THE PRIME DIRECTIVE CLEARLY STATES THAT—
AND DON'T QUOTE THE PRIME DIRECTIVE TO ME.
DON'T TRY TO MOVE TOO MUCH, JIM. YOU'RE IN NO SHAPE...

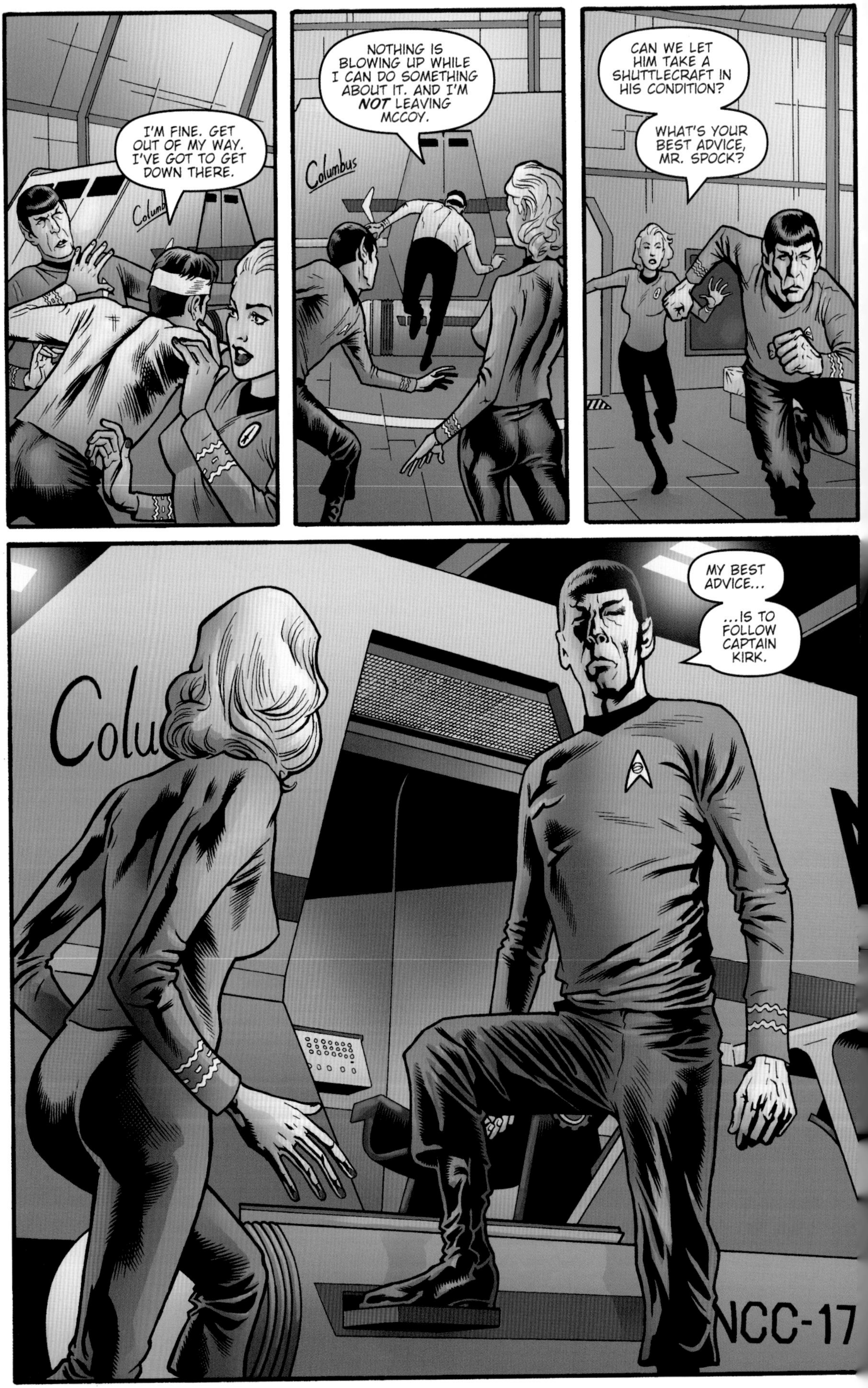
I'M FINE. GET OUT OF MY WAY. I'VE GOT TO GET DOWN THERE.
Columb
NOTHING IS BLOWING UP WHILE I CAN DO SOMETHING ABOUT IT. AND I'M **NOT** LEAVING MCCOY.
Columbus
CAN WE LET HIM TAKE A SHUTTLECRAFT IN HIS CONDITION?
WHAT'S YOUR BEST ADVICE, MR. SPOCK?
MY BEST ADVICE...
...IS TO FOLLOW CAPTAIN KIRK.
Colu
NCC-17

CHAPTER FIVE

CAPTAIN'S LOG, STARDATE 6011.7

EVERYTHING HAS GONE WRONG WITH THE DIPLOMATIC POSTING TO ARCHERNAR IV—EVEN BEFORE THE MISSION WAS CONCEIVED.

THE TWO SENTIENT RACES HERE—THE SPIDERS AND THE CRAWLERS—ARE ENGAGED IN A RELIGIOUS WAR OVER WHO SHOULD POSSESS THE "HEART OF GOD"— THE INDIGENOUS NAME FOR AN ENGINE OF NEARLY LIMITLESS POWER THAT RUNS THIS ARTIFICIAL WORLD.

HOURS AGO, A SECTION OF HEART OF GOD WAS REMOVED BY CRAWLERS AND STOLEN AWAY.

THE MISSING SECTION MUST BE REPLACED WITHIN 90 MINUTES OR THE HIGH LEVELS OF QUADRAPHASIC ENERGY NOW BEING EMITTED FROM THE GENERATOR WILL BREAK DOWN ALL MOLECULAR MATTER IN A THREE BILLION CUBIC KILOMETER AREA.

BECAUSE THIS CRISIS IS THE RESULT OF A CIVIL WAR, THE PRIME DIRECTIVE GAVE US NO CHOICE BUT TO ABANDON THE PLANET AND LET THE LOCALS SORT IT OUT.

REGARDLESS OF THE OUTCOME.

Columbus

MY CONCERN RIGHT NOW IS DOCTOR MCCOY, AND FOUR OTHER MEMBERS OF MY CREW STILL MISSING IN THE PLANET'S JUNGLE REGIONS...

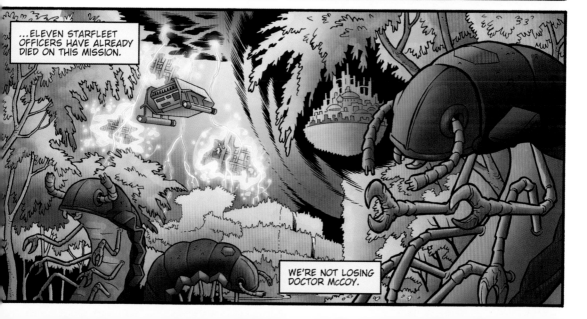

...ELEVEN STARFLEET OFFICERS HAVE ALREADY DIED ON THIS MISSION.

WE'RE NOT LOSING DOCTOR MCCOY.

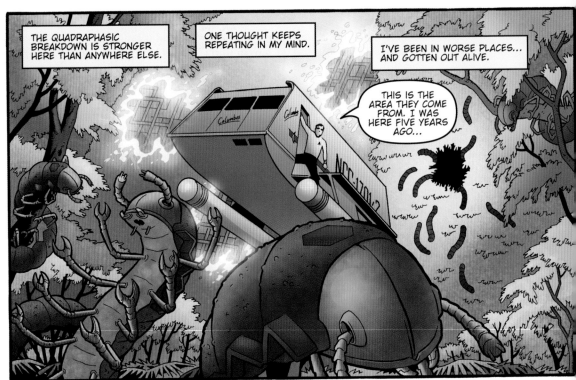

THE QUADRAPHASIC BREAKDOWN IS STRONGER HERE THAN ANYWHERE ELSE.

ONE THOUGHT KEEPS REPEATING IN MY MIND.

I'VE BEEN IN WORSE PLACES... AND GOTTEN OUT ALIVE.

THIS IS THE AREA THEY COME FROM. I WAS HERE FIVE YEARS AGO...

...IT'S WHERE THE TRIBE OF CRAWLERS WITH THE RED PAINTED FOREHEADS LIVE. THE ONES WHO ATTACKED US IN THE ENGINE CHAMBER...

IF IT'S THE SAME TRIBE, THEY WOULD TAKE THEIR PRIZE *HERE*...

THE LIGHT SHOW'S TERRIFYING THEM. THEY DON'T UNDERSTAND WHAT'S GOING ON.

NOR DO I.

THE ODDS OF FINDING THE MISSING SECTION ARE APPROXIMATELY SEVEN THOUSAND, TWO HUNDRED AND EIGHTY THREE TO ONE.

WE *HAVE* TO TRY *SOMETHING*, SPOCK.

THEY'RE NOT RUNNING IN RANDOM CIRCLES, CAPTAIN KIRK. THEY SEEM TO BE CENTERED OVER THERE, WHERE THE GROUND MEETS THE WALL.

YES, AMBASSADOR CASSADY, I SEE IT..

SPOCK, SWING AROUND THIRTY DEGREES. LET'S GET A LOOK.

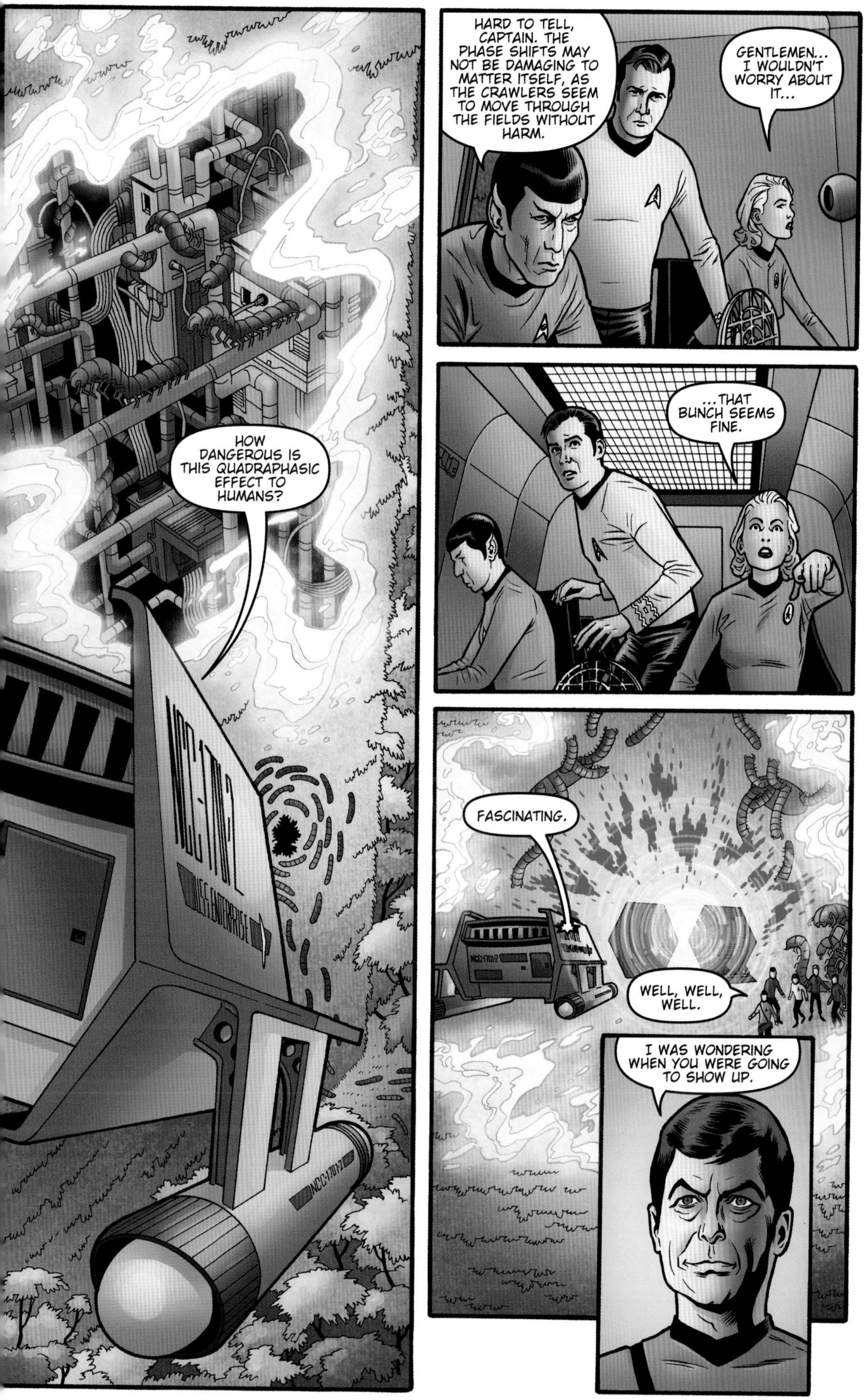
HOW DANGEROUS IS THIS QUADRAPHASIC EFFECT TO HUMANS?
HARD TO TELL, CAPTAIN. THE PHASE SHIFTS MAY NOT BE DAMAGING TO MATTER ITSELF, AS THE CRAWLERS SEEM TO MOVE THROUGH THE FIELDS WITHOUT HARM.
GENTLEMEN... I WOULDN'T WORRY ABOUT IT...
...THAT BUNCH SEEMS FINE.
FASCINATING.
WELL, WELL, WELL.
I WAS WONDERING WHEN YOU WERE GOING TO SHOW UP.

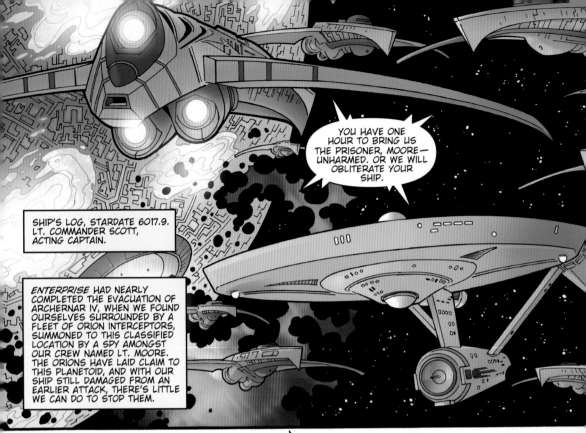

YOU HAVE ONE HOUR TO BRING US THE PRISONER, MOORE— UNHARMED. OR WE WILL OBLITERATE YOUR SHIP.

SHIP'S LOG, STARDATE 6017.9. LT. COMMANDER SCOTT, ACTING CAPTAIN.

ENTERPRISE HAD NEARLY COMPLETED THE EVACUATION OF ARCHERNAR IV, WHEN WE FOUND OURSELVES SURROUNDED BY A FLEET OF ORION INTERCEPTORS, SUMMONED TO THIS CLASSIFIED LOCATION BY A SPY AMONGST OUR CREW NAMED LT. MOORE. THE ORIONS HAVE LAID CLAIM TO THIS PLANETOID, AND WITH OUR SHIP STILL DAMAGED FROM AN EARLIER ATTACK, THERE'S LITTLE WE CAN DO TO STOP THEM.

I DON'T THINK SO, LAD. IF YOU WERE GOING TO FIRE ON ME, YOU'D HAVE DONE IT BY NOW.

YOU'RE NOT READY FOR WAR WITH THE FEDERATION.

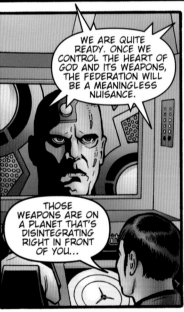

WE ARE QUITE READY. ONCE WE CONTROL THE HEART OF GOD AND ITS WEAPONS, THE FEDERATION WILL BE A MEANINGLESS NUISANCE.

THOSE WEAPONS ARE ON A PLANET THAT'S DISINTEGRATING RIGHT IN FRONT OF YOU...

EXACTLY HOW ARE YOU GOING TO CONTROL THAT?

SCOTT OUT.

ORDERS, MR. SCOTT?

STEADY ON. SO LONG AS CAPTAIN KIRK IS DOWN THERE—AND THERE'S STILL A PLANET BENEATH HIM—

—WE STAY PUT.

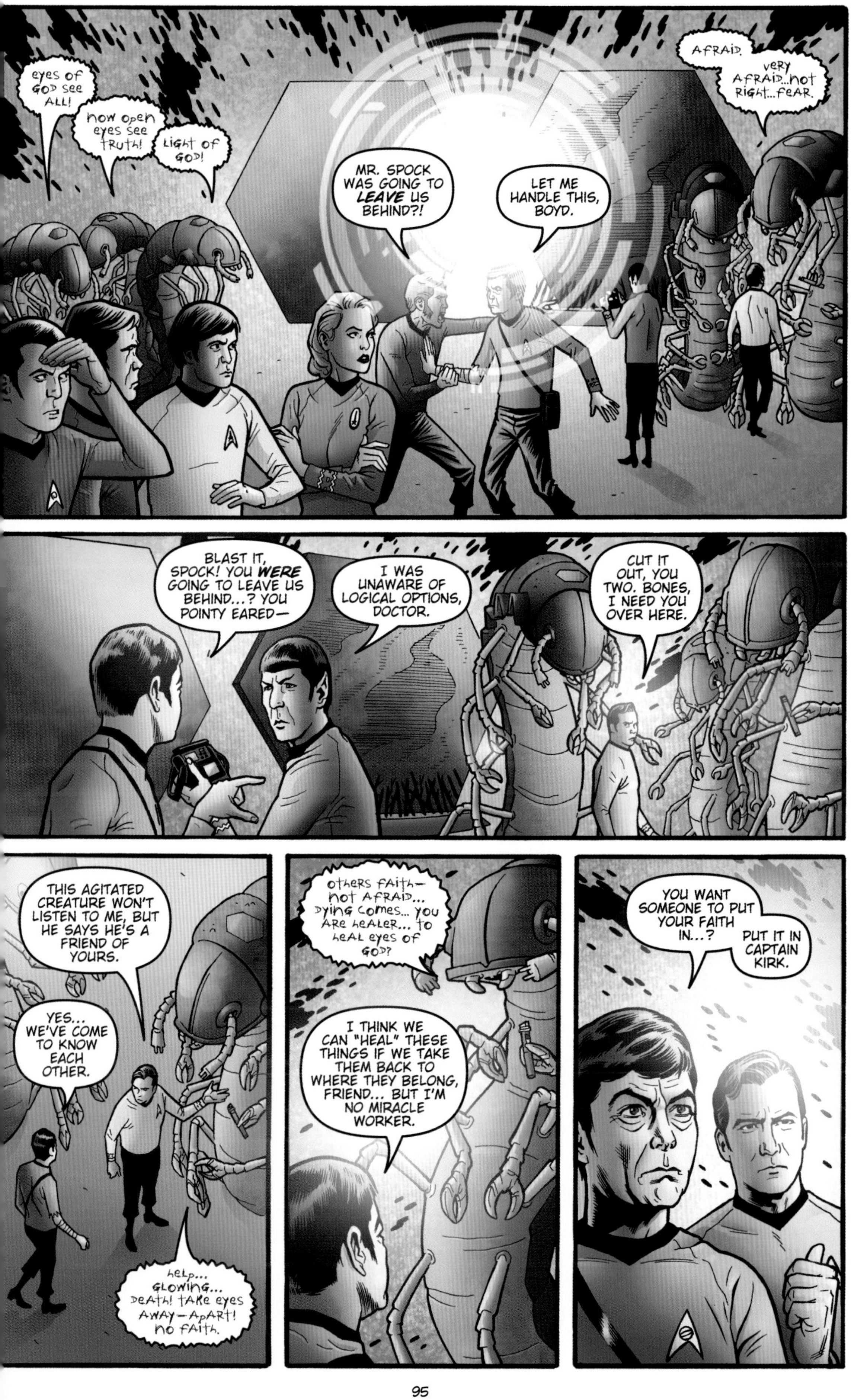
eyes of GOD see ALL!
now open eyes see TRUTH!
LIGHT OF GOD!
MR. SPOCK WAS GOING TO LEAVE US BEHIND?!
LET ME HANDLE THIS, BOYD.
AFRAID.
very AFRAID...not RIGHT...FEAR.
BLAST IT, SPOCK! YOU WERE GOING TO LEAVE US BEHIND...? YOU POINTY EARED—
I WAS UNAWARE OF LOGICAL OPTIONS, DOCTOR.
CUT IT OUT, YOU TWO. BONES, I NEED YOU OVER HERE.
THIS AGITATED CREATURE WON'T LISTEN TO ME, BUT HE SAYS HE'S A FRIEND OF YOURS.
YES... WE'VE COME TO KNOW EACH OTHER.
help... GLOWING... DEATH! TAKE eyes AWAY—APART! no FAITH.
others FAITH—not AFRAID... DYING comes... you ARE healer... to heal eyes of GOD?
I THINK WE CAN "HEAL" THESE THINGS IF WE TAKE THEM BACK TO WHERE THEY BELONG, FRIEND... BUT I'M NO MIRACLE WORKER.
YOU WANT SOMEONE TO PUT YOUR FAITH IN...?
PUT IT IN CAPTAIN KIRK.

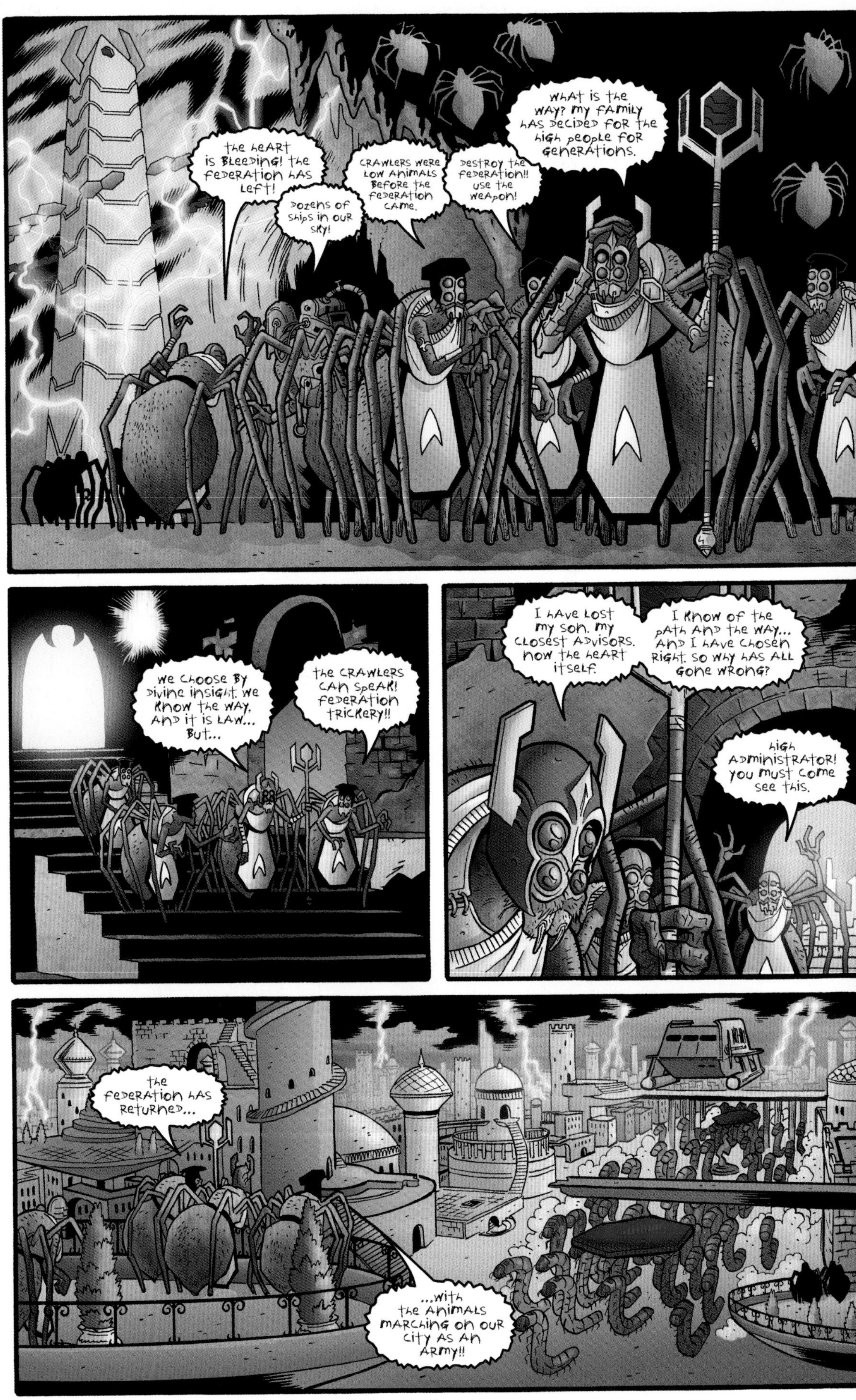

the heart is bleeding! the federation has left!
Dozens of ships in our sky!
Crawlers were low animals before the federation came.
Destroy the federation!! use the weapon!
What is the way? my family has decided for the high people for generations.
We choose by divine insight. we know the way. and it is law... but...
the crawlers can speak! federation trickery!!
I have lost my son. my closest advisors. now the heart itself.
I know of the path and the way... and I have chosen right. so why has all gone wrong?
high administrator! you must come see this.
the federation has returned...
...with the animals marching on our city as an army!!

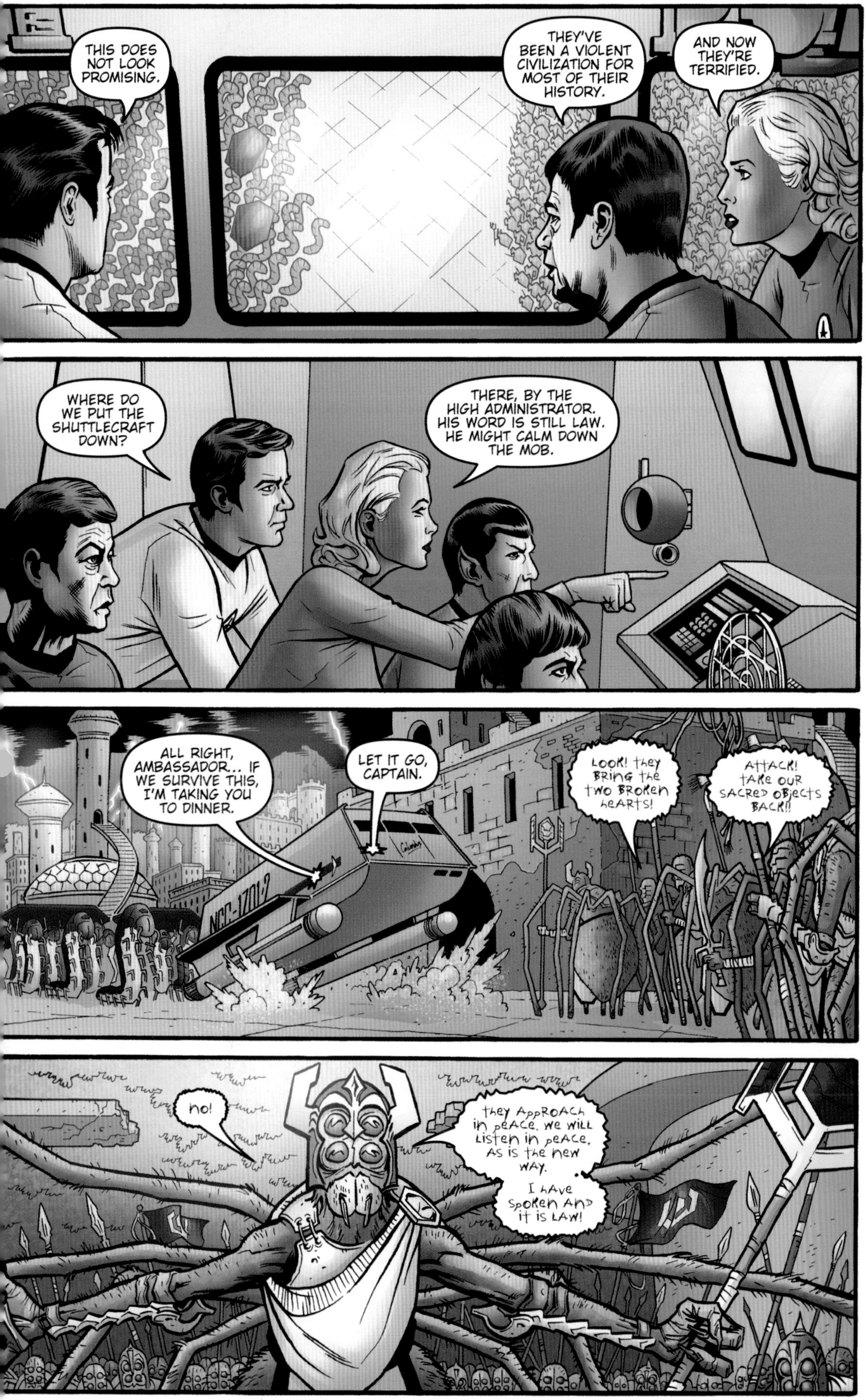
THIS DOES NOT LOOK PROMISING.
THEY'VE BEEN A VIOLENT CIVILIZATION FOR MOST OF THEIR HISTORY.
AND NOW THEY'RE TERRIFIED.
WHERE DO WE PUT THE SHUTTLECRAFT DOWN?
THERE, BY THE HIGH ADMINISTRATOR. HIS WORD IS STILL LAW. HE MIGHT CALM DOWN THE MOB.
ALL RIGHT, AMBASSADOR... IF WE SURVIVE THIS, I'M TAKING YOU TO DINNER.
LET IT GO, CAPTAIN.
LOOK! THEY BRING THE TWO BROKEN HEARTS!
ATTACK! TAKE OUR SACRED OBJECTS BACK!!
NO!
THEY APPROACH IN PEACE. WE WILL LISTEN IN PEACE, AS IS THE NEW WAY.
I HAVE SPOKEN AND IT IS LAW!

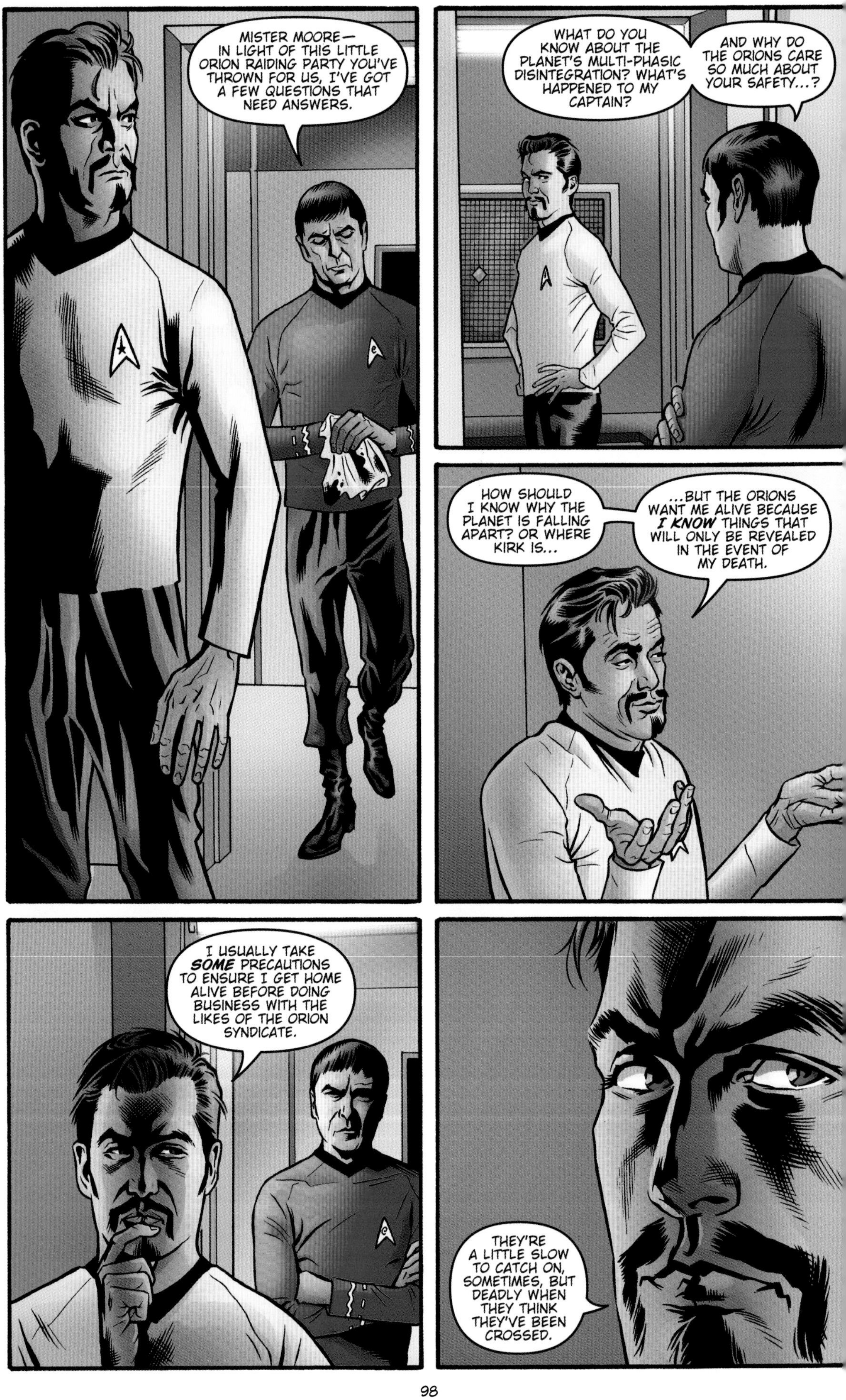
MISTER MOORE— IN LIGHT OF THIS LITTLE ORION RAIDING PARTY YOU'VE THROWN FOR US, I'VE GOT A FEW QUESTIONS THAT NEED ANSWERS.
WHAT DO YOU KNOW ABOUT THE PLANET'S MULTI-PHASIC DISINTEGRATION? WHAT'S HAPPENED TO MY CAPTAIN?
AND WHY DO THE ORIONS CARE SO MUCH ABOUT YOUR SAFETY...?
HOW SHOULD I KNOW WHY THE PLANET IS FALLING APART? OR WHERE KIRK IS...
...BUT THE ORIONS WANT ME ALIVE BECAUSE *I KNOW* THINGS THAT WILL ONLY BE REVEALED IN THE EVENT OF MY DEATH.
I USUALLY TAKE **SOME** PRECAUTIONS TO ENSURE I GET HOME ALIVE BEFORE DOING BUSINESS WITH THE LIKES OF THE ORION SYNDICATE.
THEY'RE A LITTLE SLOW TO CATCH ON, SOMETIMES, BUT DEADLY WHEN THEY THINK THEY'VE BEEN CROSSED.

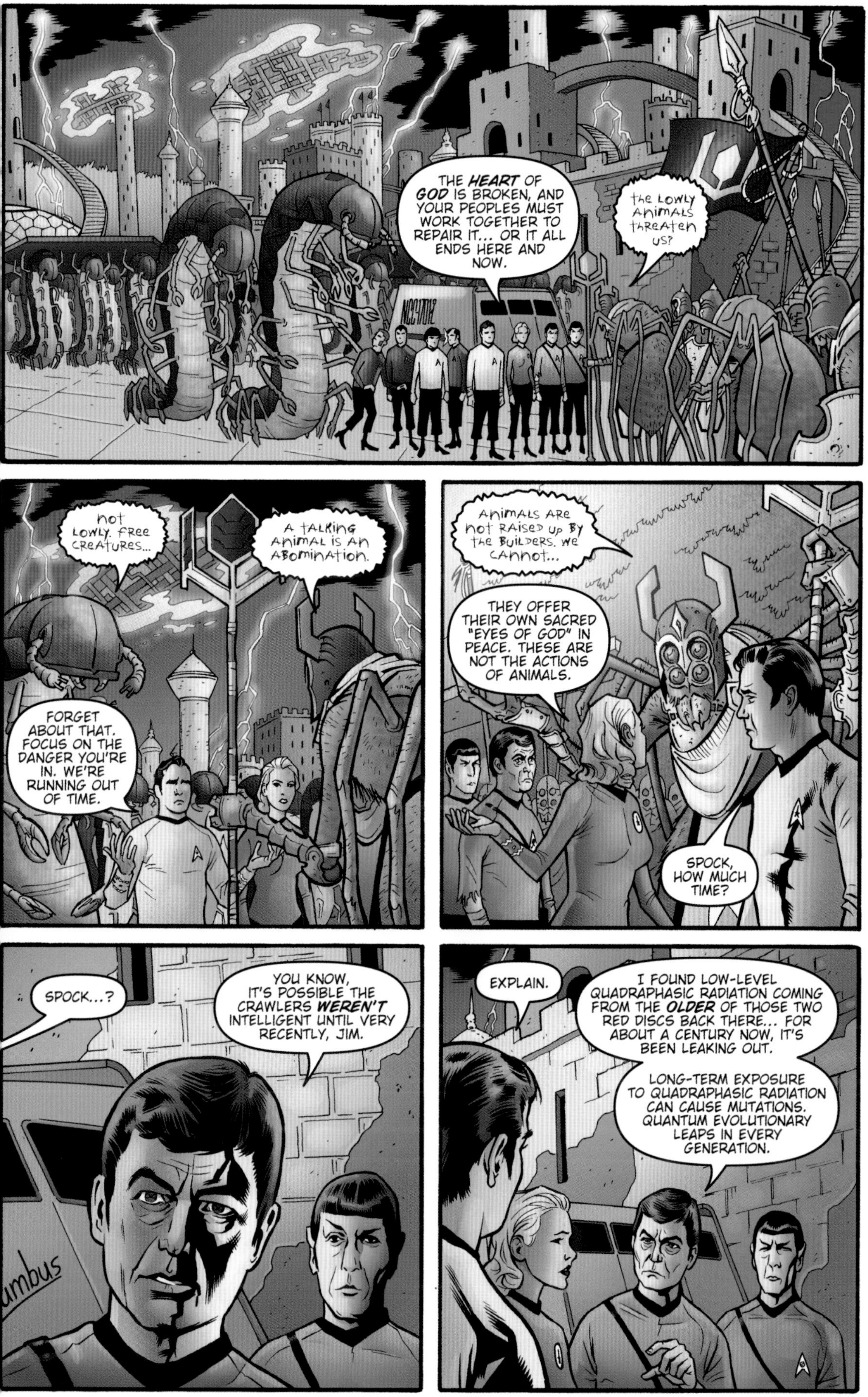
THE HEART OF GOD IS BROKEN, AND YOUR PEOPLES MUST WORK TOGETHER TO REPAIR IT... OR IT ALL ENDS HERE AND NOW.
the lowly animals threaten us?
not lowly. free creatures...
A talking animal is an abomination.
FORGET ABOUT THAT. FOCUS ON THE DANGER YOU'RE IN. WE'RE RUNNING OUT OF TIME.
Animals are not raised up by the builders. we cannot...
THEY OFFER THEIR OWN SACRED "EYES OF GOD" IN PEACE. THESE ARE NOT THE ACTIONS OF ANIMALS.
SPOCK, HOW MUCH TIME?
SPOCK...?
YOU KNOW, IT'S POSSIBLE THE CRAWLERS WEREN'T INTELLIGENT UNTIL VERY RECENTLY, JIM.
EXPLAIN.
I FOUND LOW-LEVEL QUADRAPHASIC RADIATION COMING FROM THE OLDER OF THOSE TWO RED DISCS BACK THERE... FOR ABOUT A CENTURY NOW, IT'S BEEN LEAKING OUT.
LONG-TERM EXPOSURE TO QUADRAPHASIC RADIATION CAN CAUSE MUTATIONS. QUANTUM EVOLUTIONARY LEAPS IN EVERY GENERATION.

THE CRAWLERS MAY HAVE BEEN DUMB BEASTS UNTIL ONLY A DECADE AGO. MAYBE ONLY A FEW YEARS—
BUT BECAUSE THEY WERE LIVING NEAR THE EYES OF GOD...
THEY HAVE BECOME RAISED UP...?
I BELIEVE SO, YES.
THAT IS— DEVASTATING. IT IS WRONG TO MISTREAT THOSE WHO HAVE BEEN RAISED UP BY THE DIVINE BUILDERS.
FORGIVE US.
WE SHALL WORK TOGETHER TO HEAL THE BROKEN HEART!
AS EQUALS. I HAVE CHOSEN. NOW IT IS LAW!
FASCINATING.

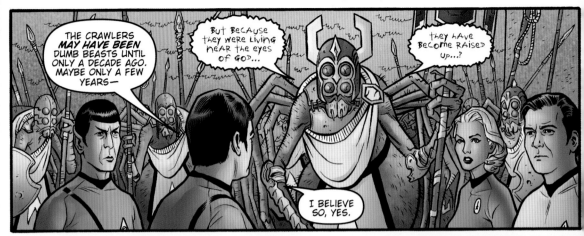

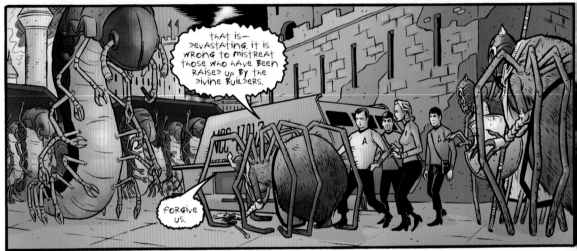

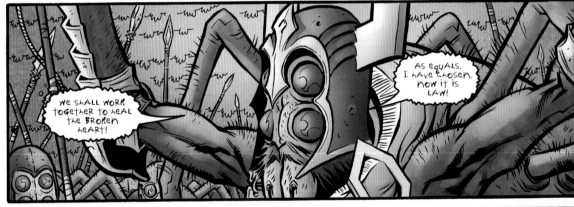

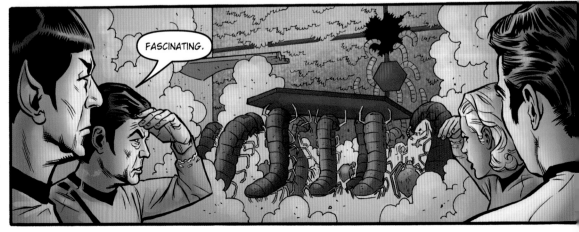

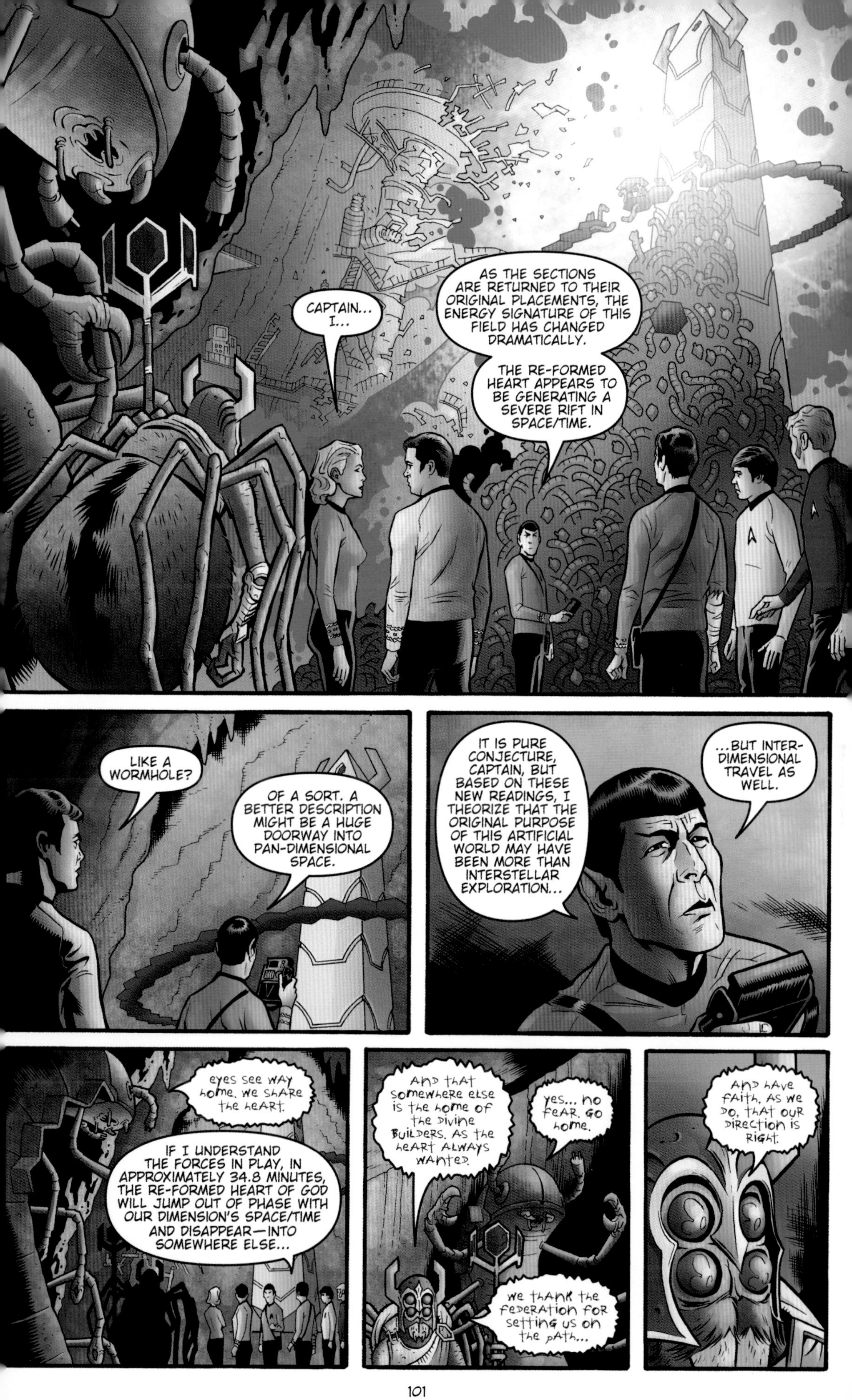
CAPTAIN... I...
AS THE SECTIONS ARE RETURNED TO THEIR ORIGINAL PLACEMENTS, THE ENERGY SIGNATURE OF THIS FIELD HAS CHANGED DRAMATICALLY.
THE RE-FORMED HEART APPEARS TO BE GENERATING A SEVERE RIFT IN SPACE/TIME.
LIKE A WORMHOLE?
OF A SORT. A BETTER DESCRIPTION MIGHT BE A HUGE DOORWAY INTO PAN-DIMENSIONAL SPACE.
IT IS PURE CONJECTURE, CAPTAIN, BUT BASED ON THESE NEW READINGS, I THEORIZE THAT THE ORIGINAL PURPOSE OF THIS ARTIFICIAL WORLD MAY HAVE BEEN MORE THAN INTERSTELLAR EXPLORATION...
...BUT INTER-DIMENSIONAL TRAVEL AS WELL.
eyes see way home. we share the heart.
IF I UNDERSTAND THE FORCES IN PLAY, IN APPROXIMATELY 34.8 MINUTES, THE RE-FORMED HEART OF GOD WILL JUMP OUT OF PHASE WITH OUR DIMENSION'S SPACE/TIME AND DISAPPEAR—INTO SOMEWHERE ELSE...
And that somewhere else is the home of the Divine Builders. As the heart always wanted.
yes... no fear. go home.
we thank the federation for setting us on the path...
And have faith, as we do, that our direction is right.

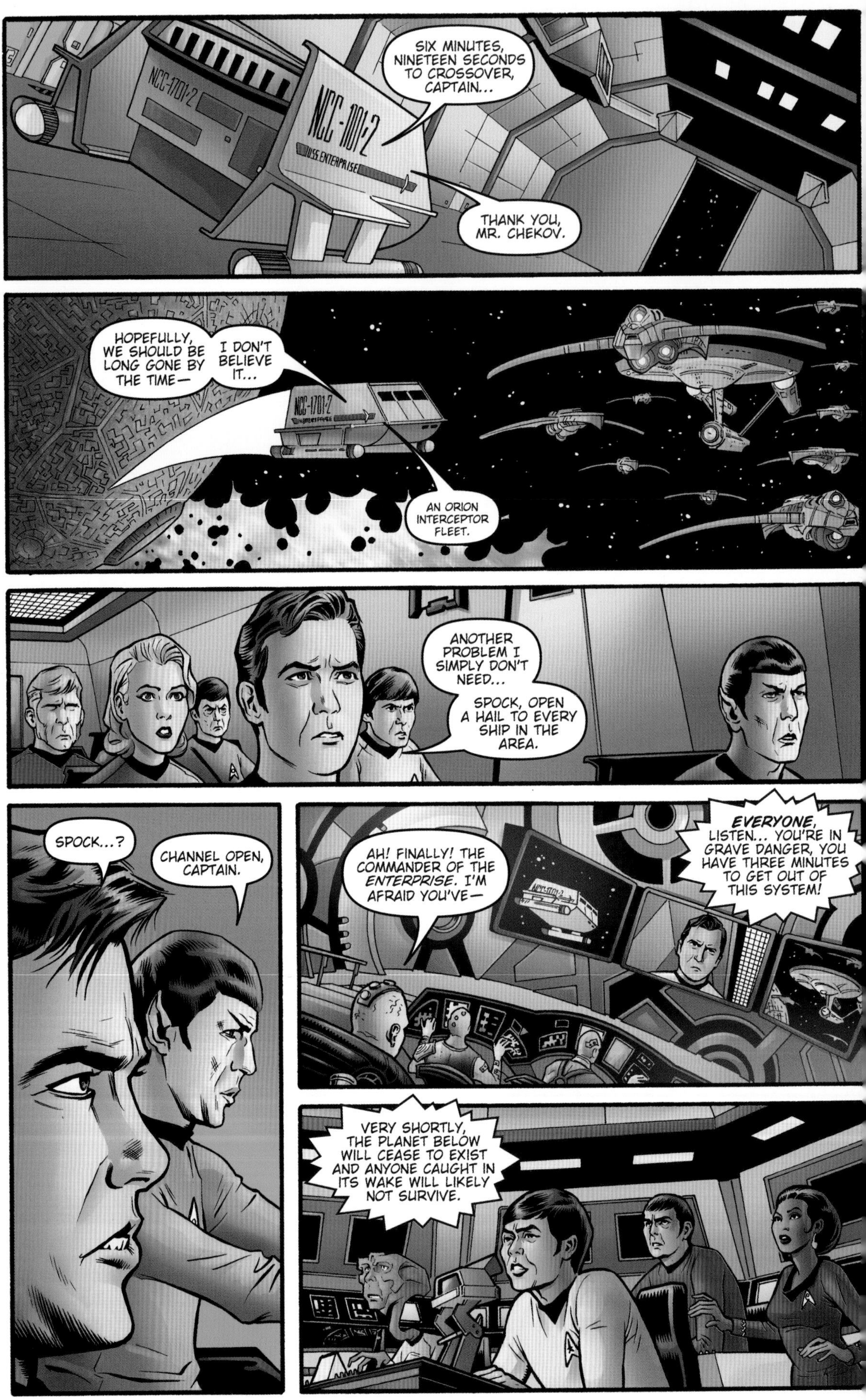
SIX MINUTES, NINETEEN SECONDS TO CROSSOVER, CAPTAIN...
NCC-1701-2
USS ENTERPRISE
THANK YOU, MR. CHEKOV.
HOPEFULLY, WE SHOULD BE LONG GONE BY THE TIME—
I DON'T BELIEVE IT...
NCC-1701-2
AN ORION INTERCEPTOR FLEET.
ANOTHER PROBLEM I SIMPLY DON'T NEED...
SPOCK, OPEN A HAIL TO EVERY SHIP IN THE AREA.
SPOCK...?
CHANNEL OPEN, CAPTAIN.
AH! FINALLY! THE COMMANDER OF THE *ENTERPRISE*. I'M AFRAID YOU'VE—
EVERYONE, LISTEN... YOU'RE IN GRAVE DANGER, YOU HAVE THREE MINUTES TO GET OUT OF THIS SYSTEM!
VERY SHORTLY, THE PLANET BELOW WILL CEASE TO EXIST AND ANYONE CAUGHT IN ITS WAKE WILL LIKELY NOT SURVIVE.

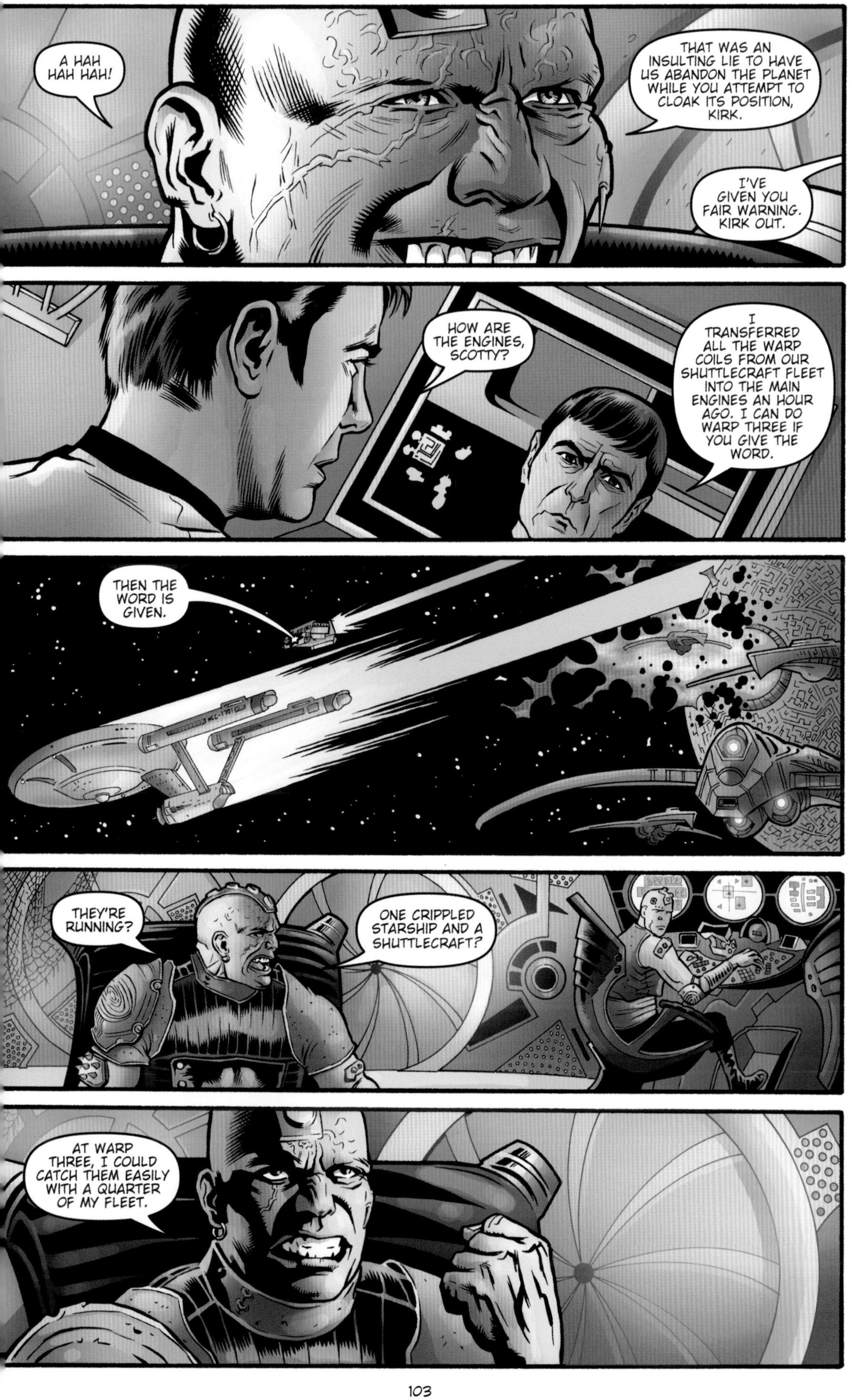
A HAH HAH HAH!
THAT WAS AN INSULTING LIE TO HAVE US ABANDON THE PLANET WHILE YOU ATTEMPT TO CLOAK ITS POSITION, KIRK.
I'VE GIVEN YOU FAIR WARNING. KIRK OUT.
HOW ARE THE ENGINES, SCOTTY?
I TRANSFERRED ALL THE WARP COILS FROM OUR SHUTTLECRAFT FLEET INTO THE MAIN ENGINES AN HOUR AGO. I CAN DO WARP THREE IF YOU GIVE THE WORD.
THEN THE WORD IS GIVEN.
THEY'RE RUNNING?
ONE CRIPPLED STARSHIP AND A SHUTTLECRAFT?
AT WARP THREE, I COULD CATCH THEM EASILY WITH A QUARTER OF MY FLEET.

CAPTAIN! ENERGY SPIKES FROM THE PLANET SURFACE LIKE—

WHAT?! BUT—

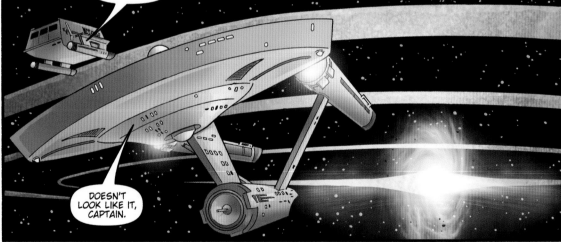

DID ANY OF THE ORION SHIPS MAKE IT AWAY IN TIME?

DOESN'T LOOK LIKE IT, CAPTAIN.

THAT'S TOO BAD. I GAVE THEM A CHANCE.

BUT AT LEAST IT'S CLEAR SAILING HOME.

NEVER DOUBTED YOU FOR A SECOND THERE, SIR!

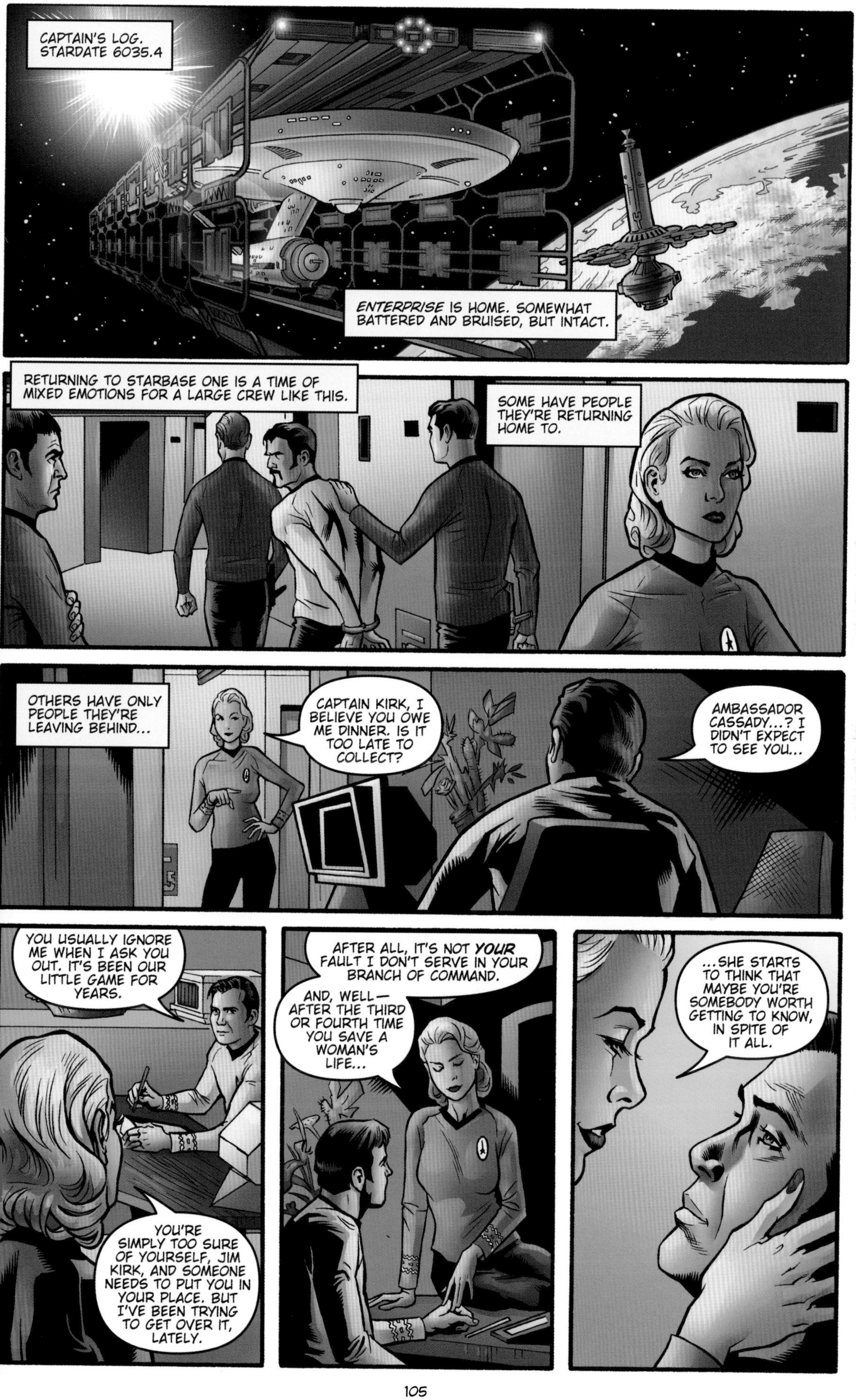
CAPTAIN'S LOG. STARDATE 6035.4
ENTERPRISE IS HOME. SOMEWHAT BATTERED AND BRUISED, BUT INTACT.
RETURNING TO STARBASE ONE IS A TIME OF MIXED EMOTIONS FOR A LARGE CREW LIKE THIS.
SOME HAVE PEOPLE THEY'RE RETURNING HOME TO.
OTHERS HAVE ONLY PEOPLE THEY'RE LEAVING BEHIND...
CAPTAIN KIRK, I BELIEVE YOU OWE ME DINNER. IS IT TOO LATE TO COLLECT?
AMBASSADOR CASSADY...? I DIDN'T EXPECT TO SEE YOU...
YOU USUALLY IGNORE ME WHEN I ASK YOU OUT. IT'S BEEN OUR LITTLE GAME FOR YEARS.
YOU'RE SIMPLY TOO SURE OF YOURSELF, JIM KIRK, AND SOMEONE NEEDS TO PUT YOU IN YOUR PLACE. BUT I'VE BEEN TRYING TO GET OVER IT, LATELY.
AFTER ALL, IT'S NOT YOUR FAULT I DON'T SERVE IN YOUR BRANCH OF COMMAND.
AND, WELL— AFTER THE THIRD OR FOURTH TIME YOU SAVE A WOMAN'S LIFE...
...SHE STARTS TO THINK THAT MAYBE YOU'RE SOMEBODY WORTH GETTING TO KNOW, IN SPITE OF IT ALL.

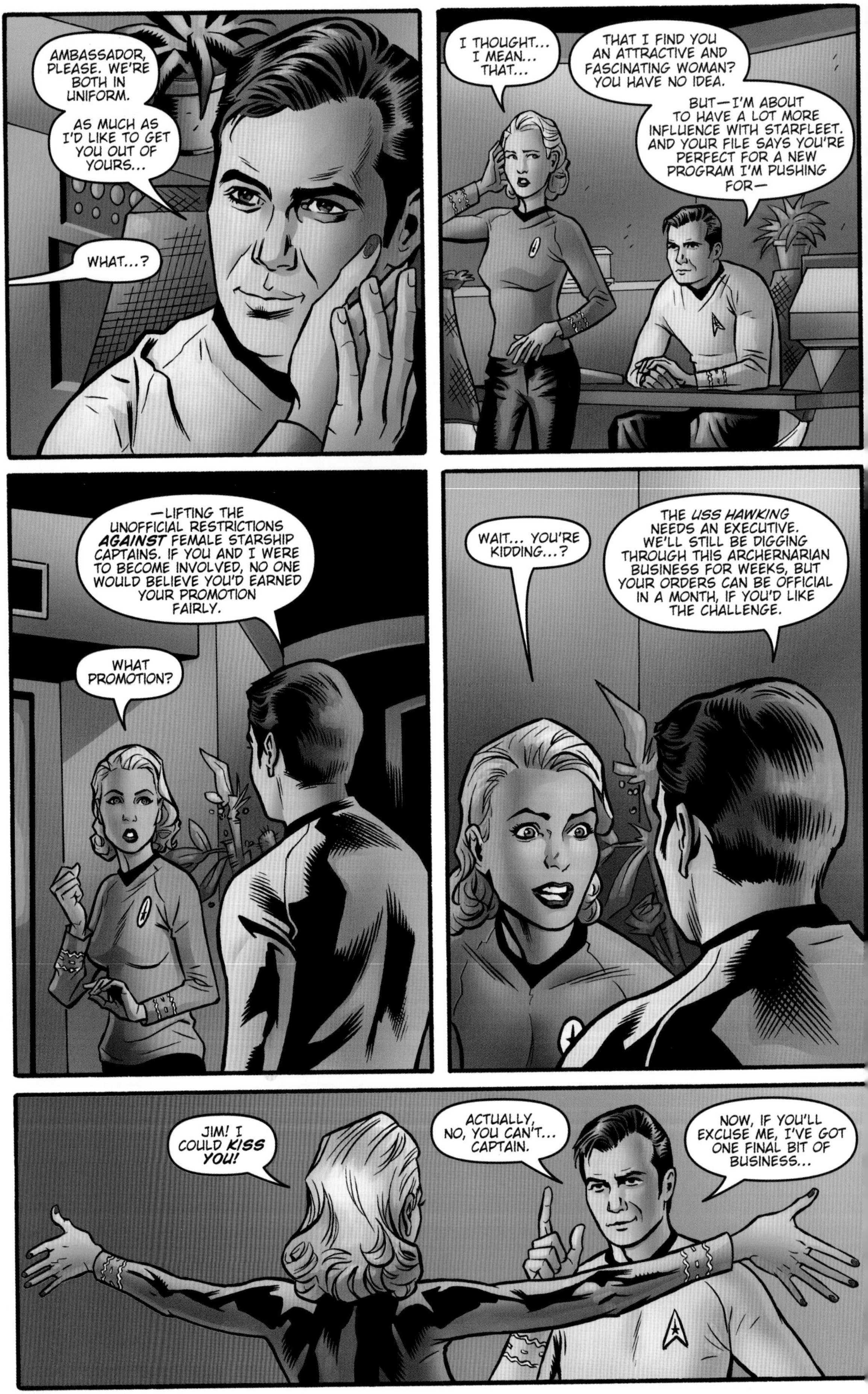
AMBASSADOR, PLEASE. WE'RE BOTH IN UNIFORM.
AS MUCH AS I'D LIKE TO GET YOU OUT OF YOURS...
WHAT...?
I THOUGHT... I MEAN... THAT...
THAT I FIND YOU AN ATTRACTIVE AND FASCINATING WOMAN? YOU HAVE NO IDEA.
BUT—I'M ABOUT TO HAVE A LOT MORE INFLUENCE WITH STARFLEET. AND YOUR FILE SAYS YOU'RE PERFECT FOR A NEW PROGRAM I'M PUSHING FOR—
—LIFTING THE UNOFFICIAL RESTRICTIONS AGAINST FEMALE STARSHIP CAPTAINS. IF YOU AND I WERE TO BECOME INVOLVED, NO ONE WOULD BELIEVE YOU'D EARNED YOUR PROMOTION FAIRLY.
WHAT PROMOTION?
WAIT... YOU'RE KIDDING...?
THE USS HAWKING NEEDS AN EXECUTIVE. WE'LL STILL BE DIGGING THROUGH THIS ARCHERNARIAN BUSINESS FOR WEEKS, BUT YOUR ORDERS CAN BE OFFICIAL IN A MONTH, IF YOU'D LIKE THE CHALLENGE.
JIM! I COULD KISS YOU!
ACTUALLY, NO, YOU CAN'T... CAPTAIN.
NOW, IF YOU'LL EXCUSE ME, I'VE GOT ONE FINAL BIT OF BUSINESS...

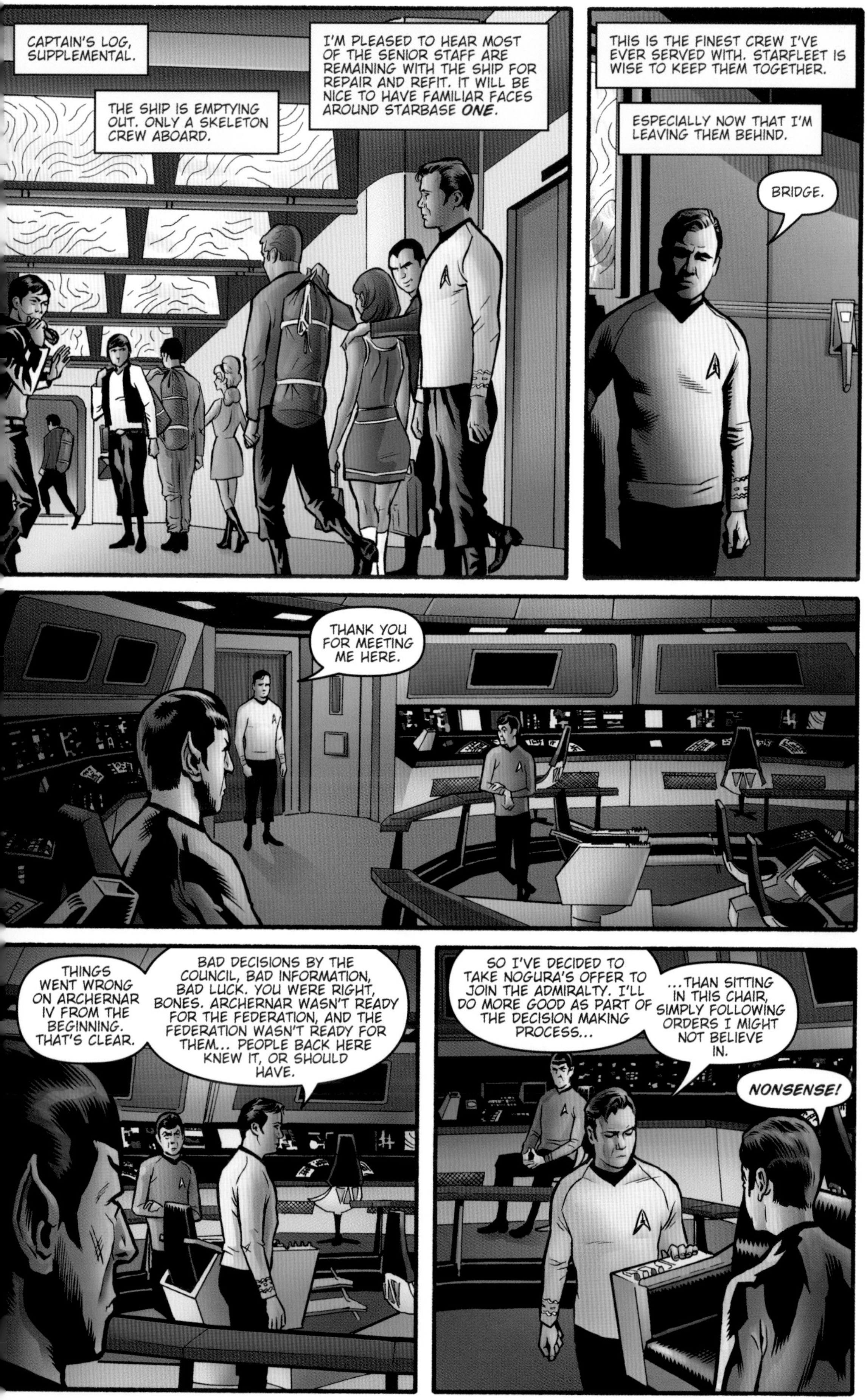
CAPTAIN'S LOG, SUPPLEMENTAL.
THE SHIP IS EMPTYING OUT. ONLY A SKELETON CREW ABOARD.
I'M PLEASED TO HEAR MOST OF THE SENIOR STAFF ARE REMAINING WITH THE SHIP FOR REPAIR AND REFIT. IT WILL BE NICE TO HAVE FAMILIAR FACES AROUND STARBASE *ONE*.
THIS IS THE FINEST CREW I'VE EVER SERVED WITH. STARFLEET IS WISE TO KEEP THEM TOGETHER.
ESPECIALLY NOW THAT I'M LEAVING THEM BEHIND.
BRIDGE.
THANK YOU FOR MEETING ME HERE.
THINGS WENT WRONG ON ARCHERNAR IV FROM THE BEGINNING. THAT'S CLEAR.
BAD DECISIONS BY THE COUNCIL, BAD INFORMATION, BAD LUCK. YOU WERE RIGHT, BONES. ARCHERNAR WASN'T READY FOR THE FEDERATION, AND THE FEDERATION WASN'T READY FOR THEM... PEOPLE BACK HERE KNEW IT, OR SHOULD HAVE.
SO I'VE DECIDED TO TAKE NOGURA'S OFFER TO JOIN THE ADMIRALTY. I'LL DO MORE GOOD AS PART OF THE DECISION MAKING PROCESS...
...THAN SITTING IN THIS CHAIR, SIMPLY FOLLOWING ORDERS I MIGHT NOT BELIEVE IN.
NONSENSE!

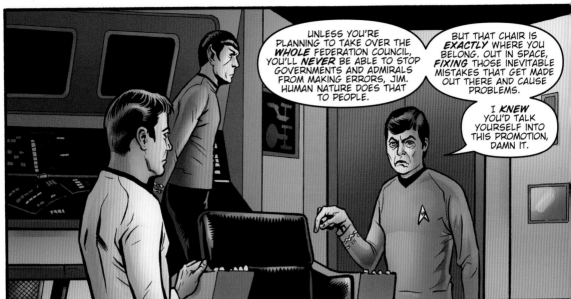

UNLESS YOU'RE PLANNING TO TAKE OVER THE *WHOLE* FEDERATION COUNCIL, YOU'LL *NEVER* BE ABLE TO STOP GOVERNMENTS AND ADMIRALS FROM MAKING ERRORS, JIM. HUMAN NATURE DOES THAT TO PEOPLE.

BUT THAT CHAIR IS *EXACTLY* WHERE YOU BELONG. OUT IN SPACE, *FIXING* THOSE INEVITABLE MISTAKES THAT GET MADE OUT THERE AND CAUSE PROBLEMS.

I *KNEW* YOU'D TALK YOURSELF INTO THIS PROMOTION, DAMN IT.

I WAS HOPING I COULD GET EACH OF YOU INTO THAT CHAIR FOR ME.

MCCOY—AS CAPTAIN OF THE MEDICAL SHIP, *GALEN.*

AND SPOCK, I WANT YOU AS CAPTAIN OF THE *ENTERPRISE.*

I RESPECTFULLY DECLINE, CAPTAIN.

I'M SORRY, JIM, BUT SO DO I.

WHAT...?

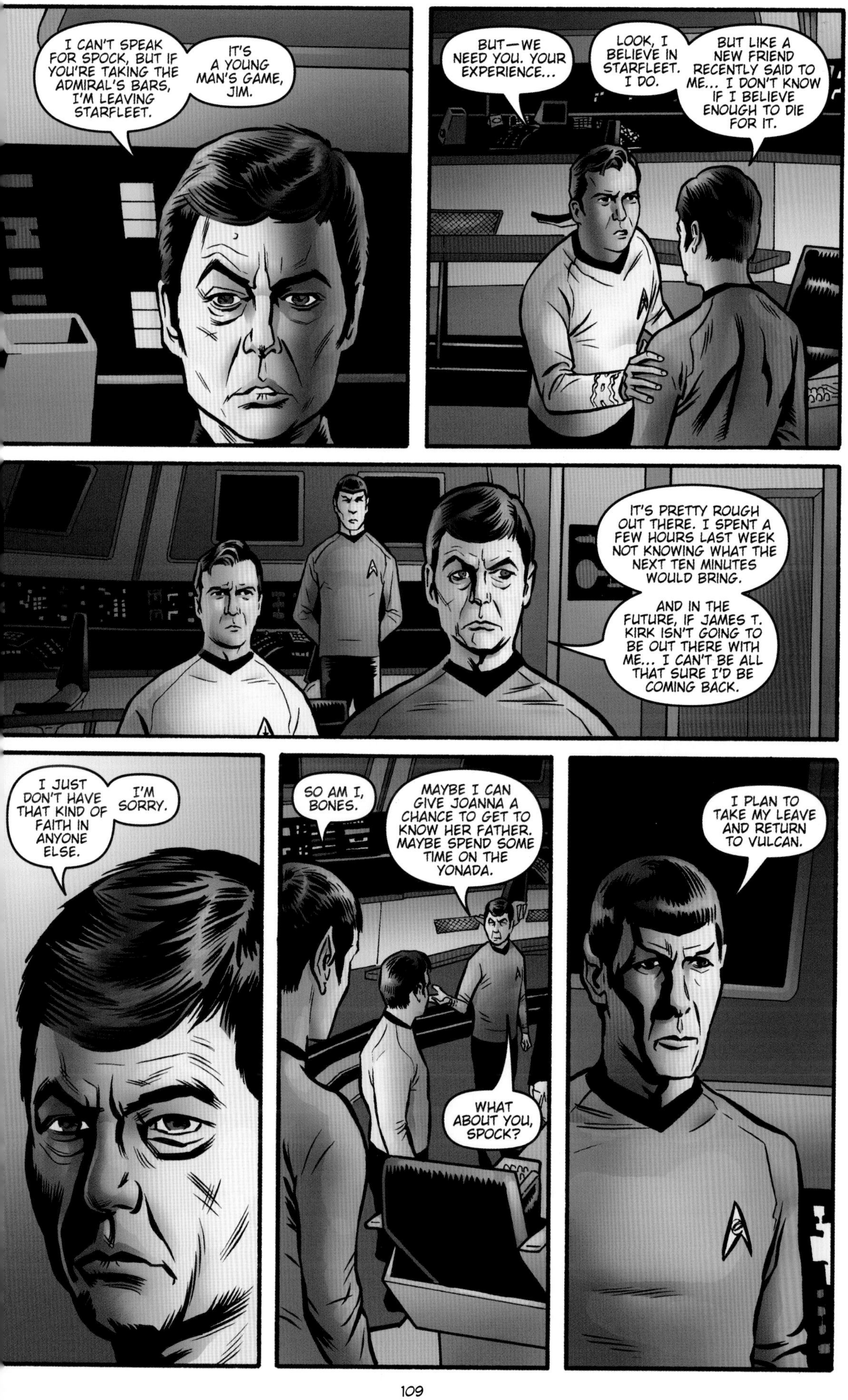
I CAN'T SPEAK FOR SPOCK, BUT IF YOU'RE TAKING THE ADMIRAL'S BARS, I'M LEAVING STARFLEET.
IT'S A YOUNG MAN'S GAME, JIM.
BUT—WE NEED YOU. YOUR EXPERIENCE...
LOOK, I BELIEVE IN STARFLEET. I DO.
BUT LIKE A NEW FRIEND RECENTLY SAID TO ME... I DON'T KNOW IF I BELIEVE ENOUGH TO DIE FOR IT.
IT'S PRETTY ROUGH OUT THERE. I SPENT A FEW HOURS LAST WEEK NOT KNOWING WHAT THE NEXT TEN MINUTES WOULD BRING.
AND IN THE FUTURE, IF JAMES T. KIRK ISN'T GOING TO BE OUT THERE WITH ME... I CAN'T BE ALL THAT SURE I'D BE COMING BACK.
I JUST DON'T HAVE THAT KIND OF FAITH IN ANYONE ELSE.
I'M SORRY.
SO AM I, BONES.
MAYBE I CAN GIVE JOANNA A CHANCE TO GET TO KNOW HER FATHER. MAYBE SPEND SOME TIME ON THE YONADA.
WHAT ABOUT YOU, SPOCK?
I PLAN TO TAKE MY LEAVE AND RETURN TO VULCAN.

SPOCK...? ARE YOU ALL RIGHT?

I DO NOT KNOW.

TWO DAYS AGO, I REACHED WHAT I BELIEVED TO BE THE ONLY SOLUTION TO THE SITUATION AT HAND, AND CHOSE TO EVACUATE ARCHERNAR IV ACCORDING TO THE RULES SET OUT IN THE PRIME DIRECTIVE.

I MADE MY DECISION WITH LOGIC, AND BALANCED THE NEEDS OF THE MANY AGAINST THE NEEDS OF THE FEW.

IT WAS THE BEST SOLUTION I COULD SEE. EVEN WITH THE CASUALTIES INVOLVED.

BUT YOU, CAPTAIN, QUICKLY FOUND A SOLUTION THAT HAD NO CASUALTIES, AND THAT ADDRESSED EVERY POSSIBLE CONCERN.

A SOLUTION I DID NOT SEE.

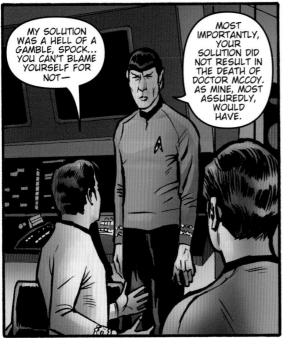

MY SOLUTION WAS A HELL OF A GAMBLE, SPOCK... YOU CAN'T BLAME YOURSELF FOR NOT—

MOST IMPORTANTLY, YOUR SOLUTION DID NOT RESULT IN THE DEATH OF DOCTOR MCCOY. AS MINE, MOST ASSUREDLY, WOULD HAVE.

I FIND I AM DWELLING ON THIS ERROR OF JUDGMENT AND LOGIC—

—FAR MORE THAN I SHOULD.

IS THAT IT?

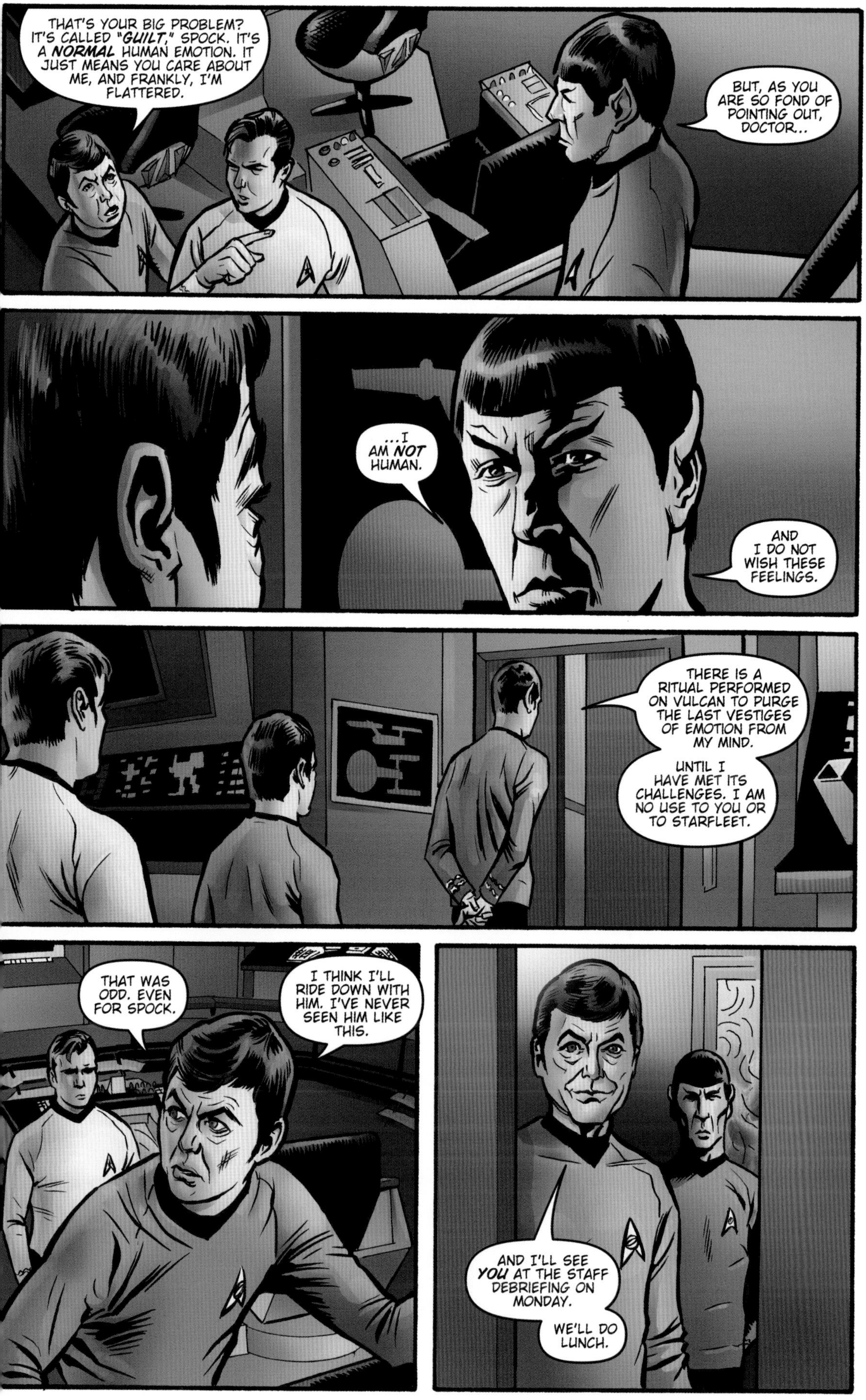
THAT'S YOUR BIG PROBLEM? IT'S CALLED "GUILT," SPOCK. IT'S A NORMAL HUMAN EMOTION. IT JUST MEANS YOU CARE ABOUT ME, AND FRANKLY, I'M FLATTERED.
BUT, AS YOU ARE SO FOND OF POINTING OUT, DOCTOR...
...I AM NOT HUMAN.
AND I DO NOT WISH THESE FEELINGS.
THERE IS A RITUAL PERFORMED ON VULCAN TO PURGE THE LAST VESTIGES OF EMOTION FROM MY MIND.
UNTIL I HAVE MET ITS CHALLENGES. I AM NO USE TO YOU OR TO STARFLEET.
THAT WAS ODD. EVEN FOR SPOCK.
I THINK I'LL RIDE DOWN WITH HIM. I'VE NEVER SEEN HIM LIKE THIS.
AND I'LL SEE YOU AT THE STAFF DEBRIEFING ON MONDAY.
WE'LL DO LUNCH.

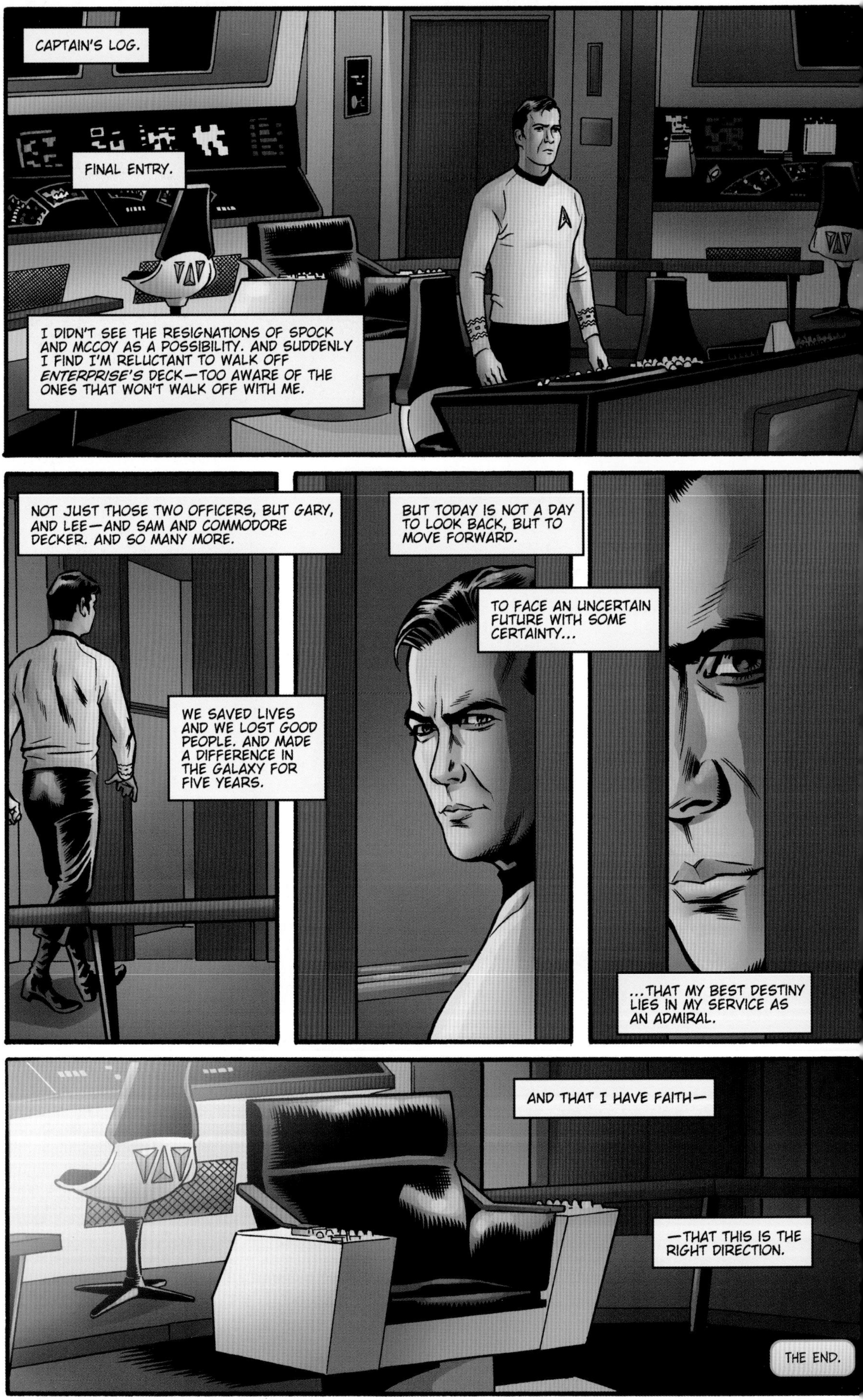
CAPTAIN'S LOG.
FINAL ENTRY.
I DIDN'T SEE THE RESIGNATIONS OF SPOCK AND MCCOY AS A POSSIBILITY. AND SUDDENLY I FIND I'M RELUCTANT TO WALK OFF *ENTERPRISE'S* DECK—TOO AWARE OF THE ONES THAT WON'T WALK OFF WITH ME.
NOT JUST THOSE TWO OFFICERS, BUT GARY, AND LEE—AND SAM AND COMMODORE DECKER. AND SO MANY MORE.
WE SAVED LIVES AND WE LOST GOOD PEOPLE. AND MADE A DIFFERENCE IN THE GALAXY FOR FIVE YEARS.
BUT TODAY IS NOT A DAY TO LOOK BACK, BUT TO MOVE FORWARD.
TO FACE AN UNCERTAIN FUTURE WITH SOME CERTAINTY...
...THAT MY BEST DESTINY LIES IN MY SERVICE AS AN ADMIRAL.
AND THAT I HAVE FAITH—
—THAT THIS IS THE RIGHT DIRECTION.
THE END.

ART GALLERY

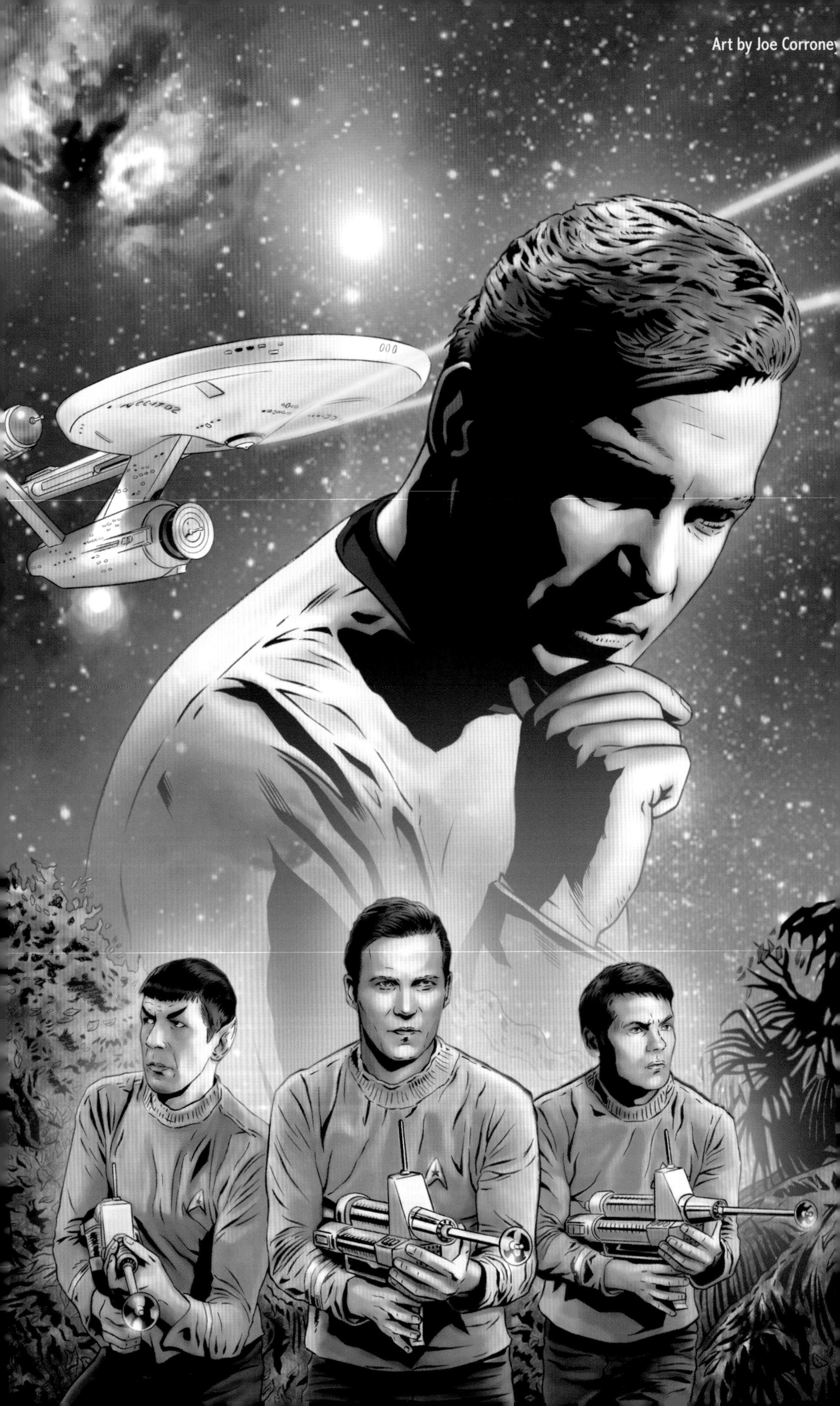
NCC-1702

Art by Joe Corroney

Art by Kevin Maguire
Colors by Chris Sotomayor

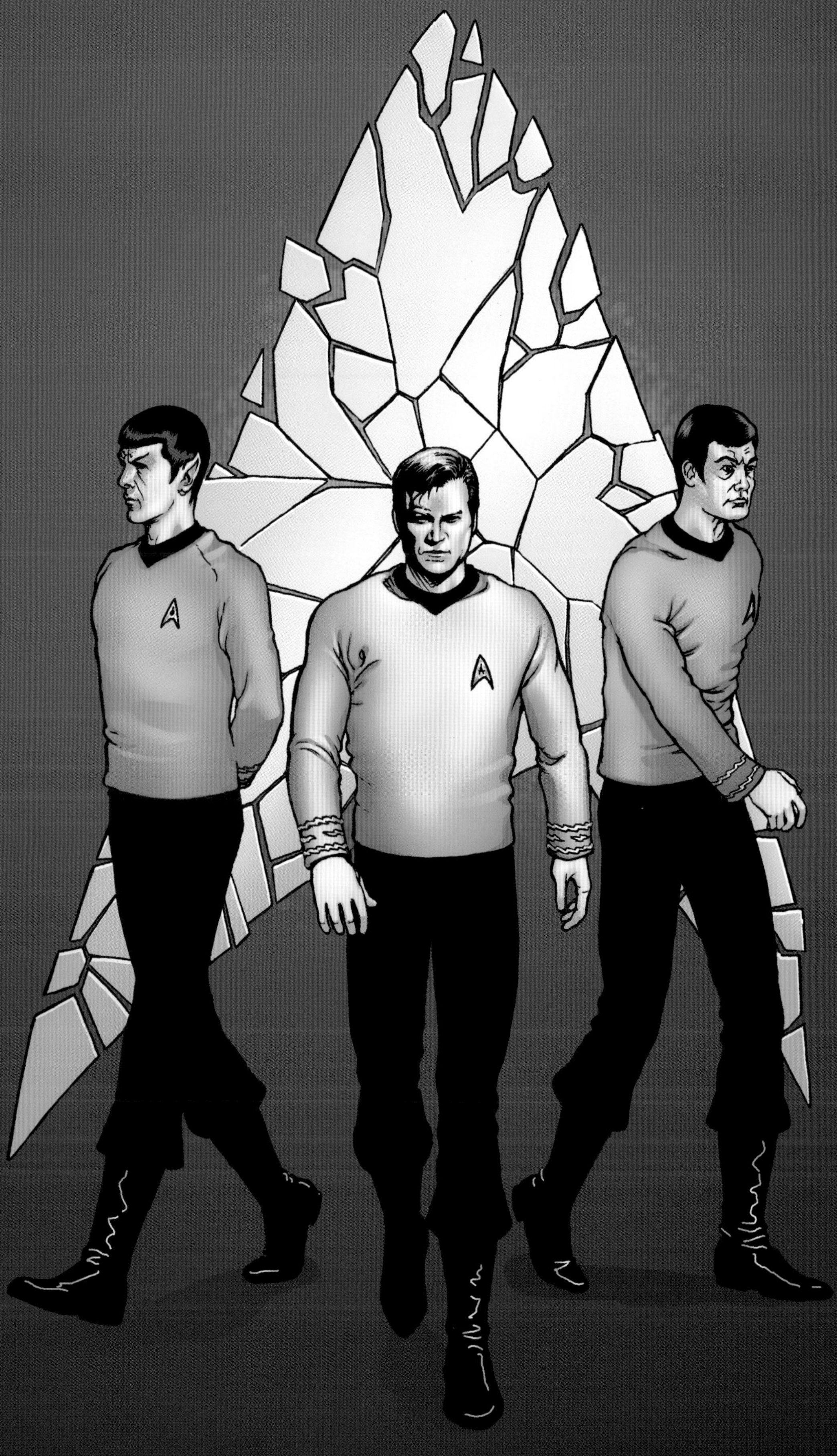

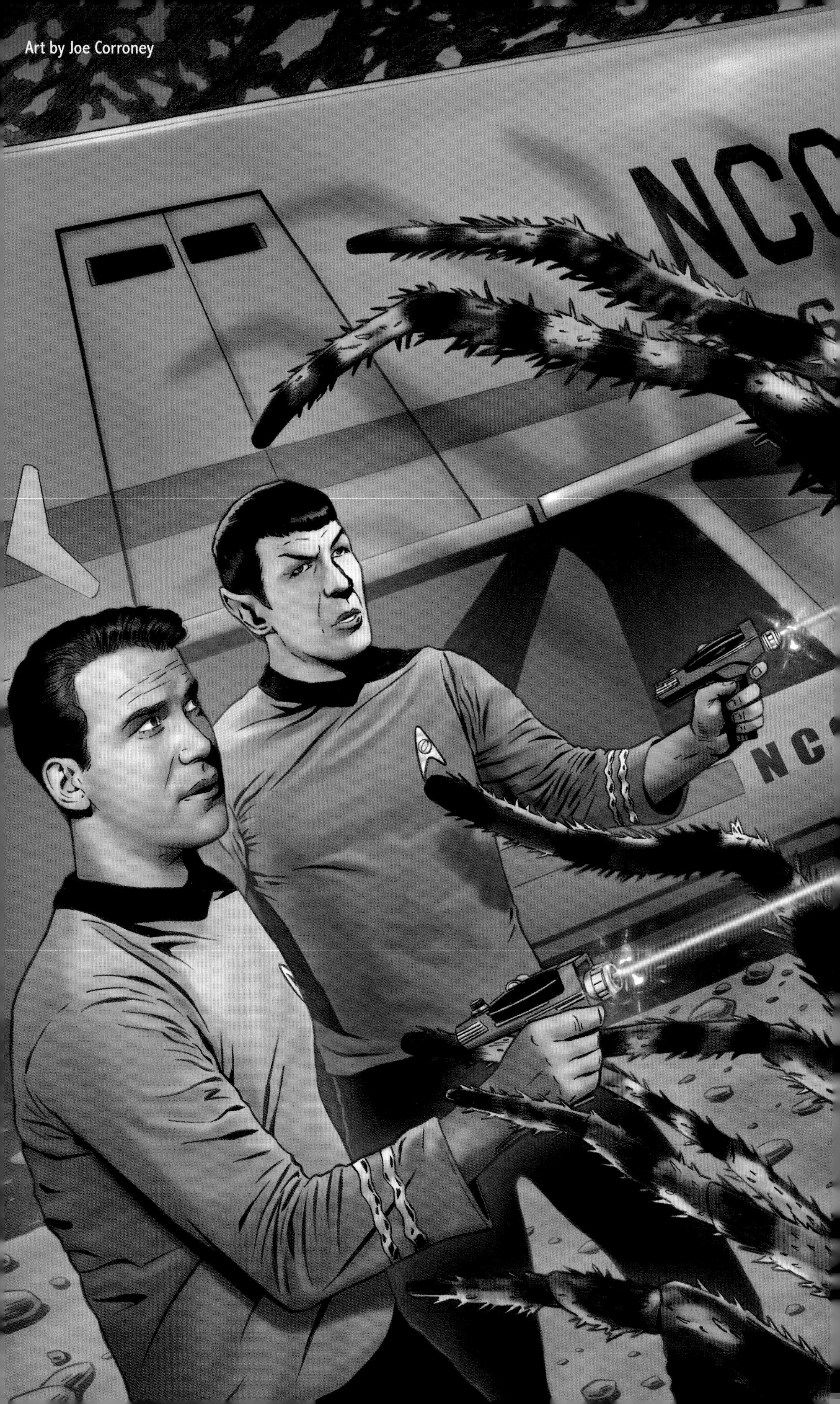
Art by Joe Corroney

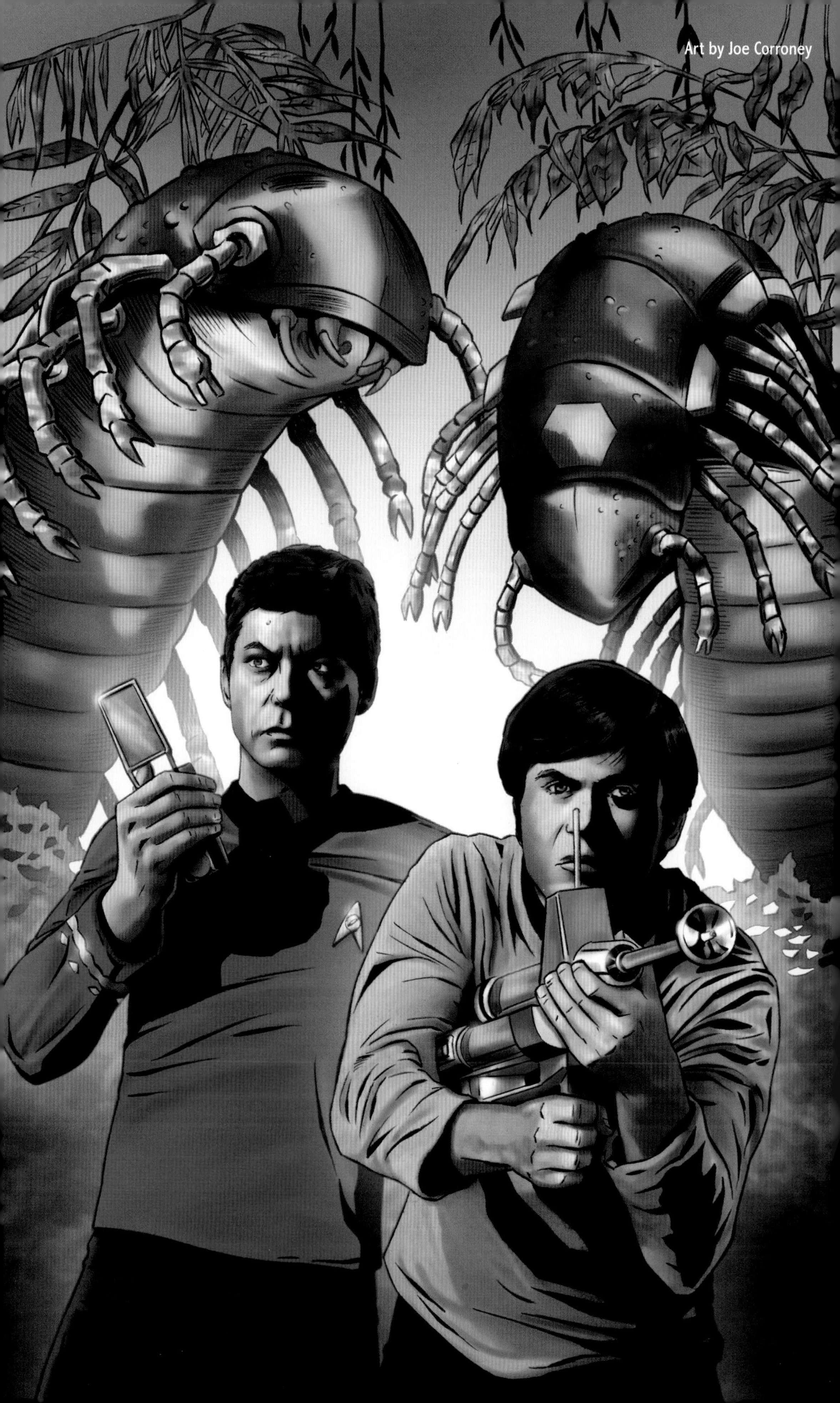
Art by Joe Corroney

Art by Joe Corroney

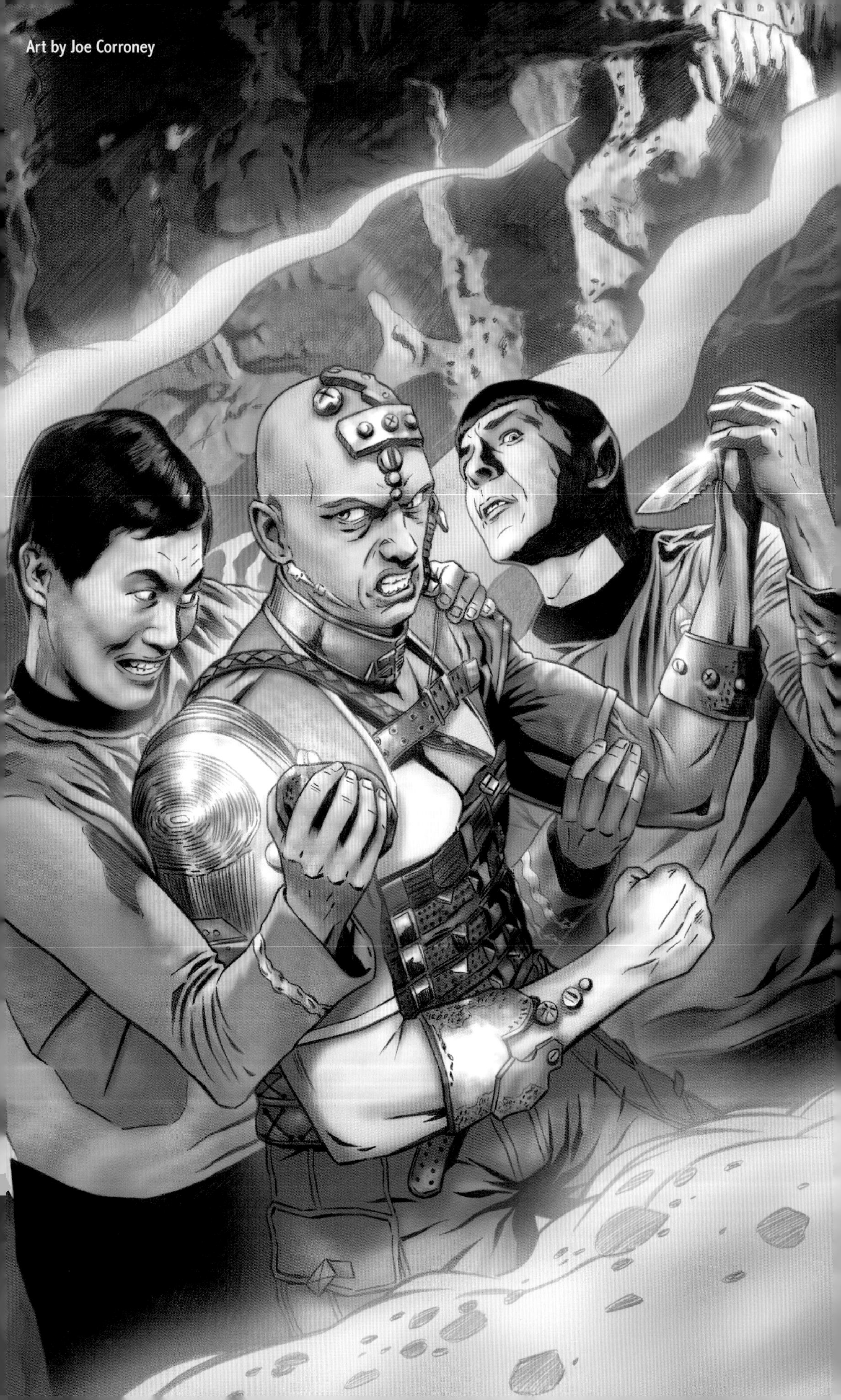

Art by Joe Corroney

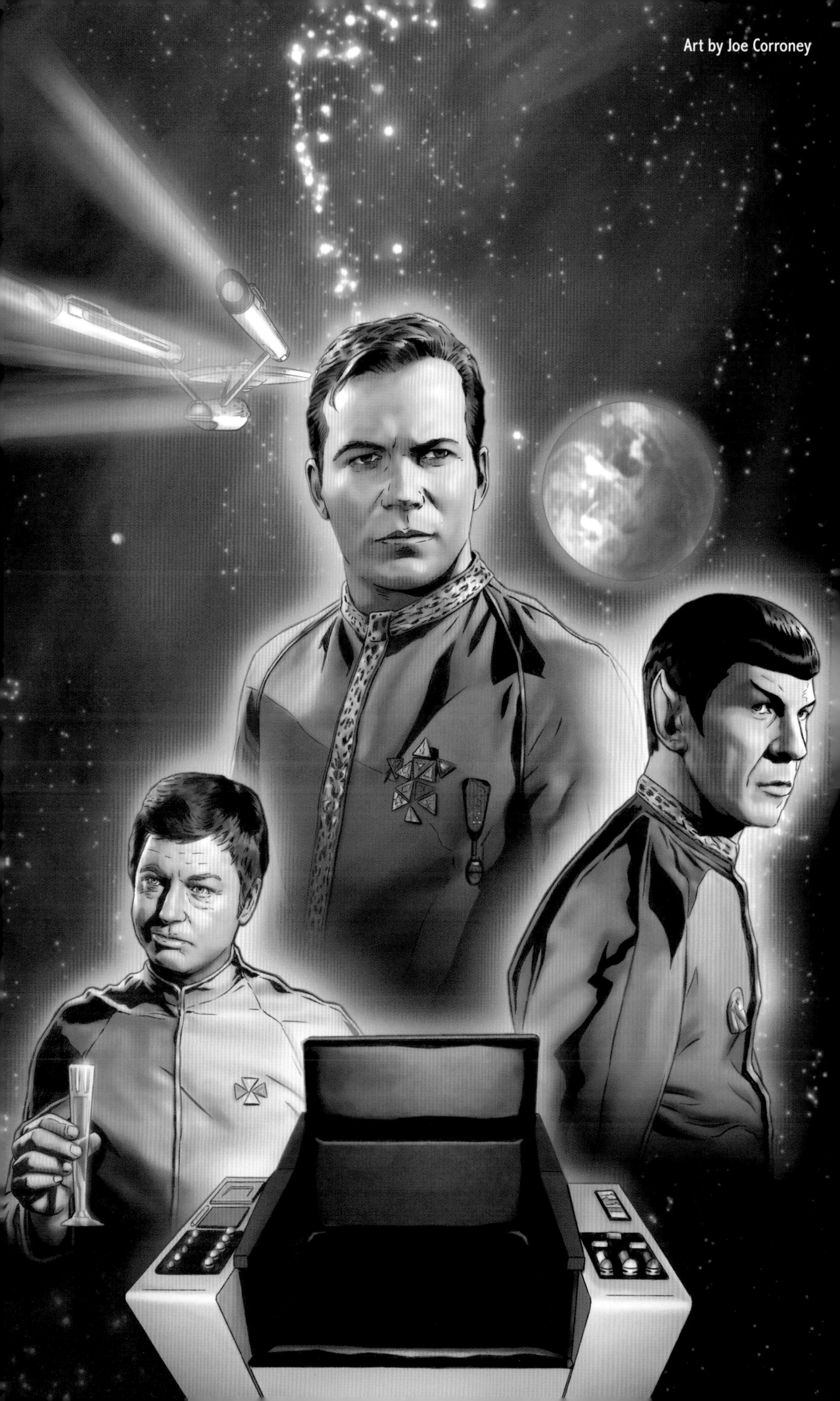

Character Sketches by **Stephen Molnar**

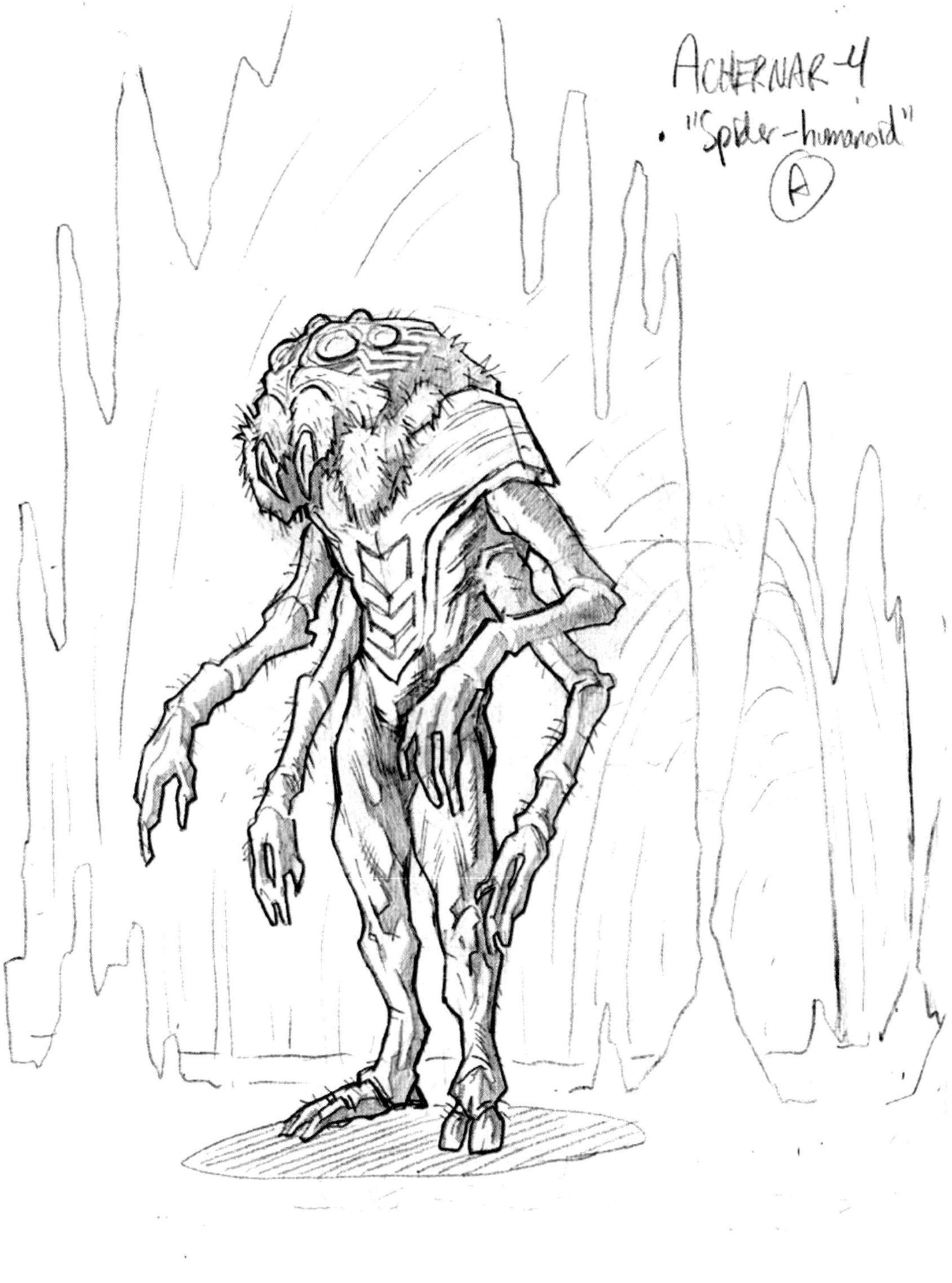
ACHERNAR-4
• "Spider-humanoid"
A

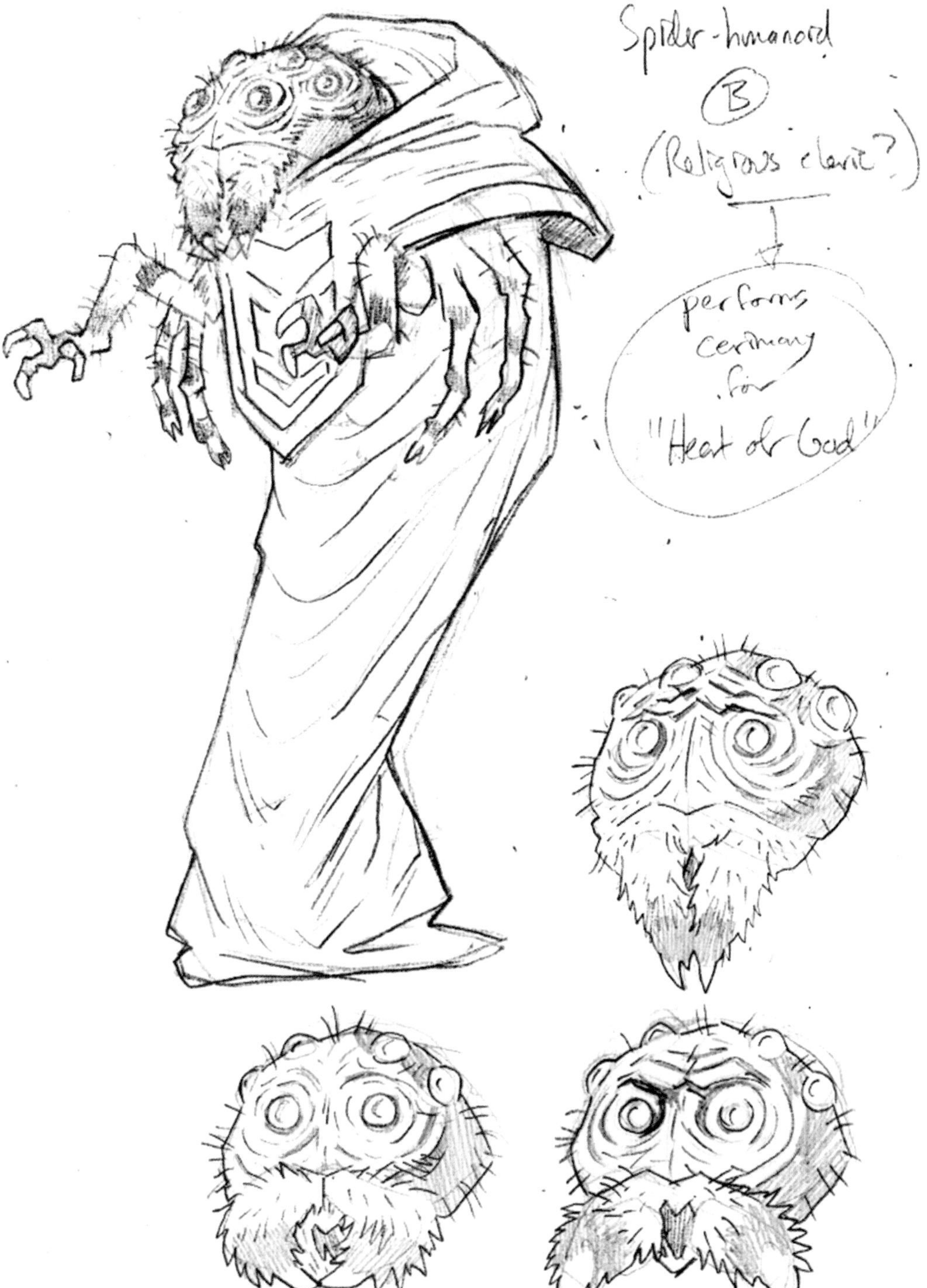
Spider-humanoid
B
(Religious cleric?)
performs cerimony for "Heart of God"

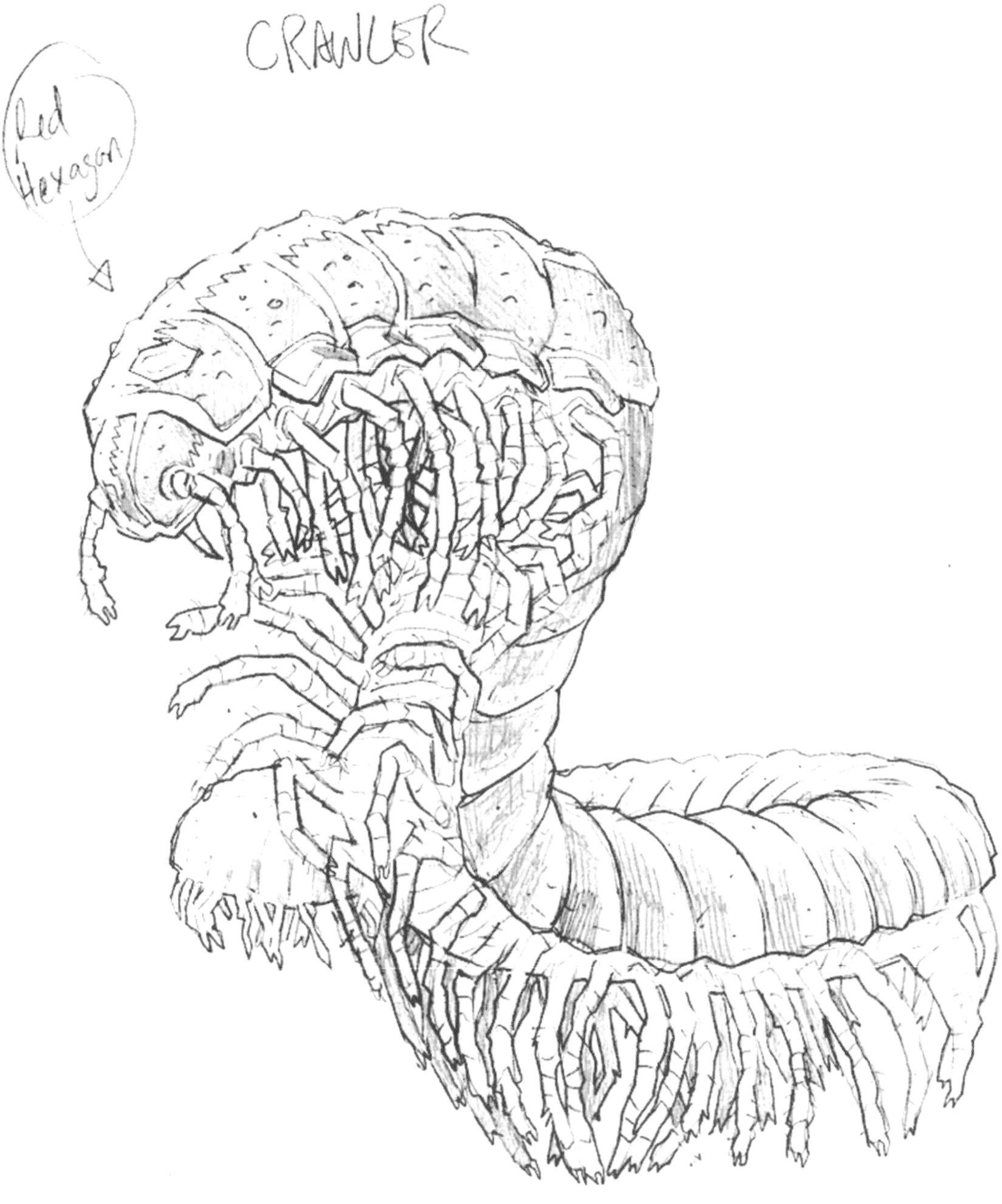
CRAWLER
Red Hexagon

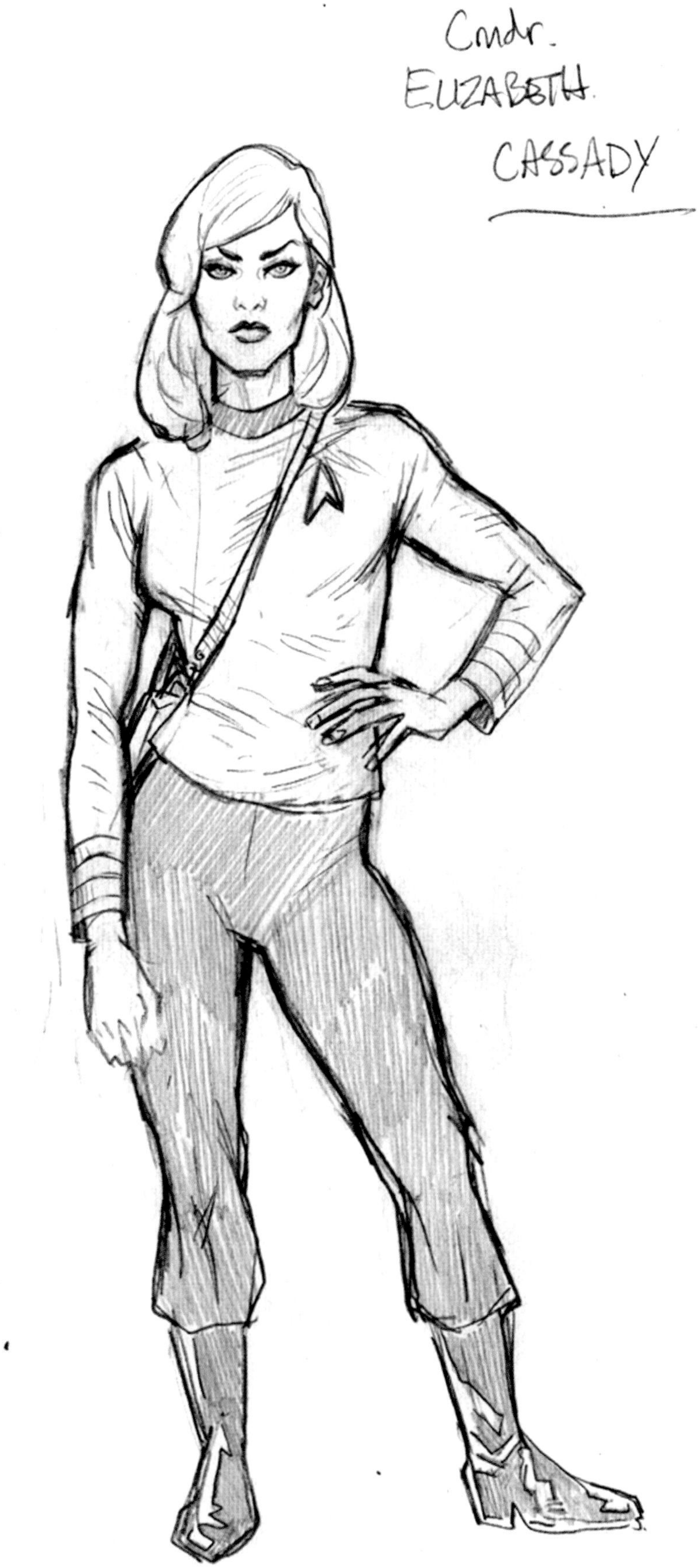
Cmdr.
ELIZABETH
CASSADY

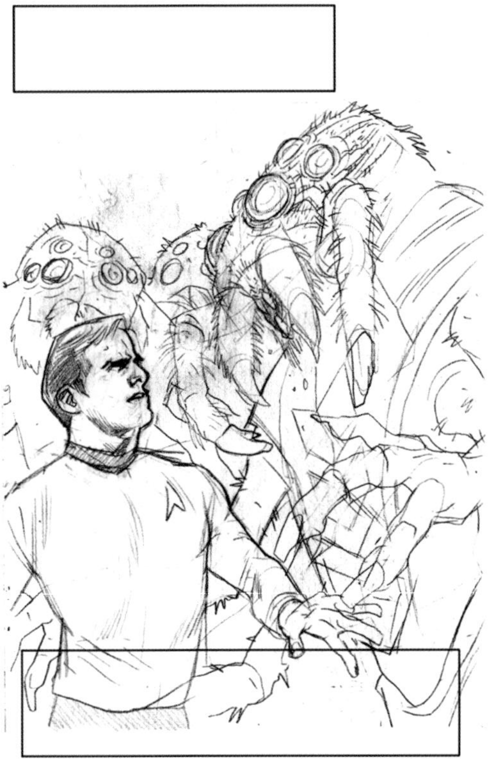

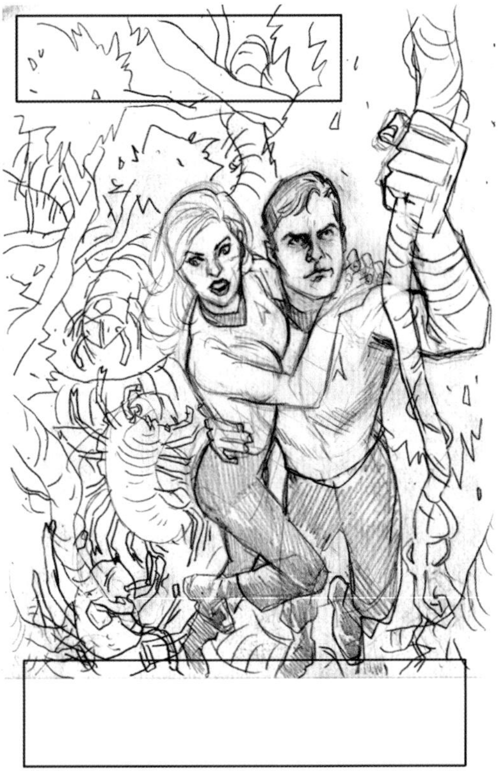

Cover Concepts by **Stephen Molnar**

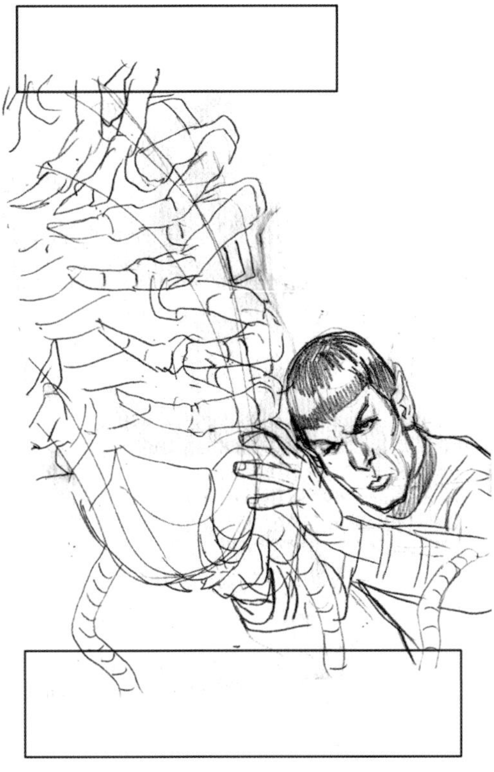

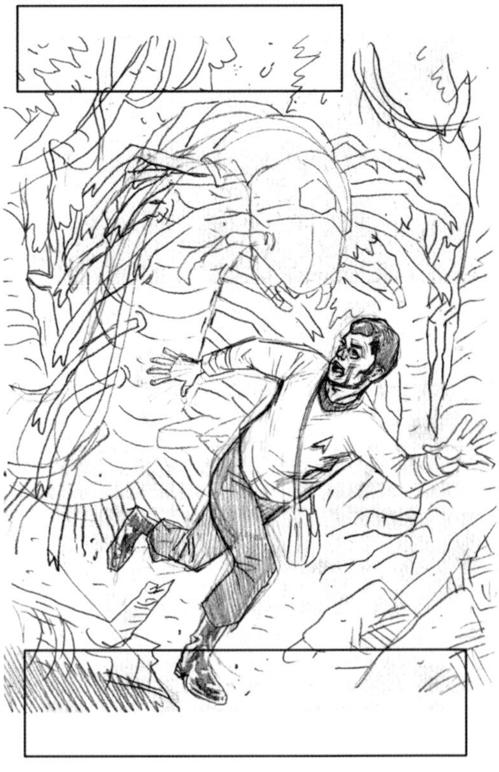